A Surgeon's
DEVOTIONS

For Bob Plimpton

With Admiration
&
Affection

Joe VanderVeer
Nov '05

A Surgeon's
DEVOTIONS

Joe Vander Veer, Jr. M.D.

Pleasant Word

ISBN 1-4141-0082-5
Library of Congress Catalog Card Number: 2003114776

TABLE OF CONTENTS

FEBRUARY

MARCH

APRIL

MAY

AUGUST

SEPTEMBER

OCTOBER

NOVEMBER

FOREWORD

These daily devotions had their beginning in 1999 as part of the Dial-A-Prayer ministry of Shepherd of the Valley Lutheran Church in Phoenix, Arizona. That year was an important one for me.

In 1999 I retired after practicing surgery for 27 years (fourteen in Portland, OR and thirteen in Phoenix, Arizona). That year I also married Diane Budd, who'd been a widow for seven years. She and I were pinned in college forty years before, but we broke up and I went on to medical school. She is a member of Bryn Mawr Presbyterian Church in Bryn Mawr, PA, the church where I grew up. After we were married and I retired, we sold our home in Phoenix, bought a condominium and have since divided our time between winters in Arizona and the rest of the year in suburban Philadelphia.

Over the years I've been part of many different churches as I have moved about through college, medical school, residency and surgical practice. That experience has been quite ecumenical—embracing such diversity as Quakerism, High Anglicanism, Methodism, Presbyterianism and charismatic Baptist. For my spiritual life, the variety of ways to worship and the varied manifestations of God's Spirit have been enriching and educational. Some of that diversity is apparent in the devotions that follow.

I dedicate this work to the Lord and to three who have been "my encouragers:"

Ethel VanderVeer, Diane E. VanderVeer, Pastor Leo Schlegel
Phoenix, AZ
October 2003

JANUARY 1

ALL THINGS MADE NEW

(Scripture to ponder: Revelation 21:1–5)

There is a story about a man from London who owned a Rolls Royce, who went for a driving trip through the provinces of France. On a dark night, on a winding, narrow road, he ran off the shoulder and into the ditch, breaking the axle of the car. The next day, with a farmer's help, the car was hauled back on to the road and into the shop for repairs. It took about a week to get the needed parts and restore the automobile, during which time the owner enjoyed the French countryside and hospitality.

After returning to England, he was surprised that he never received a bill. He sent a letter to Rolls Royce stating the facts, asking them to check into it. A few days later he got back a letter on official Rolls Royce stationery, which stated, **"We are sorry, sir, but we have checked all the records, and there is no record of there ever being a broken axle on a Rolls Royce."**

Today is New Years Day, and with the new year I am reminded that through Jesus we have been given newness of life: Through Him, it will be as though there is no record of our sins.

Hear the wonderful words of the Revelation of St. John:

I heard a great voice from the throne saying, "Behold the dwelling of God is with men. He will dwell with them and they shall be his people, and God Himself will be with them; he will wipe away every tear from their eyes, and death shall be no more, neither shall there be mourning nor crying nor pain any more, for the former things have passed away."

And he who sat upon the throne said, "Behold I make all things new." Also he said, "Write this, for these words are trustworthy and true." [Revelation 21:3–5]

PRAYER: With this New Year we praise you, our Lord and our God, for you do indeed make all things new. Through you we have forgiveness of our sins and newness of life. AMEN.

JANUARY 2

TRANSFORMING THE WORLD

(Scripture to ponder: Romans 12:2)

"As thou art in church or cell, that same mind carry out into the world, into its turmoil and its fitfulness."

—Meister Eckhart

When I read those words of the XIVth century Christian mystic Meister Eckhart, I wonder just how much fitfulness and turmoil there was in life six centuries ago, compared to our own times. Certainly in many ways life has become more hectic. Indeed, we are assaulted on all sides by the media and our senses encroached upon by the noise of modern transportation.

But the principle Meister Eckhart expounded is the same today as then: Inner peace must be achieved from an inner, spiritual base, and must be carried out into the world, if we are to do God's will.

"Do not be conformed to this world," St. Paul wrote to the Roman Christians, *"but be transformed by the renewal of your mind."* [Romans 12:2] As someone once said, "Most books are for information; the Bible is for *transformation*." And we can be transformed within by the Holy Spirit, through corporate worship and private devotions, to do Christ's work of transforming the world.

PRAYER: Let Thy Holy Spirit transform us, O Lord, so we in turn may be your workers in the world, that Your Will may be done, and Your Kingdom come. AMEN.

JANUARY 3

BUILDING ON A FIRM FOUNDATION

(Scripture to ponder: 1 Corinthians 3:11)

Frank Lloyd Wright is among America's greatest architects. He is renown for such structures as the Guggenheim Museum in New York City and the famous home, "Falling Water," near Pittsburgh, PA.

But Wright was not always held in high esteem. For years he struggled to make his architectural principles and philosophy known. Then one of his buildings, the Imperial Hotel in Tokyo, won acclaim not just for its appearance, but because it was one of the few structures that survived the devastating earthquake of 1924. Wright's special foundation and design allowed the hotel to withstand the worst stresses that nature could produce.

Our own foundation in life is equally important to help us withstand the stress and turmoil that inevitably come our way. The Lord Jesus in a parable contrasted two men, one who built his home on sand, the other on solid rock. When the rains and floods came, one house was washed away; the other was able to stand because of its firm foundation on the rock. *[Matthew 7:24–27]*

In our scripture reading for today, Saint Paul wrote to the Church at Corinth, *"No other foundation can anyone lay than that which is laid in Christ Jesus."* He is the only secure foundation on which to build our lives. He alone can save.

PRAYER: Thank you, Lord, for being the rock on which we can build, to withstand all the stresses and sorrows of this life. AMEN.

JANUARY 4

THE LIGHT OF THE WORLD

(Scripture to ponder: Matthew 5:14–16)

When I was a boy my father had a new gas furnace installed. He put in an additional line for a gaslight in the garden. I helped bury the long aluminum tubing from the basement window frame, under the lawn, to a post supporting the gaslight in the garden.

This light burned all the time but was barely visible during the day. As dusk came and darkness fell, the area of the garden walkway was suffused with a marvelous, silvery light. It was the highlight of our back yard, and it only cost about a penny a day.

One evening we noticed the light no longer burned. I checked the mantles and they were intact. But I could smell gas around the base of the lamppost. We discovered that a new gardener who had dug up the flowerbed that day had chopped through the line with a spade. Severed from its source, our lovely light went out.

In today's Scripture, Jesus says we Christians are the light of the world. If we stay connected to the source, to God, we can indeed shine brightly for Him. We do that by prayer and by meditating on His Word. But if we become severed from the source, our light goes out. Since God would have our light shine to His glory, we need to stay connected to the source.

PRAYER: **Help us always be connected to You, Lord, so our light shines out so others may see and also glorify You. AMEN.**

JANUARY 5

SINGLE COALS GO OUT

(Scripture to ponder: Hebrews 10: 24–25)

When I was a medical student living on a limited budget, I saved money by separating the burning barbecue briquettes after grilling hamburgers so they'd cool off and I could use them again.

One Sunday after I'd barbequed hamburgers the night before, a medical missionary spoke in our church about his work in Southeast Asia. He described the fate of persons who had traveled many miles to be treated at their hospital and had been converted to Christianity in the course of their recovery. As new Christians they were nurtured in the warmth of the fellowship of the medical center, but when they returned to the pagan, inhospitable environment of the villages from which they had come, their faith faltered.

"**Single coals go out,**" was the expression the missionary used—and with my barbecue experience, I knew just what he meant. We need the warmth and encouragement of fellow Christians in the church to help us grow and to stoke the fires of our faith. St. Paul speaks of this in our Scripture selection for today, when he writes,

> "In response for all he has done for us, let us outdo each other in being helpful and kind to each other and in doing good. Let us not neglect our church meetings as some people do, but encourage and warn each other, especially now that the day of his coming back again is drawing near."
>
> [TLB]

PRAYER: Help us dear Lord to seek fellowship with other members of Christ's body, so our faith grows and glows with your love, to do your will. In Jesus' name we pray, AMEN.

JANUARY 6

BEING WATCHED

(Scripture to ponder: Matthew 10:26–33)

Refugees who emigrated from the Soviet Union during the years of the repressive Communist regime have almost universally commented about how unpleasant it was to live in a society where you're constantly being watched. The network of reporting, of accusation and of KGB agents produced a situation that was the fulfillment of George

Orwell's novel *1984.* Russian society was stifling and pervaded by mediocrity. It seems nobody likes being watched.

But there is another sense of being watched that is a good sense, one that Christians are especially aware of and grateful for. It is the belief that someone is watching over us, someone is looking out for us. We are being watched by God, who protects us. It is the Christian's great source of comfort, joy and happiness. In today's Scripture passage from the Sermon on the Mount, Jesus asserts that even a sparrow is of value in the sight of God *[Matthew 10:29],* and we are more valuable than sparrows. Do you remember the song?

I sing because I'm happy, I sing because I'm free!
His eye is on the sparrow, and I know He watches me!

PRAYER: We are blessed and grateful that indeed you do watch over us. Thank You for being our Lord, our God and our Protector. AMEN.

JANUARY 7

AN ATTITUDE OF GRATITUDE

(Scripture to ponder: Colossians 3:15)

Twice in my life I have had the privilege of living abroad, once in the 1950s in rural Austria and again in the 1960s in India. Both times I lived with families, as a member of a program called The Experiment in International Living. Each time the circumstance in which I lived was very different from my home life in America. I was raised in a much more affluent environment and had many more possessions and advantages than those with whom I lived abroad.

I realized each time that my home circumstances had nothing to do with me, nor with my accomplishments: it was rather by the Grace of God that I was well off. Though not so affluent, the families with whom I stayed were full of joy and were very generous to me. From that experience, I realized, as the scripture says, that *happiness does not consist of the abundance of one's possessions. [Luke 12:15]*

I realized, too, that an *attitude of gratitude* characterized those families. They were happy, despite meager circumstances. It's the opposite of an *attitude of entitlement*, which unfortunately too many of us have in this country. Compared to most of the people in the world, we have so much.

In our Scripture passage for today, St. Paul urges the Church at Colossi to be thankful, to have an attitude of gratitude.

PRAYER: **Heavenly Father, help us to be grateful for the many gifts You have given us. Make us ever mindful of the blessings we have and help us to share our time, our talents, and our possessions with others. Place within our hearts an attitude of gratitude. We ask it in Jesus' name. AMEN.**

JANUARY 8

PLOUGHING LOOKING BACKWARD

(Scripture to ponder: Luke 9:57–62)

I was once a coxswain on a high school rowing team that won the National Championship. I got a bit of advice from the coach early on that was helpful, and I've cherished it ever since: "**Pick a distant landmark and steer for that.**" It's a secret of success in crew races, and in life.

Jesus was speaking in a similar vein when He said, *"No one who puts his hand to the plough and looks back is fit for the kingdom of God." [Luke 9:62]* To plough a straight furrow, just as to steer a straight course, one must look forward, look ahead, not behind.

In our lives, we Christians indeed look ahead and not back. The writer of the Letter to the Hebrews says, *"Let us look therefore to Jesus, the author and finisher of our Faith." [Hebrews 12:2]* We look to Him, the Son of God, the Risen Christ, as our leader and our Lord. Following His example we can indeed steer a course that is unwavering, if we keep our eyes on Him. Recall Peter, *[Matthew 14:28]* who was able to walk across the waves so long as he kept his eyes on the Master. And we, too, in these perilous times, must focus our gaze not on the troubled waters around us but upon our Savior and our God, who shows us the way.

PRAYER: Help us keep our eyes upon you, dear Lord, no matter what our circumstances. Lead us and show us your way. AMEN.

JANUARY 9

SMALL THINGS

(Scripture to ponder: Zechariah 4:10)

At breakfast recently, while opening a new box of cereal, my wife Diane told me a story
about her youth. As a child she liked a certain cereal called *Krumbles*. One day she asked
her mother if she could send away for a special spoon featured on the box, obtainable for
a dollar and a box top. She sent for it and for years used that spoon at breakfast. Reflecting on it, Diane said, "**I cherished that spoon for years. It had no material value whatsoever, but to me it was a treasure.**"

I got to thinking about the toys that children often bring to the hospital with them
when they undergo major surgery. A stuffed animal, a teddy-bear, or similar favorite
toy has little intrinsic value, but it can has great meaning to the child. The smart surgeon or anesthesiologist knows its importance in insuring a smooth induction of general anesthesia for a child. Any doctor scorns such small things at his peril.

Our Scripture passage speaks of small things. The prophet Zechariah asks,

"Who has despised the day of small things?"

Isn't it marvelous that our God, who has created the Cosmos and set the stars and
planets in their orbits, who's created the vast realm of Nature with all its diversity,
who makes no two sunsets nor any two snowflakes the same, that this God of ours is
also concerned for the fall of a sparrow? That He's not just involved with vastness, but
with small things as well? That He runs the universe, yet cares for you and for me?
That He loves each of us?

PRAYER: We bless and praise You O Lord, for You are indeed the God of great and small things. We give You thanks that You care for each of us. Help us do Your will. AMEN.

JANUARY 10

CALLED BY GOD

(Scriptures to ponder: Mark 1:16; Luke 22:31–34; John 21:15–18)

What does it mean to be called by God? It's a puzzling, even a vexing question for many of us. We gain insight if we look at the life of the Apostle Peter, when he was called by Christ. I see three lessons.

First, as we read in *Mark 1:16, Christ meets us where we are.* Peter was a fisherman, and it was in a boat by the Sea of Galilee that he encountered the Lord and received the call. We don't need to look here or look there, or travel to exotic places to meet the Lord, for he meets us right where we are.

Second, *because we are called doesn't mean we'll never falter.* St. Luke [22:31–34] relates Christ's prediction that Peter will falter, and then Luke quotes Peter's rejoinder that he's ready to go to prison or even die for his sake. But Luke gives Jesus' blunt assertion that Peter will deny him three times before the night is through. But he also tells Peter that when Peter has once again turned back to the Lord, Peter will go on to strengthen his brothers.

Finally, *God's call produces Godly action and encouragement.* His call never means we are called to act against God's will as revealed in Scripture. It *does* mean we'll act to encourage others in their Christian walk. After his resurrection, as related in *John 21*, Christ once again encounters Peter and his brothers fishing. Three times the Lord asks Peter if he loves him, and each time Christ responds to Peter's affirmations with the same charge: *"Feed my sheep"*—recalling his earlier prediction that Peter would strengthen his brothers.

PRAYER: Make us sensitive, O Lord, to hear your call, just where we are. Forgive us when we falter, and strengthen us to encourage others in the Faith, that we may all do your will. AMEN.

JANUARY 11

CLEARING THE CLUTTER

(Scripture to ponder: Matthew 8:18–22)

When I was a medical student I learned a great lesson, one that helped me later in my career. I learned it from my pastor, Dr. Arthur M. Adams, who at the time was senior pastor of Central Presbyterian Church in Rochester, NY.

I sought Dr. Adams' counsel about a problem I was having, the nature of which I don't even remember now as I write years later. But I distinctly recall the manner in which he received me, and therein was the lesson that stuck with me. We met in his office. I was used to the offices of my medical professors, whose desks were piled high with journals, books and mail.

But Dr. Adams' desk was immaculately clean. It wasn't that he didn't have journals, books and mail in his office; he did. But they weren't on his desk. Instead, they were stacked on a long table behind his desk, behind his chair. So when he spoke to me—and listened to me—across the desk, I felt he was giving me his undivided attention. No beepers went off, no phones rang, in the fifteen minutes or so that I counseled with him.

When I went into practice and set up my first office, I modeled the arrangement that I'd seen in Dr. Adams' office. In my career, I've probably not been as good a listener as he was, but taking a page from his book, I've tried to not let clutter or interruptions impair my relationship with a patient. Over the years several patients commented favorably about the setup.

I think God wants our prayer time and our devotional life to be equally uncluttered and uninterrupted, so we communicate well. Jesus wants us who have chosen to follow him to have our priorities in order, so nothing comes between us.

PRAYER: Help us unclutter our lives and remove all distractions that keep us from truly listening to you, O Lord. AMEN.

JANUARY 12

CLEANING UP OUR THOUGHTS

(Scripture to ponder: Philippians 4:8)

Do you remember the song from *South Pacific* called, "I'm Gonna Wash That Man Right Outta My Hair?" I heard it recently and it reminded me of a story told by the famous preacher Norman Vincent Peale.[1]

Before a speaking engagement in Chicago, Dr. Peale had a couple of hours to spare and at his wife's urging decided to get a haircut. He told the girl at the counter that all he wanted was a haircut, and was shown into a barber's chair. But soon someone came along and leaned the chair way back, almost flat, and pulled a plastic cover over his torso. Then he felt water on his head. He asked what was happening. The technician said he was getting a shampoo. When he protested he didn't want a shampoo, he was told there was no extra charge, and "The rules of the house say you have to have a shampoo." He assented, figuring it wouldn't hurt.

Then the barber stepped up and explained what was happening:

"We give everyone a shampoo before we work on their hair because it helps the hair respond to our treatment. Besides, our business isn't merely to cut hair. Our business is to work with the personality. We want all of our customers to walk out of this shop feeling positive and happy. In order to do that, we have to start with a shampoo. Perhaps we could do better for our customers if we could shampoo the inside of the head as well. Then, we'd wash out all those miserable, old thoughts that prevent them from the enjoyment and delights of life. We want our people to walk out of this shop not only clean on the outside but clean on the inside."

Peale was enthusiastic and said, "You and I are in the same business! I've got a place on Fifth Avenue in New York City where we do exactly the same thing. Only, we probably don't get as much money as you do."

The barber asked for his name, and on hearing it, said, "**Dr. Peale, I got my ideas from listening to broadcasts of your sermons!**"

It's a cute story that does point up the importance, in this New Year, of cleaning house in our thoughts and minds, and of thinking on good things, as St. Paul urges in our Scripture passage from his Letter to the Philippians.

PRAYER: **Help us, O Lord, to think on those things that are true, honorable, just, pure, lovely, gracious, excellent, and praiseworthy. Help us be imitators of Your Son Jesus, our Savior. AMEN.**

JANUARY 13

HIS GLORIOUS INHERITANCE

(Scripture to ponder: Ephesians 1:18 & Colossians 1:12)

I've had many instances of grace—that is, of unmerited favor—in my life. One in particular stands out, an unexpected inheritance I got from my Aunt Helen, the sister of my father.

Aunt Helen and Uncle John lived across the country in Pasadena, CA. Since we lived in Philadelphia, we rarely saw them. Their only child Joe, was named after my father. Joe was a year older than my oldest sister Jane. Although I saw my cousin once or twice in my childhood, I didn't know him well because he died shortly after graduating from college. He was a Phi Beta Kappa graduate of Pomona College who'd signed up for the Air Force at the time of the Korean War.

The weekend before he was to be shipped out, he made a long drive home to see his folks. He fell asleep at the wheel, ran off the road and hit a tree. His death was a crushing blow to his father, who thereafter developed severe hypertension. Uncle John died a few years later. Aunt Helen survived him for many years and I was able to visit her several times in Pasadena.

After Aunt Helen died, my sisters and I were surprised to receive an inheritance from her. For me, that inheritance came just after I finished my surgical residency, when I was at a financial low point. It enabled me to make a down payment on a home.

As Christians, we've received an inheritance far more valuable than the money my aunt left me: It's the knowledge of salvation, of our acceptance as children of God into his everlasting Kingdom. We're saved through God's grace, not because of who we are, or what we've done, but because of who Christ is and what he's done. It's a free gift we have only to acknowledge to receive. Confessing our sins and accepting God's forgiveness is all it takes to claim this wonderful inheritance.

PRAYER: We bless you, O Lord, for the glorious inheritance we have through your Son, our Savior, Jesus Christ: the Gift of Eternal Life. May we be a blessing to others. AMEN.

JANUARY 14

ESTABLISHMENT—OR FREE EXERCISE?

(Scripture to ponder: Luke 20:25)

Many legal controversies have been raised about the separation of Church and State in America. A recent one—a Federal Appeals Court decision that including the words "under God" in the Pledge of Allegiance was unconstitutional—prompted me to look at our nation's history and at its Constitution.

America was settled by immigrants, many of whom were fleeing from religious persecution in the countries of Europe. Colonial America manifested a religious diversity, that varied from the tolerance of Quaker Pennsylvania to the near theocracy of early Salem Massachusetts. Our forefathers who framed the Constitution after the Revolutionary War were certainly *not* Godless men, but they saw the evils of a church that was backed, endorsed and supported by the state, as was present in England. English history was punctuated by intolerance and bloodshed, depending on the religious persuasion of the monarch, whether Catholic or Protestant.

So the Bill of Rights—the first ten amendments of the United States Constitution— begins as follows:

"Congress shall make no law respecting an establishment of religion, or prohibiting the free exercise thereof;"

Obviously, it's the Supreme Court that will interpret those words, but it seems to me that "under God" is hardly the establishment of a religion. Not only did our patriotic forbears believe in God, but our government's history and documents are replete with allusions to God, from the motto, "**In God We Trust**" on our currency, to our swearing on the witness stand in our courts of law, "**So help me God.**"

PRAYER: **We cherish our government and its traditions, O Lord. May we ever be loyal and patriotic. But let us always render unto you our Worship and our Praise. AMEN.**

JANUARY 15

DENIAL, DECEPTION AND DETERMINATION

(Scripture to ponder: Philippians 3:13–14)

Recently I read in an excellent biography of Franklin Delano Roosevelt (FDR) about FDR's bout with polio[2]. Although most people who got that disease were children (its other name is infantile paralysis), when Roosevelt came down with it in 1921, he was 39. He had served as assistant secretary of the navy in Woodrow Wilson's administration and was gearing up to run for the U.S. senate seat from New York. His political career was just taking off.

He got sick while on vacation in northern Maine and the painful infection left him paralyzed from the waist down. At first Roosevelt's response to the disease was *denial*—initially he was sure he'd get back full use of his legs. Acceptance of his plight came only gradually.

As his career progressed, FDR's response to his disease was *deception*, a hiding of his disability from the public and the press. But through it all he manifested a fierce *determination*, one that allowed him to keep pressing on with his therapy and learn to stand on his legs with the help of metal braces, and even take a few halting steps.

Through the prism of history, we tend to overlook the denial and deception associated with Roosevelt's disease, and remember the fierce determination that pressed him on to great accomplishments.

St. Paul speaks of his "thorn in the flesh," a malady that scholars have puzzled over, some sort of health problem that kept him humble. For St. Paul, denial and deception were lacking, but he displays the same fierce determination to get on with the Lord's work. In our Scripture passage for today, he too calls it pressing on:

"This one thing I do, forgetting what lies behind and straining toward what lies ahead, I press on toward the goal of the prize of the upward call of God in Christ Jesus."

PRAYER: Give us, we pray, O Lord, the same fierce determination to press on toward the high calling of Your Son Jesus. Help us do Your will. In his name we pray. AMEN.

JANUARY 16

WHOM DO YOU BELIEVE?

(Scriptures to ponder: John 4:26; 9:37)

During a week I spent in England attending a special education course, I was browsing in Blackwell's Bookstore in Oxford. I entered the shop to look for a small copy of the *Book of Common Prayer* with which I'd followed the Eucharistic service in Christ Church Cathedral two days earlier. I found a copy but decided not to by it.

As I continued browsing, I saw a paperback book on one of the bookstore shelves, a recently published life of Jesus. Thumbing through it, I encountered a chapter entitled, "Was Jesus the Messiah?" As I scanned it, in one of the paragraphs I read this statement by the author: **"Jesus never claimed to be the Messiah."** It brought me up short, for it was patently false.

In my devotional reading just a few days earlier, I'd encountered two scriptures—our selections for today—that gave the lie to that author's assertion. The first occurred when Christ met the Samaritan woman at Jacob's well, the second when he opened the eyes of the blind man, who immediately thereafter was interrogated by the Pharisees. In both of these face-to-face encounters Jesus asserted he was the Messiah. Christ's assertion is quite plain and obvious.

I wonder how many people who read that paperback book will, not knowing better, believe the author's erroneous assertion.

We must be careful to test what we hear, as St. James counsels, and to check what we read against the authority of Scripture. Many there are who would lead us astray, some through ignorance, some through deceit. And it's sad to say that the Internet, marvelous as it is, just makes the problem worse: for there, there is no editor to cull out the errors and untruths.

PRAYER: **Through your Holy Spirit, Lord, help us discern the truth in all matters, that we may acknowledge, confess and believe in Your Son, our Savior Jesus Christ. AMEN.**

JANUARY 17

NO TURNING BACK

(Scripture to ponder: Luke 9:62; Philippians 3:13)

Do you recall the words of the old hymn?

"I have decided to follow Jesus—No turning back, no turning back."

When we choose to follow Jesus, it may mean peril and facing the unknown. Do we resolve to follow him no matter what, with no prospect of turning back? It's sometimes not an easy decision.

The Spanish explorer Hernan Cortes faced such an issue when he set out to explore Mexico in 1519. He knew some of his men had reservations about pressing on into an uncharted region, beyond the known world. He could have given his men a pep talk to increase their fortitude; but he did something far more dramatic—and irreversible. After they landed on the Mexican coast and unloaded their supplies, Cortes ordered the men to strip the ships of sails, yardage, fittings and cannon. Then he set fire to the boats. In scuttling the ships, he committed himself and his men to the future of their endeavor: Survive, prevail, or die. By that bold step he compelled his men to conquer and to overcome all future impediments and obstacles.

Cortes' action is reflected in the words of Jesus and of St. Paul in our Scriptures for today. When Jesus set his face toward Jerusalem—despite knowing what suffering and agony awaited him there—he said:

"No one who puts his hand to the plough and looks back is fit for the kingdom of God."
[Luke 9:62]

Likewise, St. Paul wrote to the Church at Philippi, of his own mission:

"Forgetting what lies behind and straining forward to what lies ahead, I press on toward the goal for the prize of the upward call of God in Christ Jesus."
[Philippians 3:13]

PRAYER: We have heard your call, O Lord, and have decided to follow you. Help us resolve, as though we had burned our own ships, to serve you and do your will, with no turning back. AMEN.

JANUARY 18

OPENING THE DOOR TO THE LORD

(Scripture to ponder: Revelation 3:20)

In today's Scripture, St. John describes Jesus as standing at the door, knocking. I believe Christ knocks at our door many times during our lives, that the opportunities are many to welcome and serve him.

Whenever I read or hear that passage from Revelation, I think of a time during one of my medical school vacations when I installed a garage door opener for one of our family friends. I'd worked for several summers as a carpenter's apprentice; I thought

I'd learned a lot, so decided to make some money doing odd jobs during that vacation. Pride goes before a fall.

I had all the tools I needed, for I'd set aside money during my summers to buy a tool each week. The installation of the automatic door went smoothly, and I was pleased with the result. The door had a special electronic remote control—a relatively new device in those days—with which the owner could open it as he drove in the driveway. I demonstrated it for him. He too was pleased.

But a few days later, I got a call from the man. He said every couple hours his garage door would open and shut, open and shut for about three minutes. Then it either stayed open or remained shut for about two hours, and then it started all over again. It was totally unpredictable. I went over to his house to check it out, and, sure enough, it soon began the cycle of *open-shut-open-shut-open shut* that went on for several minutes and then stopped with the door open. We were mystified.

I took the remote control back to where I'd purchased it and the store owner called the distributor. From him we discovered what had happened. (He'd had another remote returned fro the same reason.) The electronic frequency for the device was the same signal being transmitted by a recently launched satellite, which passed overhead for several minutes every two hours. We solved the problem by changing the frequency of the door's system. All of us got a laugh out of it.

PRAYER: **May we always be ready to open the door to invite you in when you knock, O Lord. Make our hearts receptive and responsive to your bidding. AMEN.**

JANUARY 19

THE MYSTERY OF THE TRINITY

(Scripture to ponder: Acts 1:1–8)

When I was growing up I was confused about the Trinity, and did not understand how God and Jesus and the Holy Spirit could all be one, or co-equal. As I became increasingly familiar with the Bible (by the time I finished college I'd read it through cover-to-cover twice), I realized that the Trinity was nowhere referred to by name, or as the Trinity in the Scriptures.

But as I acquired an overview of what the scriptures actually were—namely, the account of God's revealing Himself to a people, as perceived by them in the events of their history—the Trinity began to make sense. Here's how I see it.

God created the universe and within it the earth and all life on it. He created man and gave him—gave mankind—dominion over all the earth. The means by which this was accomplished was the Spirit—as in Genesis, for example, when the earth was without form and void, and the Spirit of God moved across the face of the water. God also was breathed the Spirit into man to give him life, creating him in His image.

But throughout history—from the time in the Garden of Eden up to the present—despite God's warnings and reminders, man has followed his own desires and not God's ways. Created by God to be in fellowship with Him, man's rebellion alienated him from God. So God finally sent his Son—born of the Spirit to a woman—to be the savior of mankind. After Jesus was crucified, the Spirit was again sent as counselor and helper, to empower those who heard and responded to God's will. The Spirit is still active today, empowering the church.

So although the Trinity is not mentioned per se in the Bible, it is through the action of the Trinity—by the Father, by the Son and by the Holy Spirit—that mankind will be saved.

PRAYER: We worship you, O Lord, as creator, and bless You for sending first your Son, to show us the way, and then the Holy Spirit to empower us to follow it. AMEN.

JANUARY 20

CHRISTIAN WEAKNESS

(Scripture to ponder: 2 Corinthians 12:10)

One of the great paradoxes—and also one of the great secrets—of the Christian Faith is contained in today's scripture text. St. Paul writes: *"When I am weak, then I am strong."*

How can one become strong because of weakness? How can this be? Doesn't weakness lead to exhaustion and failure?

What I believe Paul means is that if we truly acknowledge our weakness, our helplessness before God, His power through the Holy Spirit is released to work through us. It's a phenomenon that for Christians has been repeated countless times through history. Let me share one recent example.

It strengthened Martin Luther King, Jr, during his darkest hour. Philip Yancey tells the story[3]. After Rosa Parks had refused to move to the back of the bus in Montgomery, AL, King had been thrust into leading the civil rights boycott. The KKK threatened to bomb his home and harm to his family. Late one night he sat alone at the kitchen table. He could see his wife and infant daughter asleep in the next room. He was fearful. Here's how he described it later in a sermon:

> "And I sat at that table thinking about that little girl and thinking about the fact that she could be taken away from me any minute. And I started thinking about a dedicated, devoted and loyal wife, who was over there asleep . . . And I got to the point that I couldn't take it any more. I was weak.

> "And I discovered then that religion had to become real to me. I had to know God for myself. And I bowed down over that cup of coffee. I never will forget it . . . I prayed a prayer and I prayed out loud that night. I said, "Lord, I'm down here trying to do what's right. I think I'm right. I think the cause that we represent is right. But Lord, I must confess that I'm weak now. I'm faltering. I'm losing my courage."

> ". . . And it seemed at that moment that I could hear an inner voice saying to me, "Martin Luther, stand up for righteousness. Sand up for justice. Stand up for truth. And lo I will be with you, even unto the end of the world." . . . I heard the voice of Jesus saying still to fight on. He promised never to leave me, never to leave me alone. No never alone. No never alone . . ."

When king was weak and faltering, his confession to God became the source of his resolve and his strength—God's Strength—to go on, despite all the dangers. And eventually, it cost him his life.

PRAYER: O Lord, we see so much sadness, grief and evil in the world, and we are so weak and helpless without Your strength. Empower us through Your Holy Spirit to do your Will and follow Your Way. AMEN.

JANUARY 21

THE BOOK AND THE BIG SCREEN

(Scripture to ponder: 2 Samuel, Chapters 11and 12)

Ever since the invention of the movies, Biblical subjects have been popular in cinema. I recall as a teenager seeing Victor Mature play Samson, and a few years later watching Charlton Heston portray Moses in C.B. Demille's extravaganza *The Ten Commandments.*

As one reads through the Bible, many of the characters of the *Old Testament* seem larger than life; but that's no reason for filmmakers to portray them untrue to life, that is, to change their personalities by falsifying the Biblical record. But that's what happened in a 1985 movie entitled *King David.* Hear this from film critic Michael Medved:[4]

> **"This Godzilla-sized turkey cost 28 million to produce and attracted less than three million in ticket sales. It featured Richard Gere in the title role—a bizarre casting choice that led industry wags to refer to it as** *An Israelite and a Gentleman.* **Most of all, the film advanced the radical—and totally unsupported—notion that the Biblical king freed himself from his religious "illusions" at the end of his life. The concluding sequence shows a suddenly enlightened David violently rejecting God as he smashes the scale model of the temple he had previously intended to build."**

No such event occurred, of course, in the *Bible*. Rather, the scripture says that David was "a man after God's own heart." David was a complex character, a leader who sinned grievously by committing murder to cover his adultery with Bathsheba. Our Bible selection for today relates these events in 2d Samuel. As a result of David's sin with Bathsheba, the baby died; but after David turned in repentance to God, a second child of his union with her was Solomon, who succeeded David as king. During Solomon's reign the great temple was built in Jerusalem.

There was no need to alter King David's character for a movie!

PRAYER: **The mighty men of old were dear to You, O Lord, because they were real and honest. Help us to be so, too, and to love You with our whole heart. Forgive our sins, we pray. AMEN.**

JANUARY 22

GETTING INTO HEAVEN

(Scriptures to ponder: Acts 4:12; Ephesians 2:8)

Two pastors[5] told a humorous story recently about a man who appeared at the Pearly Gates, who wanted to get into heaven. Saint Peter met him and said it required a total of one hundred points and began to quiz the man about his life.

"I was a faithful husband for fifty years and never so much as looked at another woman," he told the Apostle.

"That gets you two points," replied St. Peter. The man was taken a bit back.

"I was Father of the Year and never lost touch with my children."

"Another two points," was the reply. The man grew a bit frantic.

"Well," he said, "I worked in a soup kitchen once a week for ten years." Saint Peter nodded and added on another two points.

"Wow! Only six points thus far!" exclaimed the man. **"It looks like the only way I'll get into heaven is by the grace of God!"**

"You get a hundred points for that answer," responded St. Peter. "Come on in!"

That story makes us chuckle, but it's Biblically sound. In our scripture for today, St. Paul proclaims, *"By grace are you saved, through faith; and not of yourselves: it is the Gift of God."* From the earliest times people have sought to earn their way into heaven by good works. But since we are all imperfect sinners, it's rather by God's free gift in Christ Jesus that we are saved.

PRAYER: **There is indeed no other Name by which we can be saved, O Lord, than that of your son, Jesus the Christ. AMEN.**

JANUARY 23

NOURISHING THE BODY

(Scripture to ponder: 1 Corinthians 12:12, 27)

In his first letter to the church at Corinth, St. Paul uses the analogy of the body and its members. *"You are the body of Christ and individually members of it." [1 Corinthians 12:27]* He speaks of how the body is not just one member—an eye or an ear or a foot— but is all members working together. They are all knit and tied together, so when one suffers, all suffer. And Christ is the head.

What ties them all together? I think that St. Paul, had he been a physician, would have gone on to assert that it's the nervous system that ties all the parts together. Through it we process all we take in through our senses: sight, taste, hearing, smell, touch. Through it we stimulate our muscles to move. Physiologically, the nervous system keeps all parts in touch.

But even more fundamental than the nervous system is *the blood*, for through the blood comes the very nourishment of the body. The blood is the means by which the whole body is sustained. The ancient Hebrews realized this, for they asserted, *"The life is in the blood," [Leviticus 17:14] and* formed an elaborate kosher system around it.

Under the new dispensation, under the Lordship of Christ, this concept is carried even further, for it is the Holy Spirit that sustains the body of Christ, just as it is the blood that nourishes all parts of our own human bodies. The Holy Spirit, the Counselor, the Comforter nourishes us individually, and as the Body of Christ.

Understanding that it's the Blood of Christ, through the Holy Spirit, that feeds and sustains all the members of the Body of Christ, gives new meaning to our communion and our life together.

PRAYER: Nourish us and sustain us, O Lord, through your blood, that we may all be one body to do your will. AMEN.

JANUARY 24

THE IRONY OF AFFLUENCE

(Scripture to ponder: I Corinthians 6:12–20)

I'm watching a popular T.V. show. In the center of the screen a man is sitting on an examination table in a doctor's office. He's recently been diagnosed with type II (adult onset) diabetes. The emphasis of the program is the increasing costs of medical care. They discuss specific therapy for this man, focusing on "high-tech" treatments such as implantable insulin pumps, computerized blood sugar monitors, and new, expensive drugs. What is *not* mentioned in the commentary, but what's obvious to my eye, is that **this patient is at least 50 lbs overweight.**

In a sense, he has an *illness of affluence.* Isn't it peculiar that on one hand we decry the high costs of modern medical care while on the other we simultaneously extol the great "progress" made through expensive technology and widely advertise the benefits of new, costly drugs? For the *irony of affluence* is that much illness in American society is caused by overindulgence in tobacco, alcohol and food.

Studies show that about half of Americans are obese. Millions of our citizens suffer from complications of obesity, including hypertension, coronary heart disease and diabetes. Mere lip service is paid to the relatively cheap treatment of weight loss, while great press is given to new, costly drugs and fancy surgery like gastric bypass. Yet—to return to the fat man on the T.V. screen—we doctors know that his type II diabetes would probably disappear if he lost 50 lbs. *But that's too much to ask of a self-indulgent population.* We want someone else to do it for us—the doctor with his pills, the nurse with her "patient education program," or the surgeon with his scalpel. It's a topsy-turvy world!

St. Paul asserted: *"Your body is the Temple of the Holy Spirit."* [1Corinthians 6:19] We can defile it with excess calories as surely as we can with tobacco.

PRAYER: **Simplify our lives, O Lord. Keep us from any overindulgence that defiles our bodies, the Temple of your Spirit. AMEN.**

JANUARY 25

THE TRAP OF UPWARD MOBILITY

(Scripture to ponder: Matthew 25:40; Luke 9:1–6)

America has always been regarded as the land of opportunity. In the wake of the terrorist attacks of September 11, 2001, a number of patriotic books have been published with titles like *Where We Stand*[6] or *Why We Fight*[7]. A third book, entitled *What's So Great About America,*[8] has this to say this about our country:

> **"By separating religion from government, and by directing the energies of the citizens toward trade and commerce, the American founders created a rich, dynamic and tolerant society that is now the hope of countless immigrants, and a magnet for the world."**

One characteristic of this "rich, dynamic and tolerant society" that has appealed to many is its **upward mobility**—the notion that by hard work and frugality one can better one's self.

But some folks seem to equate Christianity with American society, and in so doing, get caught in what I'd call "the upward mobility trap." Most Americans don't know that the axiom **"God helps those who help themselves"** comes not from the *Bible*, but *from Poor Richard's Almanac.*

I believe a close and careful reading of the Gospels, using the life of Jesus as our example, shows that the Christian life is what might be called "the way of downward mobility," to use the phrase of Henri J. Nouwen. Instead of striving to make it to the top, Christians follow our Lord's injunction to *"heal the sick, to feed the poor, and to visit those in prison."* Instead of expecting to be served or waited on, the followers of Jesus dedicate themselves to serving others, especially those less fortunate. So in some respects, the Christian Life is, perhaps, one of downward mobility.

PRAYER: We are grateful, O Lord, to be born in this great land. Help us to realize that "of whom much is given, much is also expected." May we always do your will in every aspect of our lives. AMEN.

JANUARY 26

THE EYE OF THE NEEDLE

(Scripture to ponder: Luke 18:18–30)

Contemporary novelist Ken Follett wrote a thriller called *The Eye of the Needle* about a German agent in Scotland during World War II. The man would call out on his secret, short-wave radio saying, "Hier is die Nadel,"—which means "Here is the Needle," his spy code name.

In today's scripture verse, Jesus alludes to the eye of a needle when he teaches about worldly riches. A rich Jewish leader has just asked what he needs to do to inherit Eternal Life. Jesus tells him to obey the commandments: *"Don't commit adultery, don't kill, don't steal, don't bear false witness, honor your father and mother."*

The ruler says he's observed all those commandments from his youth. Jesus, perceiving what his real hang-up was, says, *"Sell all you have and distribute it to the poor, and you will have treasure in heaven; and come, follow me."*

The rich ruler couldn't do it, and Jesus comments, *"It's easier for a camel to go through the eye of a needle than for a rich man to enter the Kingdom of God."*

What a peculiar phrase! What did Jesus mean by it? Some commentators believe Jesus was being witty, referring to one of the huge entry gates in the Jerusalem wall, called The Needle. In the middle of that large gate was a smaller door that would just admit a man—a door known as *the eye of the needle*. If a camel got through it at all, it would be with difficulty, and only by going down on its knees.

Do you suppose Jesus meant that those who were rich could indeed get into the Kingdom, but only with difficulty—by getting down on their knees?

PRAYER: Dear Lord, help us not let possessions or wealth or anything else keep us from loving and following You. AMEN.

JANUARY 27

THE FOUR "Rs" OF BIBLE STUDY

(Scripture to ponder: 1 Samuel 3:1–15)

We all know about the "three Rs" of education, "Reading, 'Riting and 'Rithmetic, which form the basis for elementary, and indeed are the foundation of all education. Similarly, as part of a Christian's education, "four Rs" have been described as a basis for *spiritual reading*. It is an ancient and central practice of the spiritual life that originated in the middle ages, called *lectio divina*. The "four Rs" of this discipline are: **Reading, Reflecting, Responding and Resting.**

Here's how it's done. Begin by simply **Reading** a passage of Scripture, asking God to open your heart to the message. Then, **Reflecting** on the passage, ask the Lord, *"What are You saying to me today through Your Word, Lord?"* This is done with an expectancy similar to the advice given by Eli to the boy Samuel, when Eli realized that God was calling the boy (today's Scripture, 1 Samuel 3). Eli told Samuel to respond, *"Speak, for thy servant is listening!" [1 Samuel 3:10]* As we **Reflect** on the passage of Scripture, we prepare our hearts to be attentive God's voice, and prepare our minds to **Respond** to His Word.

As we listen and enter into a particular passage of Scripture, and as we perceive the message God has for us in the Word, we will be moved to **Respond.** That response does not always mean that we will react or take action. It may even lead us to repentance or remorse, convicting us of our own sinfulness, as God draws us closer.

Finally, we **Rest,** secure in the knowledge that we belong to Christ, and that Christ is God's. We rejoice with St. Paul, who said:

"I am convinced that neither death nor life, neither angels nor demons, neither the present nor the future, nor any powers, neither height nor depth, nor anything else in all creation will be able to separate us from the love of God that is in Christ Jesus our Lord."

[Rom. 8:38]

PRAYER: Open our hearts, and by Your Spirit direct us, as we Read, Reflect, Respond, and Rest in You, O Lord. AMEN.

JANUARY 28

SEEKING AFTER WISDOM

(Scripture to ponder: 1 Kings 3:5–14)

Have you ever lost something so valuable that you stopped everything else to look for it, and didn't give up until you carefully retraced your steps and searched diligently for it? It happened to me once with my car keys, making me go back and search until I finally found them in a coat pocket in the closet. I looked long and hard!

Do you remember the parable our Lord told of the treasure hid in a field that a man sold everything he owned so he could buy that field? You can imagine how great that treasure must have been, for someone to sell all to buy that field. He must have wanted it badly.

I'm impressed that many people say they'd like to have faith, or like to have wisdom, but are unwilling to expend the energy and effort to gain them. Solomon, reputed to be the wisest man who ever lived, said this:

If you will receive my words and treasure my commandments within you, Make your ear attentive to wisdom, incline your heart to understanding; If you cry for discernment, lift your voice for understanding, If you seek her as silver, search for her as for hidden treasures; Then you will discern the fear of the Lord and discover the knowledge of God.
[Proverbs 2:1–5]

We read in Chapter 3 of First Kings that God told Solomon that He would grant whatever request he made. Solomon asked not for riches, nor honor, nor fame. Rather, he asked for *wisdom* to lead his people. And because he did so, God gave him wisdom *and* honor *and* fame *and* riches.

PRAYER: Grant us diligence, Dear Lord, to seek wisdom and understanding, through prayer and meditating on Your word. AMEN.

JANUARY 29

FROM THE CRUCIBLE OF SUFFERING

(Scripture to ponder: 2 Corinthians 1:5–8)

Thomas R. Kelly, a Quaker who taught at Haverford College near Philadelphia, is one of my favorite devotional writers. I was introduced to his major work, *A Testament of Devotion,* by my pastor, during my medical school years.

Kelly was raised on a farm in the Midwest and attended a small Quaker school, Wilmington College, in Ohio. He won a scholarship and transferred to Haverford College, where he was befriended by Professor Rufus Jones, the man who first introduced him to the mystical aspects of Quakerism.

I am always moved when I reread Thomas Kelly's *Testament* because I sense an authenticity that comes only from a heart that is close to the Lord Jesus. From Richard J. Foster[9] I gained insight as to why these writings from Kelly's final years are so stirring. He attributes it to two moving experiences. First, Kelly's hopes for a Ph.D. from Harvard were dashed in 1937, when—despite great study and preparation—his mind went blank during his oral exams and he failed miserably. He sank into a deep depression.

Within a year, however, his soul was immeasurably deepened during a trip to Germany, where he saw and shared the suffering of Christian brothers under Hitler's Third Reich. Of that trip, Kelly wrote:

> "I have never had such a soul-overturning . . . period as this. It is not merely heroism, it is depth of consecration, simplicity of faith, beauty in the midst of poverty or suffering that shames us. I have met some giant souls . . . One can't be the same again."

And, indeed, Thomas Kelly *wasn't* the same after that. For out of the crucible of suffering, his writings became suffused with enormous spiritual power, a power that draws the devotional reader into the very presence of God.

PRAYER: We praise You, O Lord, for sending saints like Thomas Kelly who transmit the power of Your Spirit to us. AMEN.

JANUARY 30

GOD'S HEALING PEACE

(Scripture to ponder: Psalm 23)

I have often reflected on the healing power of the 23d Psalm. The cadence and images evoked by that wonderful poem—of sheep cared for in lush meadows, being led beside still waters—are peaceful and healing. Indeed, through history the images of rivers running through pastures have always brought rest and refreshment to mind.

A research clinician once did a study of patients recovering from gallbladder surgery to see if the view out a hospital window could influence healing. His findings were published in the prestigious journal *Science*. He compared patients whose rooms faced out on a tree with those that viewed a parking lot. Those in the first group healed faster, required less medication postoperatively, and were discharged sooner than the group that looked out on the parking lot.

Just before he left his disciples, Jesus said, *"My peace I give unto you—not as the world gives."* [John 14:27] God's peace brings calmness, a security that prevails in the midst of a complex and tumultuous world. The quietness and confidence that comes from God is indeed the Healing Peace, so needed by individuals and society today.

PRAYER: **Amid all the bustle and hustle of this life, O Lord, grant us Your peace. Heal our bodies and restore our souls, that we may faithfully serve You. AMEN.**

JANUARY 31

GANDHI'S METHODS

(Scripture to ponder: Luke 6:27; John 15:13)

When I was in college, I had the privilege of spending a summer in India, living with five different families. I learned a lot about that vast land and its struggles. As I read the papers today about the ongoing slaughter in the Middle East, based on religious strife, and as I wonder about possible solutions, I ask myself if the methods of Mahatma Gandhi might not be relevant. But don't misunderstand me. Certainly, there has to be a political solution to the problems in Israel; eventually I suspect there will be two states in what was once the ancient Holy Land, a land populated by several ethnic groups in Biblical times. But how to stop the carnage and begin to talk peace?

The relevance of Gandhi today is often dismissed by those who say that although it worked with the British in Colonial India, it wouldn't work nowadays. I'm not so sure. For one of Gandhi's most powerful witnesses occurred not between the British and the Indians, but between the Hindus and the Muslims, engaged in terrible religious strife and killing at the time that independence was being negotiated. In 1947, as the politicians held their discussions in the elegant rooms of New Delhi, angry mobs of Hindus and Muslims began to slaughter one another in the villages of Northern India.[10]

Into the midst of that caldron of violence Gandhi went, at great risk to himself. He would stop in each village to read aloud passages from the Bhagavad-Gita, the Koran and the New Testament. In each town he persuaded one Hindu and one Muslim leader to move in together in the same house, and he asked them to pledge themselves to fast to the death if one of their own attacked an enemy. It worked. The killing subsided.

As I am sure you're aware, Gandhi was greatly influenced by the Lord Jesus, who taught, *"Love your enemies, do good unto those that hate you."* [Luke 6:27] The great sin in this world of ours is lack of love—love for God and love for one another. We must be willing to lay down our lives for one another, and follow the way of him who taught that

"Greater love hath no man, that he lay down his life for another."

[John 15:13]

PRAYER: Let us show our love for You, O Lord, by our sacrificial love for one another, even for our enemies, as Christ has loved us. AMEN.

FEBRUARY 1

LIVING IN THE PRESENT

(Scripture to ponder: Matthew 6:33–34)

Hear these words of Sir William Osler, the most respected physician of the twentieth century. It's his counsel to medical students and it is good advice to anyone:

"Live neither in the past, nor in the future, but let each day's work absorb all your interest, energy and enthusiasm. The best preparation for tomorrow is to do today's work superbly well."

Osler was born in Canada but became professor of Medicine in Pennsylvania, then at John's Hopkins and finally at Oxford, England. His writings are punctuated by allusions from classical literature and from the Bible.

Osler was the son of a clergyman and his advice on daily living comes straight from the Bible, from Jesus' Sermon on the Mount as recorded by St. Matthew. The King James Version records Jesus' words as *"Take no thought for the morrow."* Perhaps a better translation is given in the Revised Standard Version, which says, *"Be not anxious for tomorrow."* In other words, don't *worry* about tomorrow. Rather, concern yourself with doing today's tasks superbly well.

At the end of this section of the Sermon, Jesus gives us the key to successful living: *"Seek ye first the kingdom of God and His righteousness, and all these things will be given to you as well."* [Mt. 6:33]

PRAYER: Help us, O Lord, to do today's work superbly well, and seek Your kingdom and Your righteousness. AMEN.

FEBRUARY 2

THE POT OR THE PIPE?

(Scripture to ponder: Ephesians 5:18)

There's a Christian hymn popular in evangelical circles that goes:

> Fill my cup, O Lord, I lift it up, O Lord
> Come and quench this thirsting of my soul
> Bread of Heaven, feed me 'til I want no more,
> Fill my cup, fill me up, and make me whole.

It's a hymn of praise and communion that I love. Yet sometimes I sense confusion about the role of God's spirit as it relates to our lives.

I would suggest that we see ourselves not as a pot to be filled to overflowing for our own happiness and fulfillment, but rather as a pipe—a conduit—for the Spirit of God to work in the world, a channel through which His Love can flow out in service to accomplish God's will.

It is a great paradox of the Faith that in actuality, we are both pot *and* pipe. For when we are filled with the Spirit, we indeed have joy, peace and fullness of life. But it's not for our own satisfaction; it's for the purpose of building the Church and furthering the Kingdom of God. So God's Spirit not only fills us, but also flows through us. By allowing the Spirit to control us, we become truly fulfilled, and thus fulfill the law of Christ.

PRAYER: Pour into us Your Spirit and you Power, O Lord, so we become conduits of love, to serve with gladness and gratitude. AMEN.

GREATER LOVE HATH NO MAN

(Scripture to ponder: John 15:12–13.)

Our scripture for today comes from Christ's last discourse with his disciples, those chapters of St. John's gospel so full of wisdom and instruction. The mark of his followers, Jesus says, will be their love for one another:

This is my commandment, that you love one another as I have loved you. Greater love hath no man than this, that a man lay down his life for his friends.

[John 15:12–13]

On this day during the second World War, that love was manifest on the troopship, the *U.S.S. Dorchester,* in 1943 in the north Atlantic.[11] In the middle of the night, the ship was torpedoed by a German submarine. The troops that survived the explosion gathered on the listing deck, only to discover there were not enough life jackets to go around. After calming the men and distributing the available life jackets, the four chaplains on deck took off their own life jackets and gave them to four more men. The ship went down in less than a half hour. The last thing the men floating in the water saw were the four chaplains on deck, their arms around each other.

Whoever would save his life will lose it; and whoever loses his life for my sake will find it. For what will it profit a man if he gains the whole world and forfeits his life? Or what shall a man give in return for his life?

[Matthew 16:26]

We have but one life to live and one life to give in this world. What are we willing to exchange for it? Those chaplains knew the Living Lord and through God's Spirit had already received Eternal Life, so they could lay down their lives for their friends.

PRAYER: Through Your Spirit, O Lord, help us to love one another as you have loved us. We pray in Jesus' name. AMEN.

FEBRUARY 4

UNDER CONSTRUCTION

(Scripture to ponder: Philippians 3:12–14)

We have a stretch of major East-West highway near our home in Pennsylvania—US Route 30—that seems always under construction. The ride is invariably bumpy and jolting, for workmen seem forever to be tearing up the pavement to lay down new sewers or electrical lines, filling up the holes to give an uneven, bumpy blacktop surface.

It's a stretch of road near where I grew up, and over my entire life—during which I've traveled a great deal—it seems whenever I've returned home, the roadway is being worked on, is under construction.

The noted evangelist E. Stanley Jones once called the followers of Jesus "**Christians under construction**" By that he meant that in this life, as persons who have been called to follow *the Way*, we are in a life-long process of transformation into the likeness of Christ. The Apostle Paul, one of the great Saints of the Church, understood well the concept of being under construction. He writes in our selection from Philippians 3:

> *Not that I have already attained this, or have already been made perfect, but I press on to make it my own, because Jesus Christ has made me his own. Beloved, I do not consider I have made it my own; but this one thing I do: forgetting what lies behind and straining forward to what lies ahead, I press toward the goal for the prize of the upward call of God in Christ Jesus.*

So I smile whenever I drive over that bumpy, torn-up road (my wife, in proofing this, said I also grit my teeth!). I know that I, like it, I too am *under construction*, being improved by God's Holy Spirit, transformed gradually into His image, that of the Lord Jesus Christ.

PRAYER: We are indeed "Christians under construction" if we let the Spirit transform our lives. Help us, O Lord, be receptive to your will. AMEN.

FEBRUARY 5

THE LEAVEN OF THE KINGDOM

(Scripture to ponder: Matthew 13:33)

Have you ever used a bread machine? I once owned one, and I loved the smell of fresh-baking bread. When I first started making bread, however, I didn't do so well, because my first loaf turned out as dense and heavy as a brick! It would have made a good doorstop!

When I called the 1–800 help-line number listed in the recipe book that came with the machine, I reached a helpful woman who asked how I'd made the bread, step by step. In particular, she asked about the yeast I had used. That turned out to be the problem, for it was old and had lost its zip. When I tried again, using a new, foil-wrapped packet of yeast, the loaf turned out just fine.

In our scripture for today, Jesus likens the Kingdom of God to the leaven—that is the yeast—that a woman mixed with her flower to cause the whole mixture to rise. When I recalled how Christ called his followers the salt of the earth or the leaven in the loaf, I had to chuckle, thinking of my own experience trying to make bread with old yeast.

I suspect Christ would say that old yeast that's lost its zip is like old salt that's lost its savor—it's worthless. We Christians, his followers in a non-Christian world, need to be sure we haven't lost our zip, if we are to be effective bearers of the Good News. To retain our vitality, we must always remain close to Jesus, the source of our strength and power, through prayer and reading God's word.

PRAYER: **Refresh and rekindle us with the fervor and fire of the Holy Spirit, O Lord, that we may be salt and yeast in this world, to further your Kingdom. AMEN.**

FEBRUARY 6

THE ESSENCE OF DOCTORING

(Scripture to ponder: Proverbs 25:11)

Recently, when visiting my mother for lunch at her life-care facility near Philadelphia, as I walked from the car I passed a gardener kneeling beside a bed of exquisite yellow "baby" daffodils. A thought occurred to stop and comment, to congratulate him on his work, but I was in a hurry and passed on silently. When I returned after lunch, he was gone. For the rest of the day, I thought about my being too busy to say something nice. I regretted not taking time to compliment him.

The renowned Boston cardiologist Bernard Lown, in his book, *The Lost Art of Healing,* relates a trip to the Soviet Union, during which he asked a Siberian physician what the essence of doctoring was. She replied, **"Every time a doctor sees a patient, the patient should feel better as a result."** What a simple, yet profound insight!

Now, I'm a physician, and that Soviet doctor's words carry great meaning. It's an excellent maxim for the practice of medicine. But I'm also a Christian, and her words are perhaps even more meaningful in the context of everyday encounters for everyone, not just doctors. For as Christians we are called to serve others and be an encouragement to them, and the way we render that service can increase their joy. As our Scripture for today puts it,

"A word fitly spoken is like apples of gold in a setting of silver."

[Proverbs 25:11]

Expressing a heartfelt compliment is one of the best ways we can share our joy—and spread the Gospel.

PRAYER: Help us always speak fitting words of encouragement. We thank you, Lord, for your gift of salvation—and Joy! AMEN.

FEBRUARY 7

SMALL BEGINNINGS

(Scripture to ponder: Mark 4:26–28)

In the fourth chapter of St. Mark's Gospel, Our Lord relates the parable of the Kingdom, our Scripture passage for today. He likens its growth to that of a seed, which when it's been scattered and germinates, grows mysteriously, sprouting and growing even as the farmer sleeps:

> *The kingdom of God is as if a man should scatter seed upon the ground, and should sleep and rise night and day, and the seed should sprout and grow, he knows not how. The earth produces of itself, first the blade, then the ear, then the full grain in the ear.*

In much the same manner, the early Church grew. Who would have thought that the seeds sown by the Master among a dozen men—sown in the midst of the power of Rome and despite the cruelty of King Herod and Pontius Pilate—would have produced a Church that would grow and thrive, outlasting and overcoming the mighty Roman Empire?

So it is with the growth of the Spirit within each of us. Christ once said that we should not be looking here or looking there for the Kingdom—because the Kingdom of God is *within. [Luke 17:21]* As we accept Jesus as Lord, as we accept God as sovereign over our lives, His Spirit grows in this inner Kingdom. Our faith will grow mysteriously through God's grace if we set aside time to read His Word and devote time in our daily lives to prayer and meditation.

In such a life, through His Spirit, God causes our Faith to grow, even in as we sleep.

LET US PRAY: Plant within each of us the seeds of your Kingdom and let them grow, even in our sleep. AMEN.

FEBRUARY 8

"NO MAN EVER SPOKE LIKE THIS MAN!"

(Scripture to ponder: John 7: 32–46)

I recall once reading biblical commentator who was utterly familiar with the four Gospels. He made a statement to this effect: "If you read through the New Testament seriously and examine the life of Jesus closely, you are forced to one of two conclusions: he was either a deluded madman, or he was truly the Son of God." I've read the Gospels many times, as well as many secondary sources and commentaries, and I agree. Any person who made the claims that Jesus did was either crazy, or he was who he said he was, namely, the Son of God. I believe He was the latter, the Messiah, sent to be the Savior of the world.

In our passage for today, officers were sent by the Chief Priests and Pharisees to arrest Jesus during the last week of His life. After listening to Him teach in the Temple court, they returned empty-handed. When asked why they had not arrested Jesus, the officers replied,

"No man ever spoke like this!"

[John 7:46]

Indeed, as other astonished listeners noted from the beginning of his ministry, Jesus spoke with authority and not as the Scribes, who were the Jewish teachers of the Law. *[Mark 1:22]* His authority came straight from God and manifested itself in his works when he healed or cast out unclean spirits.

At the end of his ministry, Jesus' authority was again manifested in His *greatest miracle*, the raising of Lazarus from the dead. Indeed, no man had ever spoken as He did, as recorded in *John 11:43*, when He called into the tomb, *"Lazarus, come out!"* In that miracle in the closing days of His life, Jesus gave us a glimpse of God's Power, which soon was again manifest in His glorious Resurrection.

PRAYER: We know, O Lord, that no man ever spoke as Jesus did. We bless you that through faith in him and in the Power of his Resurrection, we have Eternal Life. AMEN.

FEBRUARY 9

TUNING IN—TO GOD

(Scripture to ponder: Psalm 46:10)

I grew up in the era just before television became prevalent. I first saw a T.V. set when I was 12, in the home of a Cub Scout, when I was a den chief. It was a huge object weighing about 25 pounds that had a 3" black and white screen! My family did not acquire a T.V. set for another five years, when my grandmother came to live with us.

We did listen to the radio as a family, and although I wasn't allowed to have a radio in my room, I cheated as a teenager and built myself a small crystal set, by which I could listen to radio stations with ear phones, late at night when the busy world was hushed.

Crystal sets are simple and depend on the fact that the internal structure of certain crystals—especially the lead ore galena—can rectify radio waves. Such crystals were the forerunners of the silicon computer chip. By touching a wire from an antenna to a crystal that was hooked in line with a set of earphones, I could hear a radio station. The crystal focused on one frequency, fine-tuning it and filtering out many others.

We are a lot like crystals, in that we can fine-tune our minds to hear God's voice. To do so, we need to filter out the sounds of the world around us, and focus on the Lord in meditation and prayer. He speaks to each of us on our own specific frequency, if we will but listen.

PRAYER: Help us set aside quiet times, O Lord, when we can be still, fine-tuning our spirits, that we may hear your voice. AMEN.

FEBRUARY 10

LEARNING DOMESTIC SERVICE

(Scripture to ponder: Matthew 20:27)

Did you hear about the woman in New York City who, in the midst of the booming 1990s founded a company called *The International Institute for Domestic Service*? She set up the business because she realized that even though servants nowadays were out of fashion, there was a market for them: she knew many New York families who were anxious to have domestic help and could afford it.

But she discovered that few who applied to work for her were suited to be servants. The person who told this story, Karen E. Layman,[12] said the founder of this "International Institute" discovered that nobody really knew how to take the position of servant. To the young women who applied for a job, she had to say, **"Take off the gold loop earrings, cut your long blonde hair, and get rid of the ruby red lip liner! You are not to draw attention to yourselves, but rather, you are to meet the needs of others."**

Our modern American society subtly teaches otherwise. Through advertising and the media, it celebrates leaders, and exalts those in politics, sports and entertainment, most of whom are quite self-centered, expecting to be served. And, not surprisingly, we learn from infancy to imitate them.

But that was neither the way nor the teaching of our Lord Jesus Christ, who said, in our Scripture selection for today:

"Whoever wants to be chief among you, let him become your servant."

As Christians, we are called not to be served, but to serve others, as Our Lord exemplified all through his life. But we cannot do it on our own.

PRAYER: Through the power of Your Holy Spirit, O Lord, replace our desire to be served with the desire to serve others, so that we may do Your will. We pray in Jesus' name. AMEN.

THE THIEF IN THE NIGHT

(Scripture to ponder: Luke 12:39)

Had I only known! It was so irksome and infuriating! I went out early this morning to drive to the YMCA to go swimming and found the garage door had been left open all night. In the darkness, someone had come into the garage, stolen my swim gear and rifled through the car, taking the vehicle registration and insurance papers and some loose change.

I said to myself, *"Gosh, if I had only known there was a thief in the neighborhood, I would have been ready, and made sure the door was shut."* Those thoughts of mine are, curiously similar to the words of Jesus, when he spoke about His return. St. Luke records it this way in our Scripture selection for today:

"But know this, that if the householder had known at what hour the thief was coming, he would have been awake and would not have left his house to be broken into."

In this and in other parables recorded in the same chapter, Jesus tells of his return—and urges His followers to be ready to greet him when he comes.

Are you ready? What does it mean to be ready for the Lord's return? And for whom is the parable of the robbed householder being told? I think it's told for all Christians, and is meant for a warning for us to be ready at all times for Christ's return.

PRAYER: Help us, Dear Lord, to ever be doing Your will, so that we are always ready for Your return. AMEN.

FEBRUARY 12

SEEING US THROUGH

(Scripture to ponder: John 14:18)

For all who come to him, the Lord Jesus Christ has marvelous words of consolation. He will not abandon us, but will see us through. Hear his words as St. John records them in his Gospel *[John 14:18]:*

> *"I will not leave you comfortless; I will come to you. Yet a little while, and the world will see me no more, but you will see me; because I live, you will live also."*

Those words have brought peace to millions of people down through the ages, as they have faced illness, adversity or death. God comforts us, St. Paul says in his first letter to the church at Corinth, so we can be a comfort to others. *[1 Corinthians 1:3&4]*

There is a story[13] about Abraham Lincoln that bears on this. During the Civil War, Lincoln often visited hospitals where the troops were, offering cheering words to the wounded. Once he stopped at the bed of a young soldier whose leg had been amputated and who was sinking rapidly. **"Is there anything I can do for you?"** asked Lincoln.

"You might write a letter to my Mother," the boy replied. The President wrote as the youth dictated: **"My dear Mother. I have been shot bad, but I am bearing up. I tried to do my duty. They tell me I cannot recover. God bless you and Father. Kiss May and John for me."** At the end of these words were added as a postscript, **"This letter was written by Abraham Lincoln."** When the boy read the letter over and saw the added words, he looked up with astonished gaze at the visitor, as he asked, **"Are you the President?"**

"Yes," was the quick answer; **"and now that you know that, is there anything else I can do for you?"** Feebly, the lad replied:

> **"I guess you might hold my hand and see me through."**

PRAYER: We praise You and bless You, O Lord, that You, too, hold our hand and see us through. You do not leave us comfortless, but have prepared a place for us with you through all eternity. AMEN.

FEBRUARY 13

A SERMON IN A MOTTO

(Scripture to ponder: Matthew 7:12)

When I was an adolescent I was greatly influenced by my experience in Scouting. Achieving Eagle rank was an encouragement and a motivator when I left home to face the lonely environment of a boarding school. The Scout Oath and Scout Law—memorized during those years of weekly meetings—have stuck with me my entire life.

The *Scout Law* is: A Scout is Trustworthy, Loyal, Helpful, Friendly, Courteous, Kind, Obedient, Cheerful, Thrifty, Brave, Clean and Reverent.

The *Scout Oath*—an admirable creed for anyone—is:

On my honor I will do my best to do my duty to God and my country and obey the Scout Law: to help other people at all times, and keep myself Physically Strong, Mentally Awake, and Morally Straight.

The *Scout Motto*, "Do a good turn daily," is but a paraphrase of the Golden Rule from Christ's *Sermon on the Mount*, our Scripture selection for today.

Scouting in the U.S. was started by a man named William Boyce, an American who became lost in a dense London fog when visiting England before the First World War. He was helped by a boy who gave him directions and accompanied him safely back to his lodgings. When Boyce offered him a reward, the lad said he was a Scout and told him of the Oath that moved him to be helpful. Boyce was so impressed that he brought the movement to the United States from Britain, where it had been founded about a year earlier by Sir Robert Baden-Powell.

Habits have great influence in our lives. Scouts make a habit of being helpful to others. Service to others is often habitual, as is daily reading of the Scriptures. Memorizing Bible passages, like committing the Scout motto to memory, can help us serve others in our daily lives.

PRAYER: Help us to do a good deed every day, doing unto others as we would have them do unto us. We pray in Jesus' name. AMEN.

FEBRUARY 14

GETTING ALONG SCRIPTURALLY

(Scripture to ponder: 1 John 4:7–11)

My wife and a friend were recently chatting. When she realized that we always had breakfast together, the friend asked, "What do you give your husband for breakfast."

"Anything he wants," was her reply.

"Really? But what does he usually want?"

"Usually he wants whatever I fix," Diane replied.

That little humorous exchange tells a lot about our relationship. We often defer to each other. We're blissfully happy and get along well.

I guess if I had to put my finger on one thing that makes our relationship harmonious and successful, it would be that we try to live scripturally. But what does that mean, to live *scripturally?*

We both believe that God is Love, which is what St. John says in his first letter (part of our selection for today) and we try to manifest love and forgiveness in our lives. We also try to follow God's manual on marriage, namely the Bible, by reading and reflecting on a part of it every day. We do this buy reading a brief section, usually at breakfast.

We once watched the Superbowl, when the underdog New England Patriots defeated the St. Louis Rams in the final seconds of that exciting game. We watched it on television. It would be silly to expect that we could have seen it if the set had not been plugged in, empowered to receiver the FM waves of the broadcast. Similarly, to receive the message God has for us, we need to read His word.

Diane and I believe the best way to have a loving, enduring marriage is to stay plugged in to Scripture, every day, and to try to follow its teachings.

PRAYER: Help us set aside time each day, Dear Lord, to read Your Word and receive Your message for our lives, that we may truly love one another. AMEN.

FEBRUARY 15

THE PRACTICE OF GOD'S PRESENCE

(Scripture to ponder: Psalm 17: 8&9)

One of my favorite devotional books is by Brother Lawrence, a monk who lived in the seventeenth century, whose little volume, *The Practice of the Presence of God* has been an inspiration to countless Christians through the ensuing centuries. Brother Lawrence tells how he would meditate and worship God in the midst of his everyday monastic chores, as he washed pots and pans in the kitchen of the cloister.

I was introduced to Brother Lawrence by reading Thomas Kelly, a Quaker professor at Haverford College in the 1930s, whose book, *A Testament of Devotion,* was recommended by my pastor when I was a medical student. Faced with the challenge of intense scientific study, coupled with long hours of seeing patients, I found myself physically exhausted and emotionally drained at the end of each day. Kelly's little book gave me new inspiration and revitalized my prayer life—as it has done for many others. It's still in print, published by Harper[14], and worth reading and rereading.

I am sure Kelly was influenced by Brother Lawrence, for he writes:[15]

There is a practice of the Presence of God which is done on the run, in the busiest of days, in office and in schoolroom and kitchen. Little prayers and communion; ejaculations of surrender and joy and exaltation; if it didn't sound silly to say it, little snugglings of the soul moving nearer to God.

When we practice such presence of God, we are like the Psalmist, who speaks of taking shelter under God's wings, protected by him as an eagle protects her young. We stay secure in God's enveloping love.

PRAYER: We take joy and find protection under the shadow of Your wings, O Lord. Teach us how to draw near and practice Your presence in all that we do, as we seek to do Your will. AMEN.

FEBRUARY 16

ONLY TWO LOVES

(Scripture to ponder: Luke 10: 25–28)

In his 1997 book, *Sources of Strength*,[16] Ex-President Jimmy Carter tells of speaking with the Cuban pastor Eloy Cruz, who had surprising rapport with poor immigrants from Puerto Rico. Carter asked him for the secret of his success. Cruz, a modest man, was embarrassed by the question and finally confided in Carter, saying, **"Senior Jimmy, we need only have two loves in our lives: for God, and for the person who happens to be in front of us at any time."** Carter said that simple yet profound theology was a great help to him in understanding the scriptures. For in essence, Carter reflected, the whole Bible is an explanation of those two loves.

In our scripture passage for today, the answer given by the lawyer who tested Jesus was the same as that given by Eloy Cruz:

You shall love the Lord your God with all your heart and with all your soul and with all your strength and with all your mind; and you shall love your neighbor as yourself.

The lawyer was quoting the Law of Moses as recorded in Deuteronomy 6:5 and Leviticus 19:18. Because at the time the law was given, there was a tribal mentality—that is, the Israelites treated their own differently than they treated the other nations around them—the lawyer asked for clarification about exactly who was meant by his neighbor.

Jesus answered by telling a parable, the parable of the Good Samaritan, our selection for today. In that story, the man who was neighborly was not the priest or the Levite, each of whom served in the Temple and was a pillar of Jewish society, but who passed on by the wounded man. It was instead the Samaritan, a despised person, who stopped and showed pity. Christ urged the lawyer, and he enjoins us, to do likewise. Christ's words have great relevance for us, who live in such a heterogeneous world.

PRAYER: Help us, Dear Lord, to see our neighbor as Christ and as Eloy Cruz saw him: the person in front of us, who needs our help. AMEN.

FEBRUARY 17

REMEMBERING ABRAHAM LINCOLN

(Scripture to ponder: Luke 10:25–29)

Abraham Lincoln was among our greatest presidents. He was of humble origins yet achieved greatness as a statesman and politician. His formal education, he once said, amounted to less than a year. He did not read widely, but he read well and was quite familiar with the works of Shakespeare and with the King James Bible.

Was Lincoln a Christian? Although he never joined a church, I believe he knew and loved the Lord. Allusions to God and to the Almighty in his speeches and writings are manifold.

A story, probably apocryphal but consistent with his wit, is told about Lincoln's attending a church service in Springfield, IL early in his career. The preacher got fired up and asked the congregation to stand. "**Everyone who wants to go to Heaven, sit down!**" he called out. Almost all the folks there sat down. "**Everyone who doesn't want to go to Hell, sit down!**" he cried. Only Lincoln was left standing in the back of the church. "**Well, Mr. Lincoln,** the pastor yelled, "**if you don't want to go to Heaven, and you don't want to go to Hell, just** *where do* **you want to go?**"

"**I want to go to Washington,**" Lincoln called back.

During his Presidency, a reporter asked him why he had never joined a church. Lincoln replied:

"When a church will inscribe over its portal, as the sole requirement for membership, that 'Thou shalt love the Lord with all thy heart and soul and mind and strength, and thy neighbor as thyself,' that church will I gladly join."

PRAYER: We know, Dear Lord, that to love you with all our heart and soul and mind and strength, and our neighbor as ourselves, is to truly do you will. Help us so to act. In Jesus name we pray. AMEN.

FEBRUARY 18

USING OUR TALENTS

(Scripture to ponder: Matthew 25:14–30)

Our scripture for today is the Parable of the Talents. In it Christ rewards the person who makes use of his talents but condemns the man who buries his talents. The Lord concluded, *"Unto everyone that hath shall be given."* I recently had a personal example recently of that spiritual principle.

I have a talent for home repairs, and now that I am retired from practicing surgery, I do volunteer work as a handyman for a group called VICaP, the Volunteer Interfaith Caregivers Program. Last week I went to the home of a couple who needed grab bars installed in their bathrooms. They'd been through a lot. He was recovering from a stroke and needed a bar on the wall by the bathtub, where his wife helped him with his bath.

She was about six weeks out from having a Whipple procedure, one of the biggest operations we general surgeons do, and she needed a bar in the stall shower where she bathed. When she found out I was a surgeon, she asked if I wanted to see her reports from surgery. I said yes, and on looking them over discovered she'd had removal of a cancer of her duodenum, a huge operation from which she was recovering nicely. She was a little wisp of a woman, about 5' 1" tall, weighing 100 pounds, whereas he was about 6'2". What strength! What courage, I thought as I began to do the job.

As I walked through the bedroom to the bath, I saw a crucifix over the bed, and in the bathroom pasted to the mirror was a quote from Norman Vincent Peale. I saw its relevance to the strength of this couple. It read:

"The secret of life isn't what happens to you, but what *you do* with what happens to you,"

As I finished the job and was heading home, I reflected on the inspiration I'd received, far greater than the small amount of time and talent I'd put in. It was God's way of giving back, just like the parable of the talents.

PRAYER: May we use our talents to serve others in your name, O Lord, knowing You've promised to give us even more. AMEN.

FEBRUARY 19

PEACE LIKE A RIVER

(Scripture to ponder: Isaiah 48:17–18)

The expression *peace like a river* comes from Isaiah's prophesy:

Oh that you had listened to my commands! Then you would have had peace flowing like a gentle river and righteousness rolling down like waves."
                                                    [Isaiah 48:18, New Living Translation]

A well-known hymn came from this passage. Its title is the recurrent chorus: "It Is Well with My Soul," It was composed in 1873, a time when evangelists were winning souls and preachers placed greater emphasis on eternity than they do nowadays. It has a fascinating history.[17]

Horatio G. Spafford was from Chicago, a friend of the great evangelist Dwight L. Moody. Spafford was a successful businessman by age 43, but got wiped out financially by the Great Chicago Fire of 1871. Earlier that same year he and his wife lost their son. To get away for a vacation, they planned to go to England where Moody was going to hold an evangelistic campaign.

Spafford sent his wife and daughters ahead on the *SS Ville du Havre,* but the ship went down in a freak ocean collision. All four of the Spaffords' daughters were among the 256 who drowned. Their father left to join his wife as soon as he heard the awful news. As his ship passed through the area of the tragedy, the captain pointed out the spot of the sinking. That night Spafford composed his famous lines:

When peace like a river attendeth my way
When sorrows like sea-billows roll;
Whatever my lot, Thou has taught me to say
"It is well, it is well with my soul."

PRAYER: It is indeed well with our souls, O Lord, for we trust You for our salvation. You have promised that those who love you and are obedient to you Word will have peace flowing like a gentle river. AMEN.

FEBRUARY 20

THE HARM OF CONDITIONED STRESS

(Scripture to ponder: 1 John 4:18)

The Nobel Prize winning cardiologist Bernard Lown tells of the research of the psycho physiologist Dr. Horsley Gantt, the only American who studied under the great Russian physiologist Ivan Pavlov. Gantt conditioned dogs—by delivering an electric shock to their legs just as he rang a bell—so that their heart raced and their blood pressure rose whenever the bell was rung, even though the shocks were no longer given. Even after a lapse of many months, just ringing the bell would provoke the increase in pulse and pressure. Gantt found that such conditioned responses persisted, as though deep in memory.

Lown made similar observations in some of his patients. He found that painful or threatening or fearful experiences early in life produced responses that later could be evoked by similar events, often producing cardiac disease.

It reminded me of a nineteenth century adage about cats: A cat that sits down on a hot cast iron stove will never again sit down on a hot stove. But he won't ever sit down on a cold stove, either.

Pain and fear are great conditioners. Because of painful memories we avoid many dangerous situations. But likewise, we can be conditioned to avoid reaching out to others who have needs. Do you suppose the Priest and the Levite passed by the man lying wounded on the side of the road from Jerusalem to Jericho because they feared the robbers might be lurking behind a nearby rock? Do our fears hold us back from taking risks to do God's will?

PRAYER: Fill us with Your Love, O Lord, for we know that perfect love casts out fear. Help us take risks to do Your Will, that Your kingdom may come. AMEN.

FEBRUARY 21

WATCHING THE SUNRISE

(Scripture to ponder: Psalm 8)

Most weekday mornings in Arizona, I ride my bike to the YMCA where I swim laps. Besides being good for my stamina, I find the trip inspiring, particularly pedaling back home facing the east, watching the sunrise as the moon fades. I remember the Psalmist's words (from our Scripture selection), pondering the splendor of creation:

"When I consider the heavens, the moon and the stars which Thou hast ordained, what is man, that Thou art mindful of him, and the son of man, that Thou visitest him?"

There are more stars in the universe, astronomers estimate, than there are grains of sand on the earth.

God's marvelous design is evident in His amazingly diverse creation: just as no two snowflakes are the same, so no two sunrises or sunsets are the same. Each morning is a new beginning and each evening a new ending.

As we look about and see all the evil and destruction in the world, it is tempting to ask how God, who has created all the beauty and diversity of nature, could allow the sometimes sordid ugliness of human nature.

But the scriptures also say,

"He hath showed thee, O man what is right: For what doth the Lord require of thee, but to live justly, love mercy and walk humbly with thy God?"

[Micah 5:8]

God has given us everything we need for happiness and fulfillment; it is *we* who have gone astray. As Isaiah says,

"All we like sheep have gone astray, each one to his own way."

[Isaiah 53:6]

God has clearly shown, through his Word, how we should behave and act. It is *we* who must resolve to walk in His way.

PRAYER: **Dear Lord, empower us to apply what we read in Your word to our lives. Help us realize that the order in the universe reflects the order You would have among us, as we walk Your path here on earth. AMEN.**

FEBRUARY 22

LIVING BY THE RULES

(Scripture to ponder: Romans 1:17)

Are you a person who tends to live by the rules? Do you like to have things lined up, or things lined out for you? Do you react when someone cuts into line ahead of you, or otherwise doesn't follow the rules? I tend to react negatively when that happens to me, and get angry or resentful.

One of Martin Luther's greatest insights into the Christian life came when he was a monk trying to follow the rules. He wrote:

"As a monk I tried very hard and took the greatest pains to live as the rules prescribed. I would always first repent of all my sins and then confess and enumerate them. Often I even repeated the confession, and then I would diligently perform the penance imposed on me. And still my conscience could never achieve security. I had constant doubts about the sufficiency of my efforts, saying to myself: you did not do this right, weren't contrite enough, omitted that from confession, etc. And so the longer I tried to heal my weak and troubled conscience by following human rules, the more uncertain, weak and confused it became each day."[18]

Luther, realizing he could not earn salvation by following the rules (he constantly and repeatedly fell short), came to realize it was by *faith*, not by works, that one is righteous. As it is written in Paul's letter to the Romans, our Scripture for today,

"Therein is the righteousness of God revealed from faith to faith: as it is written, The just shall live by faith."

The only rule we have to follow for salvation is to have faith in the Lord Jesus Christ. For it is by Faith that we live, and move, and have our being, and it is by faith that we receive Eternal Life.

PRAYER: So often we get trapped into thinking salvation comes from living by the rules. Help us see, O Lord, that it comes from loving You and having faith in the saving power of Your Son. AMEN.

FEBRUARY 23

SERVANTHOOD

(Scripture to ponder: John 13:1–10)

As one reads through the New Testament, it's apparent that *Servanthood*—serving one another and others out of love for God—is a crucial concept. But it's a hard for us—who live in a society with no slaves and almost no servants—to grasp its meaning. In Bible times it was clearer.

A servant in those days was always at the beck and call of his master. In *Luke 17*, Christ speaks of his disciples as servants, who prepare a meal and serve their master before they themselves consider eating. Jesus himself was the supreme example of a servant, and St. John's record of Christ's last discourse gives us some insight into how servanthood can be achieved.

What is it that allowed Jesus to be a servant, to wash the Apostles feet, for example? It is the same conviction that enables us as Christians, empowered by the Holy Spirit, to serve those around us. *It's the knowledge of who we are and where we are going.* Hear today's Gospel:

> *Jesus . . . knowing that the Father had given all things into his hands and that he had come from God and was going to God, rose from supper and laid aside his garments and took a towel . . . and began to wash his disciples feet . . .*
>
> [John 13:3–6]

As Christians, we are children of God, with a priceless inheritance, who are going to be with the Lord in Heaven for all eternity. Even in this life we can never be separated from Him, who sent his Spirit to be our Comforter. We are free, therefore, to become servants of others.

PRAYER: Dear Lord, we're used to being masters, not servants. Yet we know your way is the way of Servanthood. Empower us by Your Spirit to serve others, as you did when you walked the earth. AMEN.

FEBRUARY 24

IS IT TEN—OR TWO—COMMANDMENTS?

(Scripture to ponder: Luke 10:29–37)

We are all familiar with the Ten Commandments, given to Moses by God on Mount Sinai, recorded in Exodus Chapter 20. If you read the rest of that book and read Leviticus, the book that follows it, you discover there are not just Ten Commandments. There are scores, even hundreds of them in the first five books of the Old Testament, the part of the Hebrew Bible that the Jews called the Law.

The Pharisees were a Jewish sect that sought to keep those many laws and statutes and ordinances, and they accused Jesus of seeking to *abolish* the Law because he did things like heal the sick on the Sabbath, which was a holy day and one on which no work was to be done. Indeed, definitions of actions that constitute *work* take up many verses of the Old Testament.

But Jesus refused to be constrained by a rigid, narrow interpretation of the Law. He said he came not to abolish, but to fulfill the Law, and it's apparent that his teachings go beyond the *letter* of the law, to the *spirit* behind the law. Two examples: Where the Sixth Commandment forbids murder, Christ enjoins us to not even get angry, for anger leads to violence. And regarding the Seventh Commandment, he goes beyond the act of adultery to proscribe looking lustfully on a woman, for lust leads to sexual sin.

I believe Jesus would tell us there are not scores of commandments, not even ten, that we must observe, but only *two: **Love God and love our neighbor.*** From his Parable of the Good Samaritan in Luke Chapter ten, our Scripture for today, it's apparent that our neighbor is not to be defined narrowly as the person next door, but is anyone we encounter who needs our help.

Our Lord said, *"On these two commandments hang all the Law and the Prophets."* *[Matthew 22:40]* Observing them, we fulfill the Law.

PRAYER: **Help us show our love for You, O Lord, by loving all those we encounter in our daily lives. In Jesus' Name we pray. AMEN.**

FEBRUARY 25

SENT FROM GOD

(Scripture to ponder: John 1:6–8; 3:17)

Enrico Caruso, the renowned Italian tenor, was born on this day in Naples in 1873. As a youth, he hoped to become a singer but was told he had neither the talent nor the necessary voice. He persisted and got instruction at first by observing the music lessons of other students.

It's told that when he desired to sing the role of Rudolfo in *La Boheme,* he had to first audition before Puccini himself. The maestro listened to Caruso sing a few pages of the score, then leaped from his chair, exclaiming, **"Who sent you to me? God?"** Caruso made his debut in Covent Garden in 1902 as the Duke in *Rigoletto.* His Metropolitan Opera debut York occurred in New the following year and he sang there for the next eighteen years. Caruso was the first major tenor to be recorded.

"Sent from God" was Puccini's exclamation. The expression, *"Sent from God,"* was also the proclamation of our first Scripture passage for today:

> *There was a man sent from God whose name was John. He came for testimony to bear witness to the light that all might believe through him. He was not the light but came to bear witness to the light.*

Puccini saw Caruso as God-sent because he had such a stunning voice. The writer of the forth Gospel records that God sent John to bear witness to Jesus, and the Gospel goes on to say about Jesus, whom John the Baptist was announcing, (in our second selection) that

> *"God sent the son into the world not to condemn the world, but that the world might be saved through him."*

Caruso and Puccini have given us divine music, but Jesus Christ gives us salvation. Through him we have Life Eternal.

PRAYER: We thank you, Lord, for beautiful music. But most of all, we bless you for the gift of Eternal Life we have through Jesus. AMEN.

FEBRUARY 26

THE BIBLE IN CHAINS

(Scripture to ponder: Psalm 119:105)

When I served on a medical school teaching faculty there was a cart in the emergency department that held a selection of the latest textbooks—textbooks of medicine, surgery, pediatrics, obstetrics and emergency medicine. Each of these large tomes had a chain from its binding to the cart, an insurance that the books—which contained the latest, valuable information about the practice of medicine—would not wander off. There was always a tendency for medical students or residents to want to carry the books away somewhere else so they could read them in quiet, but then they rarely came back; hence the chains.

In a similar manner, when the Bible first was translated and printed in English, many years before individual Bibles were printed and universally available, the large Bibles in the churches and cathedrals of England were chained to the pulpit. Formerly the scriptures were available only in Latin and therefore could only be read by the clergy or someone with a university education. Publishing a translation in the vernacular—in English—made the public eager to read the book, which became valuable, for such volumes were initially rare.

The Bible today is available in many translations and editions, and it's the most widely printed book in the world. It's ironic, for despite its availability, it's one of the least read. It is a treasure chest of exciting stories, poetry and history. Most important, it is the record of God's message to mankind, the "manufacturer's guide" to right living. Its wisdom is available to anyone who takes time to read it. It sheds light on the path for our daily walk.

PRAYER: Give us, O Lord, a desire to read your Word and acquire your wisdom, so freely available to us today. AMEN

FEBRUARY 27

TAKING PRUDENT REFUGE

(Scripture to ponder: Proverbs 22:3)

We were cruising along in a bus—one of those tall busses that tourist groups use, the ones that have a huge windshield about sex feet off the ground. Suddenly the driver announced, "Uh-Oh, it looks like trouble ahead." He slowed, then turned off the highway and took a back road route instead of the main road. Later we discovered from the news that the traffic snarl that he saw from his higher vantage point had tied up traffic in that area for several hours. By his prudent and timely action he spared his passengers much delay.

The wisdom of the Proverbs, our selection for today, states,

"The prudent sees danger and takes refuge."

Who are the prudent? The dictionary defines them as those who exercise sound judgment in practical matters. The Bible—particularly the Book of Proverbs—is full of prudent wisdom. Prudence also comes to those who are led by the Spirit of God. For the Lord Jesus promised his followers that He would send God's Spirit, to be our comforter and also to be our counselor, to give us spiritual discernment.

It seems that in the history of humanity there have been few times as troubled as ours. We are today in greater need than ever of the wisdom and insight that God's Spirit can provide. More than ever, we need to set aside time each day for prayer, meditation and reflection, time to read God's Word and to hear His Voice.

PRAYER: **We thank You, Lord, that you have sent Your Spirit to be our counselor and our comforter, and that you are our refuge and our strength. AMEN.**

FEBRUARY 28

CHEAP AND COSTLY GRACE

(Scripture to ponder: John 15: 9–13)

Dietrich Bonhoeffer was a German pastor hung by the Nazis because he continued teaching in an underground seminary and was part of a plot to overthrow Hitler. He coined two phrases, **Cheap Grace** and **Costly Grace**, and in his writings he explained the important difference between the two.

St. Paul wrote that we are saved by grace, through faith *[Ephesians 2:8]*, and Bonhoeffer would surely acknowledge that. Salvation is by grace and is a gift of God, but it's not free: it was purchased through Christ's suffering and death on our behalf.

So what's the difference between **Cheap Grace** and **Costly Grace**? **Cheap Grace** is what I'm afraid what many believe in who have not been tested in the crucible of suffering, who believe they are spiritually blessed and saved because they are secure and live in a land—America—that is materially blessed, a land "flowing with milk and honey," where we live lives of ease and enjoyment.

To recognize and accept **Costly Grace** is to follow Christ by living a life of dedicated sacrifice, even unto death. The **Costly Grace** of Dietrich Bonhoeffer was epitomized by something he said—and lived: **"when Christ calls a man he bids him come and die."** Bonhoeffer knew that when we truly give our lives over to the Master to control and use for His kingdom, we effectively die to ourselves, so that we may live to God.

But it's not a one-time thing. Rather it involves constant renewal and returning to God, for in our own sinfulness we constantly want to go our own way, not God's way.

PRAYER: **Help us count the cost, Dear Lord, the price you paid for our salvation, and help us follow you in all that we do. Forgive our sins and help us turn to You in prayer each day. AMEN.**

FEBRUARY 29

PUMPING UP NUMBER ONE

(Scripture to ponder: John 13:1–17)

I was recently in a well-known department store to pick up some goods I had ordered. As I passed the teens department I noticed a bunch of T-shirts with large, self-promoting buttons that read "World's Greatest," or "I love myself" and "I love my attitude problem," (with a big red heart instead of the word *love*), or "# One," or "I stop traffic." The messages seemed to be typical of the sassy approach to advertising to youth nowadays.

It's true that Jesus taught *"Love your neighbor as yourself," [Matthew 22:39]* but I wonder what He'd think of the glorification of the self that we see all about us nowadays.

People who are secure in God's love don't need to go parading around proclaiming, "I'm the greatest!" or "I love myself!" Indeed, Christians who are secure in God's love, who seek to do His will, are persons who look out for others, not just themselves. Indeed, Christ would have us be servants to one another, following his example, when he washed his disciples feet at the Last Supper as described in our Scripture selection for today.

It's true, we've been created with an instinct for self-preservation: we naturally look out for ourselves. And that's what I believe Christ means by self-love. He asks that we accord our neighbor the same concern that we give to ourselves. But He does not say—as advertisers imply, to sell their products—that we should *glorify* ourselves. Rather, we should glorify God.

PRAYER: We bless You, Heavenly Father, that You look out for us. Keep us secure in Your love, so we can look out for others. AMEN

MARCH 1

TREASURE IN EARTHEN VESSELS

(Scripture to ponder: 2 Corinthians 4:7–10)

As a surgeon, I am often called to deal with the ravages of illness or injury as it affects the human body. In caring for trauma victims especially, St. Paul's words to the Church at Corinth, our selection for today, come to mind:

"But we have this treasure in earthen vessels, that the transcendent power belongs to God and not to us."

Human flesh houses the human spirit, which is the essence of us as persons. The body can be crippled by disease or crushed by trauma, yet God's Spirit within a person can still shine forth.

St. Paul's words are also a reminder that there is more to life than our bodies, and that our real life is held close to God in Christ, our real home in heaven.

"If in this life only we have hope," said St. Paul, *"we are indeed the most miserable of all men." [1 Corinthians 15:19]* But thanks to God, our Hope is not here in this material world, but in Heaven, in the healing and renewal that comes with resurrection and rebirth.

The great Mystery—and the great Joy—of the Christian Life is that eternal life can begin *right now*, if you surrender your will and your life to Jesus Christ. *Do you lack Joy? Does you life lack vibrancy?* You need only confess Jesus as your Lord and Savior and ask God to fill you with His Spirit, to receive fullness of life.

PRAYER: **Dear Lord, help us to see that this material world is not all there is, nor are our bodies but the vessels that can house your heavenly treasure. Fill us with Your Spirit. In Jesus' name. AMEN.**

MARCH 2

GENEROSITY

(Scripture to ponder: 2 Corinthians 9:6–10)

Generosity is a Christian virtue that is extolled in the teachings of Jesus and St. Paul, but is perhaps best learned by experience. A generous gift is one that exceeds expectations. Sometimes it involves a gift that is unexpected.

Such an example occurred in my own life, when at the death of an aunt—who lived thousands of miles away and whom I had rarely seen—I received a bequest of several thousand dollars. That generous and unexpected gift enabled me to do something I would otherwise been unable to do: buy a home with some acreage and woods, a property along a river in Oregon. It came at a time in my life when I had just finished my surgical residency and had no savings. I reflected many times thereafter on her generosity, which so enriched my life.

Our pastor once told a story which bears on generosity.

"A monk once found a precious stone and kept it. One day he met a traveler. As the monk opened his bag to share his provisions with the traveler, out tumbled the jewel. The traveler asked the monk if he might have it. The monk gave it to him readily.

The traveler departed overjoyed with the unexpected gift of the precious stone. A few days later he came back in search of the monk. He found him, gave back the stone and made this request:

"Please give me something much more precious that this stone. As valuable as it is, please give me that which enabled you to give the stone to me."

PRAYER: All good and precious gifts come from You, O Lord. With grateful hearts, we ask you for the gift of Generosity. AMEN.

MARCH 3

GOING TO WALDEN POND

(Scripture to ponder: John 10:10)

The April, 2002, issue of *Smithsonian* magazine had an interesting article about a group of woodworkers who, using hand tools, rebuilt Thoreau's cabin on the shore of Walden Pond near Concord, MA. In March 1845, when he was 27, Henry David Thoreau built a small cabin and lived in it for the next two years. In *Walden*, his famous account of that experience, Thoreau wrote that he went to Walden Pond

". . . **because I wished to live deliberately, to front only the essential facts of life, and see if I could not learn what it had to teach, and not, when I came to die, discover that I had not lived.**"

Legend has it that years later, when he was on his death bed, Thoreau was asked by a clergyman if he had made his peace with God. He is said to have replied, "**I never had an argument.**"

In a sense, each of us has our own Walden Pond, for each of us lives in a cabin that we ourselves build, not of timbers and pegs, but composed of the experiences, endeavors and decisions of our lives. Will we come to the end and discover we have not lived?

Jesus dealt with the issue in our scripture selection for today:

"I am come that you may have life, and have it more abundantly."

What Christ meant by a more abundant life, I believe, was a life enriched by the love of God and of our neighbor. For he taught, "A new commandment I give unto you, that you love one another as I have loved you" [John 13:34] That love—in which he laid down his very life for us—is the secret of the abundant life that Thoreau sought, and that each of us desires.

PRAYER: **Help us always love you and love our neighbor, that we know your abundant life, O Lord. AMEN.**

MARCH 4

DELEGATING DECISIONS

(Scripture to ponder: Exodus 18:14–24)

You may have heard the story of a man who was having some trouble in his marriage, who approached for advice a friend whose marriage seemed sound. "My wife and I argue a lot over decisions," he said, and he asked his friend how he managed things at home.

"We don't have any problem at all," his friend replied. "She makes all the little decisions and I make all the big ones." When asked what sort of decisions she made, he said, "Oh, you know, like what kind of car we'll drive, or where we'll live or what sort of house to buy." His friend was intrigued and asked what sort of decisions *he* made. "Oh, like when we'll bomb Iraq, or how much to lower the prime lending rate for the Feds."

It's a silly story, but delegation of decisions can be important in life. When Moses was leading the Children of Israel in the wilderness (as described in our scripture lesson for today), he found himself burdened with constantly making decisions about disputes brought before him. His father-in-law Jethro saw the toll it was taking and suggested that Moses delegate the adjudication of minor disputes to able, God-fearing men who would bring the major disputes to Moses for Judgment. Moses thought the advice sound and followed it. Good managers today follow suit.

Sharing our decisions with our spouses and with God is an important aspect of the Christian life. Staying in the Word—regular reading and study of the Bible—lets our spirit align with God's Holy Spirit as we approach life's decisions.

PRAYER: Help us make time each day, O Lord, to study Your Word and share with You all the decisions of our lives, little or big. AMEN.

MARCH 5

A CLEAN HEART

(Scripture to ponder: Psalm 51)

Early in my surgical practice I used to do a lot of open-heart surgery, mostly assisting with revascularization of patients whose coronary arteries were blocked with deposits of fatty tissue. A patient whose heart was failing and pumping poorly because not enough blood got to the contracting muscle would suddenly get a "clean heart" when the arteries were unblocked and blood flowed to the muscle unimpeded. The organ immediately beat with renewed vigor, and such patients at once got a new lease on life. The effect was dramatic and immediate.

God tells about another type of clean heart in Psalm 51. Many people—in that instance King David—are weighed down with unclean hearts from sin: *"Create in me a clean heart, O God, and renew a right spirit within me!"* the King cries to God. If you are familiar with the account of David's sin of adultery with Bathsheba and murder of her husband Uriah (beginning @ *2 Samuel 11:2*), you know about God's power to cleanse us from sin. The confession of sin by believers, and the subsequent forgiveness by God are two of the most important aspects of Christian Faith, and they have a place in the worship service of most churches. *"All have sinned and fall short of the Glory of God,"* writes St. Paul *[Romans 3:23]*. And all of us are in need of forgiveness.

The Lord alone has the power to cleanse our hearts and release us from the power of sin. Think of the many times that the Lord Jesus forgave sins to restore people to wholeness and health. He alone can create within us a clean heart. Do you harbor any secret sin, and need a clean heart? God in his grace and mercy can grant it, if we confess our sin and ask for His forgiveness.

PRAYER: With your cleansing power, O Lord, release us from sin, restore us to your salvation, and uphold us with your Spirit, which you freely give to all who truly seek you. AMEN.

MARCH 6

WHAT TO DO?

(Scripture to ponder: James 2: 17 & 18)

"What would you like to do with the rest of your life?" I asked the 81 year old man who sat with me in the car. He suffered from macular degeneration and was legally blind. I, as a volunteer driver, was taking him to a doctor's appointment.

"I'd like to do something to help pay back. You see, I've had a good life, and I'm grateful for it. I'd like to do something like you're doing, but I can't see well enough to drive."

He told me his life story as we drove to the doctor, how he'd spent many years in the Navy after enlisting during the Second World War, then had his own heating and refrigeration business for 20 more years.

I asked my question about what he'd like to do as we drove back from the appointment. His answer made me wonder how many others there are like him, who would like to do something, but cannot? How many of us have good intentions that we don't pursue because we're too caught up in our own busy lives?

Let's not wait until retirement or until we're incapacitated, to act on good intentions! We can set aside time—we can *make time*—for that's what we always do for things we really want to do—we can make time to help others, if we really want to. We can show our faith by our works, as the Apostle James wrote in our Scripture selection for today. Resolve **today**, to do it!

PRAYER: We do indeed have good intentions, Lord. Help us translate them into action, to show our gratitude and to do Your will. AMEN.

MARCH 7

FILLING MY PEN EVERY DAY

(Scripture to ponder: Luke 12:22–32)

I like to write with fountain pens. I like the way they feel and the way they write. Unfortunately nowadays there are so many forms to fill out with multiple copies that require pressing down hard, I have to carry a ballpoint pen, too. But I still carry my old Parker 51 fountain pen with me, 'cause I write a lot of letters and like the feel of that pen. But there's another reason I use it, besides finding it comfortable.

The reason is: *it's a reminder.* You see, I have to fill it with ink anew each day so I don't run out. And each time I fill it up, I'm reminded, that's how God wants us to live our lives: fill up anew each morning with his love and his spirit. By morning prayer and meditation, using *Daily Guideposts* or *The Upper Room*, for example, or regular Bible readings, one gains strength for the day.

A famous physician once counseled, "Live your life in day-tight compartments." He found success in life was related to living life one day at a time, doing each day's work well, and not worrying about tomorrow. He was echoing what Jesus said: *"Who, by taking thought"*—that is, by worrying—*"can add a cubit to his stature?"[Luke 12:25]* As the Bible also says, *"Sufficient unto the day is the evil thereof."* [Matthew 6:34] Each day has worries enough of its own!

PRAYER: **Heavenly Father, fill us anew each day with your Spirit. Grant us the wisdom and the discipline to live our lives one day at a time, starting afresh each morning. Fill us with your love. Keep us free from worry. Help us do your will. AMEN.**

MARCH 8

THE $64,000 QUESTION

(Scripture to ponder: Matthew 16: 13–19)

Back in the early days of television there was a quiz show called *The $64,000 Question.* The contestants competed for cash prizes by answering questions. The question that carried the biggest reward—and the one that was the toughest to answer—was the $64,000 question. The program finally went off the air amid a scandal of cheating. But while it was on the air, it stimulated a lot of thinking.

What's *your* $64,000 Question, the one that asks what's most important to you? I believe the most important question any one can ask is the one recorded in our Scripture for today, the one that Christ asked his disciples: *"Who do you say I am?"* *[Matthew 16:19]*

How we answer that question depends, of course, on how we see the Lord Jesus. Some see him as a great teacher, but nothing more. Some see him as a prophet, in the Old Testament tradition. Some, such as the Hindus, see him as a special reincarnation—which puts him up on a shelf with all the other gods of the vast Hindu pantheon.

But Simon Peter gave the answer that Christians hold dear, the one that proclaims Christ as unique: *"You are the Savior of the World, the Son of the Living God !"* *[Matthew 16:16]* Only if we believe that, can we manifest a living faith, a faith worth dying for, faith that has the power to change hearts and transform the world.

How do *you* answer that $64,000 question?

Prayer: **Heavenly Father, we acknowledge Jesus as your son and our Lord. Grant us through the power of your Holy Spirit to serve others in love, and to and proclaim his Lordship as savior of the world. AMEN.**

MARCH 9

REPENTING AND REPEATING

(Scripture to ponder: Mark 1:1–8)

Imagine a lank man wearing a camel skin girded around his waist with a rough leather belt, sandals on his feet, a man who eats locusts and wild honey. Hear his rough voice call for repentance, and denounce the Sadducees and Pharisees as a brood of vipers! John the Baptist must have been thunderous as he spoke to the responding crowds, proclaiming that although he baptized with water, he was only a messenger preparing the way for one who would baptize with fire and with the Holy Spirit. It would have been a sight to behold! The account, from Mark's Gospel is our selection today.

A contemporary counterpart for John the Baptist might be the Reverend Billy Graham, who also exhorted crowds for the Lord. He spoke to millions around the world and brought many to repentance and to Christ.

A story is told about a reporter who did some follow up studies on Graham's crusades. He found that many of the people who responded to altar calls at the end of his services were actually repeaters, that is, folks who'd come forward before on another occasion. In his article the newsman belittled Graham, and attacked the statistics showing numbers of people saved.

But I think the reporter understood neither the message, nor the Christian Life—which is, I believe, a story of repetitive turning to God to repent of our sins. We continually stumble and fall as we seek to follow his Will and His Way. If we repent, God brings renewal to our hearts, minds and spirits by the only force that can bring—indeed, that ever has brought—salvation to this wounded, hurting world. For are all sinners; but as confessing Christians, we are forgiven sinners. Through God's mercy we have reconciliation, restoration and renewal.

PRAYER: **Forgive our sins, O Lord, the many times we fall short in this life, and renew a right spirit within us, replacing our hearts of stone, so we may truly worship You to do Your will. AMEN.**

MARCH 10

WHO CAN SEPARATE US FROM GOD ?

(Scripture to ponder: Romans 8: 35–39)

It is not uncommon, when we have experienced loss of a loved one or other forms of grief, to feel separated from God. Another common source of such feelings is depression, or guilt when we have fallen short of the mark.

But just as clouds and overcast skies can hide the sun, which shines just the same, above the clouds—which we appreciate dramatically when we take off from an airport when its raining and climb above the clouds—so God is ever present, though we are shrouded in our own feelings.

God's Love is always there. Thus can the Psalmist write,

Let us sing his praises, for he has not despised my cries of deep despair; he has not turned and walked away. When I cried to him, he heard and came.

[Psalm 22:24]

And hear what comfortable words St. Paul has for us who believe:

For I am sure that neither death, nor life, nor angels, nor principalities, nor things present, nor things to come, nor powers, nor height, nor depth, nor anything else in all creation will be able to separate us from the love of God in Christ Jesus our Lord.

[Romans 8:38–39]

I am convinced that just as an airplane taking off can lift us above the clouds, so *PRAISE* is how we can lift our souls unto God, how we come into His presence. Praise lifts us out of our everyday circumstances into His Light.

LET US PRAY: Dear Lord, sometimes we feel far from you through grief or guilt or depression. Lift us into Your presence, show us your face, reminding us that nothing can ever separate us from your love, through Christ Jesus. AMEN.

MARCH 11

CRACKED—OR—CRUSHED?

(Scripture to ponder: Luke 20:18)

My wife and I usually travel together between our home in Philadelphia, and Phoenix, where we spend winters. But as we drove to the airport to leave Arizona in the spring of 2002, she was headed east and I was flying west to help my daughter who had just had knee surgery.

"Oh, I left some eggs in the fridge that you need to use up," she said as we were parting. I was going to return to Phoenix for one day to close up before I myself flew back to Pennsylvania a week later.

On the flight to Portland, I got thinking about eggs. An egg is interesting—it's useful if you crack it, utterly useless if you step on it. In one instance it's valuable, in the other, worthless. If it is broken by being cracked, it can become something delicious, but if it is crushed, it's no good whatsoever.

Do you remember the passage in Luke where Jesus quotes Psalm 118, telling of the stone which the builders rejected becoming the head of the corner? It's our Scripture for today. In the very next verse he says, *"Everyone who falls on that stone will be broken, but when it falls on any one, it will crush him."* It reminded me of the egg.

For, just as it's necessary for an egg to be broken to be useful, so we, too, must be broken if we are to be useful to God. Out of brokenness comes God's strength. Conversely, those who reject God will be crushed—like an egg that's been stepped on. I believe that is what Christ was getting at, and it's sobering. It's our choice.

PRAYER: **We know that it's in being broken that we become useful to you, O Lord. In our brokenness make us instruments of your will and of your peace. Release your spirit within us. AMEN.**

MARCH 12

WILL IT BE JUSTICE OR MERCY?

(Scripture to ponder: Romans 3:21–25)

Have you ever gotten into trouble and got what you deserved? Have you ever gotten into trouble and got *not* what you deserved—that is, what would have been *just*, but instead received *mercy?*

Recently I've been reading quite a bit of Shakespeare in preparation for taking a course about his plays. There's a marvelous passage about the quality of mercy in *The Merchant of Venice.* In that play the merchant Antonio has borrowed 3000 ducats from Shylock, who makes the loan with the stipulation that if it is not repaid by the due date, he may cut a pound of flesh from whatever part of Antonio's body he wishes.

When Shylock demands payment, which Antonio cannot meet because his fortunes have changed, Portia, disguised as a lawyer defending Antonia, makes the famous "Quality of Mercy" speech. Shylock presses his case, insisting he only wants justice done. In pleading for mercy, Portia says:

". . . consider this, that in the course of justice none of us should see salvation."

"Mercy," asserts Portia, *"is mightiest in the mightiest,"*
"It is an attribute to God Himself."

If you recall the play, you remember that Shylock refuses to be merciful, but Portia saves Antonio on a technicality: Shylock may have his pound of flesh, but in doing so, he may not spill one drop of blood.

The Bible speaks to the same issues in today's Scripture passage, asserting: *"All have sinned."* If we were to be judged by justice alone, none of us could be saved. Almighty God is most merciful, and through the sacrifice of Jesus, we receive that mercy as the free gift of salvation.

PRAYER: We do indeed believe the Scriptures, O Lord, and know your mercy is from everlasting to everlasting to those that reverence you. We praise and bless You for the gift of salvation through Jesus Christ our Lord. AMEN.

MARCH 13

THE APPEAL OF ODORS

(Scripture to ponder: Genesis 8:21)

We probably use our sense of smell the least of all our senses. But it can be one of the most evocative of our five senses. I was reminded of this as I rode my bike to the YMCA recently to swim laps and passed several blossoming orange trees emitting their sweet, pleasant odor.

As part of morning devotions today I encountered the famous hymn written in 1913 by George Bennard[19], "The Old Rugged Cross:"

**On a hill faraway stood an old rugged cross,   the emblem of suffering and shame; and
I love that old cross where the dearest and best for a world of lost sinners was slain.**

I never sing that old hymn but what I smell the strong odor of cedar, and I never smell cedar without thinking of that hymn. For when I was a boy, we hade a summer place in Medford Lakes, NJ, a community in which all the buildings were made out of cedar logs. I first heard that hymn in the Community Church there, and we sang it at least once each summer in that little cedar-smelling log church we attended on Sunday every summer for about ten years.

In the Old Testament there are many references to the "sweet savor" of burnt offerings to the Lord, beginning with Noah's offering after the flood (our scripture for today), continuing down through the other books of Moses. Although sacrifices are no longer offered to God as in the days of old, if it's not too sacrilegious, do you suppose the Lord would be pleased with the pleasant odor of backyard barbeques today?

PRAYER: Your Word describes the sacrifice of Christ as a sweet-smelling savor. *[Ephesians 5:2]* May our lives also be pleasing to you, O Lord, as we seek to do your Will in this strife-torn world. AMEN.

MARCH 14

FISHING FOR PEOPLE

(Scripture to ponder: Mark 1:16–17)

It seems to me there was great method in our Lord's decision to choose fishermen as his first four disciples. Fishermen are usually savvy and patient, and both are worthwhile if you're fishing for people.

There are many ways to fish. One method that I learned about when I served in the Indian Health Service in Washington State is called *gill netting*. To do it, the Indians string a net across a river when the salmon are migrating in from the ocean to spawn upstream. The net has gaps about the size of your hand: smaller fish swim through it, but the larger salmon get stuck around their middle at the dorsal fin, and in their struggle to get free, their gills get caught and hold them fast.

I thought of today's Scripture when I read in Jimmy Carter's book, *Sources of Strength* about a truck driver who was asked to address the 1976 Southern Baptist Convention. Although this man shared the podium with Carter and Billy Graham, he wasn't an accomplished speaker at all. In fact, he was terrified as he rose to the lectern and slowly began his story.

He told of being a drunk, and how his life changed after hearing about Christ. He joined a church, but didn't know anybody there and he felt more at ease at the pub. So he cast his net there, and began to talk to the customers, answering their questions about his faith. At first he was looked on with curiosity and was treated as a joke; but he kept up with their questions, and if he didn't have an answer, he'd go and look it up.

As he finished his halting testimony, this humble truck driver looked out over the seventeen thousand delegates at the convention and quietly closed his short speech by saying *"Fifteen of my friends became Christians."* Then he sat down. He was indeed a true fisher of men for God.

PRAYER: Just as there are many ways to fish, O Lord, so there are many ways to serve You and share the Good News of the Gospel. Help us never be afraid to tell others of the hope that is within us. AMEN.

MARCH 15

HOW MANY KEYS DO YOU NEED?

(Scripture to ponder: Matthew 16:13–20)

Have you got some old keys lying around? I do, and I suspect most people do, too.

I once encountered a bunch of old keys in a drawer in my workshop. I smiled as I sorted through them, for they brought back memories. There was a key to a home I'd sold several years earlier. Several small keys were there, to luggage locks I'd long since discarded when I replaced them with combination locks. I found a pair of car keys to a vehicle I'd traded in, and even a small key to a motor scooter that had been stolen from me years before!

After my father died a few years ago and I went through his things, I found a bunch of old keys, none of which I recognized. The keys had no meaning for me, and for all intents and purposes, they were worthless.

We don't need many keys as we go through life, and most of them get replaced or become outmoded. Yet we seem to hang on to them, don't we?

I think we really only need one key, and that's one from St. Peter's key ring. After he made his great proclamation of who Jesus was (recorded in our selection from Matthew 16), Jesus gave Peter *the Keys to the Kingdom.* Peter's great confession, recorded in today's selection, is the key to life eternal:

"Thou art the Christ, the Son of the living God!"

PRAYER: O Lord, help us to realize that the only key we need in this life is to know you, the Christ, the Son of the living God. Help us always do your will. AMEN.

MARCH 16

WAITING ON THE LORD

(Scriptures to ponder: Isaiah 40; Psalm 100)

They that wait upon the Lord shall renew their strength.
They shall mount up with wings as eagles,
They shall run and not be weary,
They shall walk and not faint.

[Isaiah 40:31]

We Americans are not patient people. We are prone to action, to making things happen, to fostering change.

There used to be an expression—which came out of the hustle and production quotas of World War II—"**The difficult we do every day; the impossible takes a little longer.**" But in God's timing, in the vast framework of eternity, our human impatience means nothing.

Occasionally at night I will awaken from sleep, bothered by a particular problem. I will wait in the darkness for the morning light. But there is nothing I can do to hasten the dawn. It comes in its own time.

Besides the connotation of *patience*, there's another sense of waiting on the Lord, which is often overlooked. It is the sense of *serving the Lord*, used in the same sense as in waiting on tables by a waitress—the sense of serving, of doing another's pleasure. *"Serve the Lord with gladness, come before His Presence with thanksgiving,"* says the Psalmist. *[Psalm 100]*

In that sense of joyously waiting on the Lord with gladness and thanksgiving, we are granted the patience and perspective we need to face the problems of this world.

Prayer: Dear Lord, show us how to wait upon you and serve you with gladness
             and thanksgiving for the many blessings you bestow, all the days of our
             lives. AMEN.

MARCH 17

COMMUNING WITH THE SAINTS

(Scripture to ponder: Ephesians 1:15; Colossians 1:26)

The contemporary Christian writer Henri Nouwen, in his book, *Genesee Diary,* says this about saints: "**Without saints you easily settle for less-inspiring people and quickly follow the ways of others who for a while seem exciting but who are not able to offer lasting support.**"

There are many ways to define a saint. The Roman Catholic Church has formally recognized many saints from all eras, and the reformed tradition has many as well. St. Paul in today's scripture from Ephesians seems to imply that all who believe in Christ are the saints. I myself regard as saints all those persons—whether alive or dead— whose life and teaching is inspiring, drawing me closer to God. By that definition the words of Nouwen just quoted have great meaning and hold great promise for us in our Christian walk.

Certainly we all love to listen to great preaching; but I have to admit that in my daily intercourse I rarely encounter great preachers. But in another sense, such encounters can indeed occur every day, if I form the habit of spending a portion of each day in meditation and prayer, and in communion with the saints: by reading the writings and becoming familiar with the lives of those Christians throughout history whose lives have invigorated and renewed the Church.

There are hundreds of them. If we will but spend the time, they will give us continual inspiration in our walk with God. An excellent place to begin is with the selection of readings in a book entitled *Spiritual Classics*[20] edited by Richard J. Foster and Emilie Griffin. It's part of an excellent series called **RENOVARÈ** Resources for Spiritual Renewal.

PRAYER: We believe in the communion of Saints, O Lord, in those who know you well and have gone before us in this life. Help us to come to know them, to inspire us to do your will. AMEN.

MARCH 18

FINDING GOD

(Scripture to ponder: 1 Kings 19:9–12)

Where is God to be found? A book published a few years ago bore the title *Where is God when it Hurts?* In these painful days following the terrible destruction of the world Trade Center and other terrorist acts, many are asking that question, and are earnestly seeking God.

The Bible shows us many ways to find God. St. Paul, preaching to the Greeks, asserted that God is in the midst of us. He said, *"In Him we live and move and have our being." [Acts 17:28]* But although God has created all of nature, God is not nature. Read the selection for today, that tells about when Elijah sought the Lord. God was not in the wind, nor in the earthquake, nor in the fire, but in a still small voice that came to the prophet.

One of the best ways to find God, in my experience, is to go where He is. Psalm 22 tells us that *God inhabits the praises of His people. [Psalm 22:3]* It's a crucial concept.

Through my life, because I went to college in one state, to medical school in another, and did my residency in a third, I've been a part of many churches. I have been impressed with the variety of ways that Christians worship God. Often this takes the form of psalms and hymns and spiritual songs that lift up praise to God. By such worship we are carried into Heavenly realms where we get glimpses of the Eternal Glory. We are transported, as Isaiah was, when he said, *"I saw the Lord sitting upon a throne, high and lifted up; and His train filled the temple." [Isaiah 6:1]* Praising God brings us into His very Presence. It's a wonderful way to find and commune with Him.

PRAYER: You are Holy and indeed worthy to be praised, O Lord! Let us praise and find You in our songs and hymns. AMEN.

MARCH 19

DECAYING WOOD

(Scripture to ponder: Isaiah 40:6–8; Genesis 3:19b)

My wife and I often take walks together. This morning as we walked I noticed a split rail fence on a neighbor's property. The bottom rail was riddled with termite runs: if you had put your foot on it, it would have collapsed. A bit farther on our walk we saw another split rail fence where two of the rails were lying on the ground. These had been almost completely consumed by dry rot and termites.

All around us in nature we see evidence of decay. In the plant kingdom, everything grows, blossoms, dies and decays. The same is true of the animal kingdom: every animal—including man—is subject to disease, decay and eventually death.

In the story in Genesis from our Scripture selection, the fall of man and the casting out of Adam and eve from the Garden of Eden are described. God concludes his sermonette on the consequences of the first couple's sin by saying

"You are dust, and to dust you shall return."

Those words have been repeated countless times at Christian funerals through the ages, often accompanied by Holy Water shaken from an olive branch on to the bier. Indeed, we are all subject to death and we all eventually decay into dust.

It's a humbling thought that should help us focus our mind on eternity.

PRAYER: **All around us, Lord, we see the evidence of eventual decay. Some day we too will all be dust. But we praise You for we know that Your Word never decays. It endures forever. AMEN.**

MARCH 20

MEDICAL CHERRY PICKING

(Scripture to ponder: Luke 5:29–32)

For several years in my medical career I was chief of general surgery in a branch of a large, nationally known HMO (health maintenance organization). It was enjoyable work, but in providing medical care in that environment, things were run very much like a business: we doctors were ever and always made aware of the bottom line.

When HMOs first became popular in the 1970s under the umbrella of insurance companies, there occurred a peculiar phenomenon called *cherry picking,* until the federal government put a stop to it a few years later. *Cherry picking* involved insurance companies signing up as many healthy folks as possible—usually young, employed married couples—in whom the risk of catastrophic illness was very low. About the only common expenses for these enrollees were maternity benefits. By insuring mostly healthy folks—by *cherry picking*—and by avoiding underwriting people with advanced or chronic illnesses, the insurance companies made great profits, for they maximized income and minimized expenses.

But it's the sick, not the healthy, who need medical care. Christ said exactly that to the Pharisees in today's Scripture selection. In context, of course, he was not speaking of cherry picking of HMOs, but rather of his mission, and by extension, of the mission of his church. Were he here today, I think he might allude to cherry picking, and reiterate: The church exists to call not the righteous, but sinners to repentance, to minister to a sick and hurting humanity. Sometimes in the comfort of my denomination and my church, I find myself forgetting that principle.

PRAYER: Dear Lord, Your Son came as physician to a sin-sick humanity, to call not the righteous, but sinners to repentance. Help us to be ministers to each other and to all mankind. AMEN.

MARCH 21

GOD'S MARVELOUS PROVISION

(Scripture to ponder: Genesis 22)

Have you ever felt God's marvelous provision in your life? Our Scripture passage for today, the story of Abraham going to the mountain to sacrifice his only son Isaac at God's request, gives the faith-full reply of father to son. When the boy notes they have the wood and the fire, but no animal to sacrifice, Abraham replies, *"God will provide himself the lamb for a burnt offering, my son." [Genesis 22:8]*

I'd just graduated from medical school in Rochester, NY and was heading for my internship in Portland, Oregon. It was a choice made with much prayer, one that meant moving far from friends and relatives. After I had a hitch put on our little Chevy II wagon, we loaded all our possessions into a 5' X 8' U-Haul trailer, including a double bed, a sofa, a tandem bicycle, seventeen boxes of books and an upright Amana freezer full of frozen food from our large garden. (The electric company assured us that if we plugged the freezer in each night of the trip, the contents would stay frozen.)

All went well until the third day, when the heavy load tore the bolted hitch through the floor of the car. A welder in Iowa secured a hefty, new hitch, but cautioned us that with the load, we'd never make it over the Rocky Mountains. So we unloaded most of the trailer contents there in Iowa, shipping them to Oregon by Mayflower Van Lines. We drove on with the freezer and the trailer that we'd hired one-way to Portland. The cost of the hitch and the moving van was $400, definitely *not* part of our meager budget!

But just the previous week at graduation, God had provided a marvelous surprise for us: I won a newly established prize in memory of a classmate who had died the year before. The prize? It was a plaque and a letter—and a check for $400. Before we were even aware of what our needs would be, God had provided for us.

PRAYER: Thank you, O Lord, for Your marvelous provision for us in all the facets of our lives. Help us be a blessing to others as we seek to do Your Will. AMEN.

MARCH 22

KNOWING THE TRUTH

(Scriptures to ponder: Luke 20:25; John 8: 26–32)

The Bible often contrasts things eternal with things temporal. One example is described in our first selection, when the Pharisees tried to trap Jesus after they asked him about paying taxes to Rome. His response clearly separated things temporal from things eternal: **"Render unto Caesar the things that are Caesar's, and unto God the things that are Gods."**

In our second selection, Jesus taught **"You shall know the truth and the truth will make you free."** In the matter of ascertaining the truth, we get another contrast between the eternal and the temporal: On the night he was betrayed, Jesus was brought before Pilate. In response to the prelate's asking, "So you are a king?" Jesus replied, *"For this I was born and for this I have come into the world, to bear witness to the truth. Everyone who is of the truth hears my voice."* [John 18:37]

To this statement by the eternal, incarnate Son of God, came the cynical, temporal rejoinder of Pilate: *"WHAT IS TRUTH?"* [John 18:38]

You see, for the temporal mind, particularly one who must judge testimony given by several witnesses, truth is relative, depending on the point of view of the observer. It's a common occurrence in the courtroom.

But the Truth as presented by Jesus involves eternal, unchanging verities: Faith, Hope, Joy, Peace and Love. These have stood the test of time, and will stand forever, based on God's word. He who sees into the heart has set the standard to which we prayerfully aspire.

PRAYER: open our eyes and our ears, Dear Lord, that we may see and hear your Truth, that we may do Your will. AMEN.

MARCH 23

REMEMBERING SINS NO MORE'

(Scripture to ponder: Jeremiah 31:34)

Have you ever had a secret that you were ashamed of, one that you finally confessed? Do you recall what happened then? Here's one of mine.

When I was about nine years old we lived in the suburbs of Philadelphia. We had a refrigerator (with an upper, freezer compartment) and we had a gas stove. It happened that my mother had a cooking thermometer that fascinated me. It was made of glass, with a blue liquid in the center that moved up and down as the temperature changed.

When mother went out and I was alone, I'd get out that thermometer, turn on a burner on the gas stove and prop open the door of the upper compartment of the refrigerator. Then I'd alternately put the bulb of the thermometer into the gas flame and into the freezer, delighted by the rapid up and down movement of the bright blue fluid. One day I left the bulb in the flame a split second too long. With a plinking "pflitt" the blue fluid shot out of the top of the thermometer, making a tiny blue dot on the ceiling. I shut off the gas, shut the refrigerator door and took a shovel from the garage and buried the thermometer in the garden.

Ten years passed before I got up the courage to ask my mother about that thermometer. She said she did not remember it, even though I told her the story of its demise, which was still vivid in my own memory.

The Love of God is like that, too. In our Scripture for today Jeremiah says that if we turn to the Lord our sins will be blotted out like a cloud.

PRAYER: We Praise You, Dear Lord, that when we confess our sins and seek forgiveness, you remember our sins no more. AMEN

MARCH 24

RAISING SEEDLINGS

(Scriptures to ponder: 1 Peter 2:2; 1 Corinthians 3:2)

When I was a boy my father was an avid gardener. Each year he raised a surprising number of vegetables from a small plot behind the house.

One of his favorites was a special lettuce called Manoa, for which he got seeds from Hawaii. He'd plant them inside the house in moist potting soil in March, and after they sprouted, he'd set them outside in the daytime, during the cold days of early spring so they'd become hardy. At night they were brought back inside. With time and nurturing, he knew he could transplant them and they'd withstand cold nights in cold soil. He gave the seedlings progressively longer exposure to the harsh elements until he finally set them out all night. Then he transplanted them into the garden. As the days got progressively warmer, the plants not only survived: they became strong and vigorous.

The Apostle Peter in his first says we should long for the pure spiritual milk by which we are nourished unto salvation. St. Paul writing to the Church at Corinth indicates we are fed on milk at first but progress to solid food as we grow into Christ's likeness. God in His wisdom treats us as seedlings, feeds us milk at first, then with more substantial food. We are nourished in the Church. With time and experience, counsel and loving support, we grow strong and hardy in the family of Christ, ready to be set out into world to do His will.

PRAYER: Nourish us, Dear Lord, and strengthen us through Your word, in Christ's family, which is the church. Help us grow to maturity, so we may do your will in the world. AMEN.

MARCH 25

THE TEMPLE OF THE HOLY SPIRIT

(Scripture to ponder: 1 Corinthians 6:19)

Recently I returned to my roots in suburban Philadelphia and there looked up one of my old Scouting friends, whom I'll call Sam. He had been a superb athlete when we were Scouts, running cross-country in high school. When the troop went to the Adirondacks for a week, he set a record by climbing nine peaks in eight hours.

Sam's family ran a local plumbing business, so I stopped in to say hello to my old friend, with whom I'd not kept in touch. A tall young man who looked vaguely familiar rose and stepped up behind the counter as I entered. I introduced myself and inquired after Sam. The young man said he was Sam's son, and informed me that Sam had died of lung cancer three years earlier. He said his dad had been a heavy smoker.

My recollection was that Sam had not smoked while he was a member of the troop, so he must have begun thereafter. Indeed, when I knew him, he was what I might call a personification of the Scout Oath, for so far as I had known, he kept himself "physically strong, mentally awake and morally straight."

In our Scripture for today, St. Paul says that our bodies are the Temple of the Holy Spirit; we are to keep them clean and pure and undefiled. When I knew him in Scouts, Sam seemed to be all those things, but sometime afterward he fell under the terrible sway of tobacco addiction, which exacted a horrible price from his body.

PRAYER: **O Lord, help us realize all our life long that our bodies are the Temple of the Holy Spirit. Help us keep them clean and undefiled, so we may serve You all our days. AMEN.**

MARCH 26

EVIL THOUGHTS

(Scripture to ponder: Ephesians 4:29)

When I was a senior medical student, my wife and I flew from Rochester, NY, to spend Thanksgiving with my family in Philadelphia. After a wonderful three days we were driven to the airport by my folks, who dropped us off and went to park the car as we checked our bags.

The line was long. We were miffed when a red-headed woman cut into the line just ahead of us. Both my wife and I were muttering under our breath about rude people who cut lines, when I heard my mother's voice behind me exclaim, **"Why Edith Harkins! How nice to see you! You must meet my son and daughter-in-law."** She shook hands as she hugged the woman who'd cut in ahead of us and they exchanged pleasantries. Boy, were we embarrassed!

We would have done well to heed the words of St. Paul in his letter to the Church at Ephesus (our Scripture for today):

"Let no evil talk come out of your mouths, but only such as is good for edifying, as fits the occasion, that it may impart grace to those who hear."

We never go wrong if we use edifying words—words that build up others—not destructive, critical words. Sometimes it is Oh, so hard to refrain from snapping or backbiting. But such actions or retorts are never healing: they only cause hurt, or open old wounds.

PRAYER: Dear Lord Jesus, help us to follow You in every area of our lives, recalling that You did not respond harshly or answer back. Fill us with your peace. AMEN.

MARCH 27

HOPE

(Scripture to ponder: John 3:16–17)

As a physician, one of the most important things I bring to my encounters with patients is *hope*. Almost everyone who comes to me for help does so because of a specific need, and usually because of my faith and my surgical training, I can help them.

On occasion someone comes who has a malignancy, say advanced cancer of the breast or of the bowel, whose exam shows widespread disease. Although there is little chance of cure, I can still offer them *hope* by treating their symptoms and by listening to their problems, bringing my experience to bear from treating other advanced cases.

Even in those situations that to the patient seem hopeless, we can almost always offer help to alleviate distressing symptoms.

But the greatest gift I can share with them—indeed, with anyone—is confidence in God's gift of Eternal Life. In his first letter to the church at Corinth, St. Paul wrote:

"If in this life only we have hope in Christ, we are of all men most miserable."
[1 Corinthians 15:19]

But we have hope in another life. The joy and the comfort I have in my life in Christ comes from the assurance that he has overcome death, that when we fall asleep in death, we will wake eternally. We have that confidence because of our faith. Let us pray with St. John *[John 3:16–17]*:

PRAYER: **Dear Lord, we know that You so loved the world that You gave Your only Son, that whoever believes in Him should not perish, but have everlasting Life. For You did not send Him into the world to condemn it, but rather, through Him, the world might be saved. AMEN.**

MARCH 28

AT HOME IN CHRIST

(Scripture to ponder: Matthew 11:28–30)

Home is the place where, when you have to go there They have to take you in.

[Robert Frost]

We are a mobile society. On the average, families move every five years. I myself have moved fourteen times in my sixty-five years. Home is now where my wife and I reside. But for many years, home was the large, old house in Pennsylvania where I grew up, a home where my parents lived for forty years and where each of us four kids still had a room. As in the Robert Frost quote above, we were always welcome in the old house, loved and accepted by our folks.

After they moved into a "life-care" situation, my father died and my mother required more care as she grew older: she ended up in one room. When I retired from practicing surgery in Arizona, we sold my home and bought a condominium where we spend the winters. Diane and I have our primary home near Philadelphia, not far from where my 100 year-old mother lived.

So you could say we have two homes—one in Pennsylvania and one in Arizona. Each is comfortable, furnished with things we love. But there's a third home we have, the most precious of all.

It's the home we have in the Lord, a place in the world but not of the world, a place where we're completely accepted and loved by our Heavenly Father. It is a priceless edifice, not built with hands or of wood or stone. It's the place where Jesus is Lord—the Kingdom of God—to which He summons every one of us with gentle welcome. Its essence is well captured by the words of William Thompson's hymn:

"Softly and tenderly, Jesus is calling, Calling for you and for me; See on the portals He's waiting and watching, Watching for you and for me.

"Come home, come home, Ye who are weary, come home. Earnestly, tenderly, Jesus is calling, Calling, O sinner, come home."

PRAYER: Thank you Lord for being always with us. When we need rest unto our souls, we can come home to your open arms. AMEN.

MARCH 29

THE THIRTEENTH APOSTLE?

(Scriptures to ponder: Matthew 4:8–22; 19:16–26)

The Gospel of Matthew records Jesus calling the first four disciples, who were fishermen. They left their nets and followed him. Later in that gospel, Matthew describes Christ's encounter with a man who came to ask how he could obtain eternal life. Jesus tells him to observe the commandments. The man says he's kept them from his youth. He asks what else he lacks. Jesus replies:

> . . . *"Go and sell what you have and give it to the poor, and you will have treasure in heaven, and come and follow me"* . . . *But when the young man heard that saying, he went away sorrowful: for he had great possessions."*

Quite clearly, Jesus calls this rich young man to follow him, much as he called the original twelve. What if he'd responded by selling his possessions, and what if he'd taken up with them? Might he then have become the thirteenth apostle? For later on Judas, one of the original twelve, hung himself after he betrayed our Lord, and the others cast lots to fill his place, choosing Matthias to fill his place, as recorded at the end of the first chapter of Acts.

It's not an idle question for us, who confess Jesus as Lord today in affluent America. We, who have many possessions, claim to follow him who had no possessions, who said he had no place to lay his head *[Luke 9:58]*. Does our material wealth get in the way of following him? Do we sometimes fail to respond to his call because of worldly impediments? Is the world too much with us? By getting and spending, do we "lay waste our powers," as William Wordsworth put it?

God calls us to service. He summons us to follow where he leads. Are we ready to give it all up for him? For he is the Pearl of Great Price.

PRAYER: We have heard your call, O Lord. May we never let our possessions get in the way of responding with our whole heart and soul and mind and strength. Help us love one another. AMEN.

MARCH 30

MANAGING LIFE'S JOURNEY

(Scripture to ponder: 1 Corinthians 13:1–13)

How do we approach life? How do we respond to its vicissitudes? I thought of those questions this morning when I looked at a picture on the wall of our guest bathroom. It shows a brace of Canadian Geese in flight, and the caption beneath reads

Faith is how you know where you are going; Hope is what keeps you going; Love is how you get there.

That picture is a capsule lesson in managing life's journey.

Faith, Hope, and Love. Those words, of course, conjure up the magnificent "Hymn to Love" that St. Paul recorded in Chapter 13 of his first letter to the Corinthians, which gives many of the attributes of love. It closes with the words,

"Thus remain Faith, Hope and Love; but the greatest of these is Love."

We know love is the way because Jesus Himself said, *"A new commandment I give unto you, that you love one another as I have loved you."* [John 15:12] And the apostle John, who was so close to Jesus that he was known as the beloved disciple, says *"God is Love; and he that dwells in love dwells in God, and God in him."* [1 John 4:16]

The secret of life's journey is to love God, and to love one another.

PRAYER: Teach us through Your Word, O Lord, to love one another as You have loved us. AMEN.

MARCH 31

AN HONEST FATHER

(Scripture to ponder: Proverbs 20:7)

"When I was a boy of 14, my father was so ignorant I could hardly stand to have the old man around. But when I got to be 21, I was astonished at how much he had learned in 7 years."

[Mark Twain]

I came to a similar, new appreciation of my Dad, as I emerged from my adolescent years.

My father was a hardworking physician. Although our family schedule was arranged so we always had breakfast and supper together, we didn't see a lot of him when we were growing up. He left for the hospital to make rounds right after our early breakfast, and usually went back to see patients after supper in the evening. He never watched T.V. and I rarely saw him reading a book. We never played catch.

What a contrast was the father of one of my girl friends. He'd taken early retirement and was always at home. Whereas my father spent almost four years in an Army hospital in the South Pacific during WWII, this man made a fortune at home producing brass propellers for liberty ships. He read widely, spoke fluent French and Italian, had many interests and was a brilliant conversationalist. He was sophisticated. Even after I stopped dating his daughter, I'd go visit him, and through him I became familiar with authors such as Stefan Zweig and Albert Camus. We spent many hours chatting.

But despite my friendship and admiration for this man—who wrote a glowing letter helping me get into college—I began to notice some disturbing contrasts with my father. My Dad didn't smoke and rarely drank; but I seldom saw this man without a cigarette or a cocktail in his hand. My father spent most of his time helping others; but this man was almost completely self-absorbed. Although I did not think he was dishonest, he was not well respected, whereas I continually ran into people who sang the praises of my father. In short, as I grew up and experienced the world, my esteem for my father grew; but for the other man, it waned.

Our Scripture in Proverbs declares: *"It is a wonderful heritage to have an honest father." [Proverbs 20:7]* For me it was, indeed.

PRAYER: Thank you, Lord, for fathers who are faithful and true, for they often are the way we come to know You better. AMEN.

APRIL 1

AN UNEXPECTED HONOR

(Scripture to ponder: Luke 14:7–11)

Recently at a medical meeting in the Midwest, I sat beside a doctor from New York City. He turned out to be President of the New York Academy of Medicine, one of the oldest medical groups in the country, an academy that has a splendid collection of old medical books. I belong to a similar group in Philadelphia, and since medical history is one of my special interests, I asked if I might come for a visit to "see his shop."

I made arrangements for the visit, which included lunch in his office. He said he'd be on a tight schedule that day, for he'd been selected for Grand Jury duty. "Why don't we just share a sandwich in the office; we can chat over lunch," he said, when I called.

I planned to drive up from my home near Philadelphia, and a week before, called his secretary because I'd forgotten to ask about parking. I told her I'd be glad to bring up sandwiches for us. She responded, "You'll be able to park in the lot next to the building," and she continued, "Don't worry about lunch—he's taking care of that."

I arrived a few minutes early. Their offices were on the sixth floor. The secretary had me wait in his inner office, and as I did so, I noticed that in the adjoining room—that was like a small library—a small table was getting set with a white tablecloth and silverware. Just then he came in and greeted me. We chatted for several minutes until he said, "Let's continue to talk while we have some lunch." He then ushered me into the library-like room. At the small table we were served a Caesar Salad and deli sandwiches by the white-coated waitress who'd set the table. It was a far cry from what I'd expected or what I'd have brought.

Reflecting on it later, I was reminded of Christ's parable of the feast where the guest who came took a humble seat and was brought to the head table to be honored by the host. The story is told in today's Scripture passage. It was a variation on Jesus' teaching that in his Kingdom, the *first shall be last, and the last first. [Mark 10:31]*

PRAYER: Help us always, O Lord, to not have grand expectations for ourselves, but rather to seek a lowly place, serving others, and trusting in Your Divine Providence. AMEN.

APRIL 2

FILL YOUR MIND WITH GOOD THINGS!

(Scripture to ponder: Philippians 4:8–9)

Through the ages there has always been a recognition that we become what we take in through our eyes and our ears. The ancient philosophers believed in the concept of the *tabula rasa,* that the mind was like a blank slate on which our experience—that which we take in through our eyes and ears—would write. Human beings were born with a *tabula rasa,* a blank slate, they believed. Although science has since shown that heredity also exerts a strong influence, still the strongest influence by far is what we experience in life.

In modern times, when computers have become so universal, the same phenomenon is recognized in the catchword *GIGO,* by which is meant *Garbage In, Garbage Out,* namely whatever you program into a computer is what you'll get out! We are not computers, but our minds work in similar ways, and what we take in through our senses tends to become a part of us and often later comes out through our mouth.

This was vividly brought home to me when I was twelve years old. I was a den chief in a Cub Scout pack. One day a Cub Scout's little six-year-old sister met me at the door of their home singing a beer commercial she'd learned by watching television. She had no idea what the jingle meant, but she had taken it in through her ears and brought it out through her mouth.

"Fill your mind with good things," is excellent advice. In our Scripture selection for today, St. Paul urges us to think about things that are lovely and pure and honorable. Nowadays with all the tintinabua of the media and the assault on our senses that we endure each day, it's imperative that we Christians consciously work at filling our minds with good things.

Prayer: Dear Heavenly Father, help us set aside time each day to read your word and meditate on it, filling our mind with good things from the joy and peace of the Gospel. In Jesus' name we pray. AMEN.

APRIL 3

WHO ARE THE MINISTERS?

(Scripture to ponder: Ephesians 4:11–12)

It is common to speak of the ministry as a synonym for the Clergy. Someone who enters the ministry is usually one who becomes ordained as a pastor of a church. But the Latin noun *minister* actually means *servant*, and the Latin verb *ministrare* means *to serve*.

On the back of our church bulletin there's a column that lists the clergy and staff of the church. Under the heading of "Ministers" it reads: "All the members of the church." Below that are listed the names of the pastors and the staff.

Our Scripture selection indicates that the ministers of the church are actually the members of the congregation who follow Jesus, who take his life as the model for their lives, namely to serve the needs of others. Being a Christian is not a spectator sport!

St. Paul, in his letter to the Church at Ephesus is quite clear as he differentiates between the clergy, that is, the full time employees, and the ministers:

And He gave some as apostles and some as prophets, and some as evangelists and some as pastors and teachers, for the equipping of the saints for ministry, to the building up of the body of Christ.

It's apparent that we, the members of individual congregations, are those saints, who, instructed by our church leaders, can in turn minister to one another and to the world, to carry out God's will.

PRAYER: Teach us and inspire us, O Lord, through our leaders and through Your Holy Spirit, so we may effectively minister to a suffering world. AMEN.

APRIL 4

FLYING A BEAM

(Scripture to ponder: Isaiah 30:21)

During the Second World War, my father was a major in the Army, the commanding officer of a large field hospital in the Pacific Theater. He once was summoned to meet with General Douglas Macarthur and traveled in a two-seater fighter plane across miles of ocean to the rendezvous point. On the way back the pilot lost his bearings and could not find his way. He was running out of gas, with the bleak prospect of ditching in the wide ocean. But they managed to pick up a radio beam from one of the American air bases, and using it to direct them, flew on to safely land. Dad said it was an unforgettable experience.

In flying a beam, a pilot is guided by what he hears in his earphones, a certain tone being emitted if he strays to the right, another if he goes off to the left. The pilot constantly listens and makes small corrections to stay on his course.

So it is with the Christian life. The journey we are on is our life's course, and as Christians the beam we listen for is God's Word. We hear it by reading the Bible and by praying every day. If we stray to the left or to the right, we can make small corrections so we stay on course. But to do so, we must always be attentive to his voice, telling us the way in which we should go.

PRAYER: **Dear Lord, guide us as we go about our everyday activities. Make us always attentive to hear your word and stay on the beam of your will, as we continue on life's course. AMEN.**

APRIL 5

CACOPHONY OR HARMONY?

(Scripture to Ponder: 1 Corinthians 14:33)

Does your life sometimes seem to be an unrelated jumble of events?

The composer George Gershwin was once walking with a friend along a crowded popular beach resort near New York City. Their conversation was pierced by the shrieks and sounds of hundreds of voices. Hucksters on the boardwalk barked out their wares. The crashing roar of the sea was audible on one side and on the other, the deep rumbling roar of the subway. In the midst of it all could be heard the clanking tunes of a merry-go-round.

Gershwin remarked to his friend, **"All of this could form such a beautiful pattern of sound—a musical piece expressive of almost every human activity. But it is all disorganized, discordant and exhausting as we hear it now."**

Gershwin knew that mere disorganized sounds produced cacophony not harmony, for he was a master at arranging and blending sounds.

Modern life itself can seem a cacophony, a jumble of unrelated events. But I do not believe that is what God has in store for his people. As our Scripture selection for today proclaims, he is not a God of confusion, but of harmony and peace. Through daily prayer and meditation on the scriptures, we can allow our lives to be arranged and blended by God into his master plan, and we will find harmony for our souls.

PRAYER: Dear Lord, we live in a jumbled, often frenetic world. Through your Spirit, arrange our lives harmoniously, blending them into Your will. In Jesus' name we pray. AMEN.

APRIL 6

DIRECTED STEPS

(Scripture to ponder: Proverbs 16:9)

"A man's mind plans his way, but the Lord directs his steps."

RSV

When I was a boy I was a member of an active Boy Scout troop near Philadelphia that was steeped in tradition and went on many exciting trips. I got interested in mountain climbing when we spent a week in the Adirondacks and I got to climb Mt. Marcy, the highest point in New York.

After I grew up and moved away, one of my old friends became Scoutmaster. Under his guidance the troop took many thrilling trips, including kayaking white water and mountain climbing abroad. One of these trips had been to Switzerland where they planned to climb the Matterhorn.

I didn't know about the Matterhorn trip at the time because I was out west. But over the years I had done quite a bit of mountain climbing. I spent a summer in the Austrian Alps where I did a lot of rock climbing, and as a surgical resident I scaled several of the snow-covered peaks in the Northwest, including Mt. Rainier, Mt. Adams, and Mt. Hood.

I'd always wanted to climb the Matterhorn, and at age 58, that wish came true when I traveled to Zermatt, hired a Swiss guide and made the ascent. We set out at 3:30 A.M from a hut at 10,500 feet and climbed the first six hours in darkness, using head-lamps. The trail was hard to see, and if I'd not had an experienced guide, I'm sure I would have gotten off it. Reaching the summit about 10 AM, it was glorious.

So when I ran into my old Scouting friend and found he'd led some of the troop on the trip up the Matterhorn, I asked how it went.

"Well," he said, "it was O.K., but we never got to the top. In the darkness we got off the trail, and by the time the sun was up, it was too late to make the summit."

He and I had both made plans to climb the Matterhorn, but only one of us had made it to the top. The difference was I'd had an experienced guide directing my steps.

PRAYER: We know the value of making plans for our lives, O Lord; we pray that You may always direct our steps. AMEN.

APRIL 7

GIVING UP MARBLES

(Scripture to ponder: I Corinthians 2:1–10)

Non-Christians—and even some Christians—see the call of God as one that would have us *give up* certain things, and they are reluctant to respond. But that misses the point. The famous Philadelphia preacher Donald Gray Barnhouse told a story that illustrates the point.

As a boy, he'd play marbles on the street with his pals. Every afternoon in the summer as they sat on the sidewalk and shot marbles, the older boys would pass by, swinging their bats and socking their mitts, joshing each other on their way to the empty lot down the street.

Now Donald Barnhouse loved to play marbles. In fact, there was nothing he liked better at that time in his life. He thought that he'd never give it up. But one day as the older boys passed by, one of them called out, "Barnhouse, can you play center field?"

As he related this in his sermon, Barnhouse, snapped his fingers, and exclaimed, "I gave up marbles just like that!"

That's what the life God has in store for us too! Hear the words of Saint Paul at the end of our Scripture passage for today:

"Eye hath not seen, nor ear heard, nor hath the mind of man conceived what God has prepared for those who love him"

PRAYER: **Help us hear and respond to Your call, O Lord, for in our hearts, we know you have inconceivable joy prepared for us. AMEN.**

APRIL 8

GETTING WHIPSAWED

(Scripture to ponder: Ephesians 4:14)

I sometimes tune in to the PBS *Nightly Business Report*, a program that tracks the stock market. Although I own a portfolio of stocks, I don't follow the market minutely, but I have friends who do, and it seems they get whipsawed by its daily ups and downs.

My father taught me to invest in quality companies for the long haul, an approach that helps me avoid getting whipsawed.

It strikes me that some people seem to get whipsawed in their spiritual lives. They go through highs and lows, depending on whether they were elated or displeased by a sermon or a particular service or a piece of music, or by how they feel.

In his letter to the church at Ephesus (our Scripture passage for today), St. Paul urges the Christians there not to be tossed to and fro by every wind of doctrine. He counsels them not to be whipsawed, but to grow up into Christ.

The way to avoid getting spiritually whipsawed (continuing the stock market analogy) is to invest in quality spiritual "companies"—that is, to have as the basis of faith the classical writings of Christianity. It implies being well grounded in the Bible and being utterly familiar with the writings of our great heritage, including its devotional literature. By reading and meditation, prayer and worship, we develop a strong, unwavering faith.

PRAYER: Help us, O Lord, to invest our time and energy in your Word, that our faith may be steady and strong. AMEN.

APRIL 9

CONSIDER THE BIRDS

(Scripture to ponder: Matthew 6:26)

The little gray bird landed on the table and hopped around on one foot. "My, but they're a lot of birds here on the island!" my wife exclaimed. It was true. One of the striking things we noticed was the abundance of birds—all sorts and sizes. They made lots of noise and were most apparent at meals, where they flew in and out of the open-air restaurant where we were having breakfast.

We were vacationing on the island of Barbados, the easternmost island in the Caribbean Sea. Although it was humid, there was always a breeze. The foliage was lush, giving great cover for the birds. Sparrow-sized smaller birds had no compunction about landing on the tables after diners had left, or even when folks got up to get something in the buffet line. The waitresses didn't make much effort to shoo them away. But in the restaurant we saw none of the larger birds, doves and a pigeon-like bird that was much more colorful than those we were used to in the States.

But there were no sea birds like the gulls and pelicans we'd seen on vacation in Mexico. *I wonder who feeds those larger birds?* I mused as we finished breakfast. I soon found out.

We left the restaurant to walk back to our room. As we rounded the corner we saw a large birdbath, but instead of water, it was filled with old muffins and croissants. There were about a dozen doves and pigeons feasting away on the treats. They had indeed been provided for, just as Jesus taught in today's scripture selection.

PRAYER: When we consider the birds, we realize how you provide for us day by day. We bless you, Lord, and are thankful for your provision. Help us do your will always. AMEN.

APRIL 10

HAPPINESS IS LIKE A BUTTERFLY

(Scripture to ponder: Matthew 6:25–34)

The Declaration of Independence asserts that we have an inalienable right to the pursuit of happiness. When we step back and look at our society, we see that pursuit is going on full speed ahead! But judged by the numbers of prescriptions for tranquilizers and antidepressants that physicians prescribe each year—more than any other single category of medication—it seems there's a lot of unhappiness in our land.

But happiness is like a butterfly. When you pursue and try to catch it, it zigs and zags and is a most difficult thing to catch. But if, like a gardener you quietly go about your work, you find that it marvelously alights on your shoulder!

So it is with life. Sir William Osler, one of this century's greatest physicians, said:

Live not in the past, nor in the future, but let each day's work absorb all your interest, energy and enthusiasm. The best preparation for tomorrow is to do today's work superbly well.

In today's selection, that greatest physician of all, the Lord Jesus Christ, said:

Do not be anxious about tomorrow.

The true way to happiness is to do today's work superbly well. Shut out the past, seal off the future and live today supremely well, to the fullest and the best that we can. Then happiness, mysteriously, miraculously, will alight on us.

Prayer: **Dear Lord, help us find true happiness by doing that which you would have us do today, superbly well. In Jesus' name we pray. AMEN.**

APRIL 11

CHRIST LIFTED UP

(Scripture to ponder: John 3:14–16)

For God so loved the world that He gave His only begotten Son, that whoever believes in him should not perish but have eternal life.

That verse—*John 3:16,* probably the best known verse in the New Testament—was spoken by Jesus to Nicodemus, a ruler of the Jews. It follows immediately after the verse when Jesus predicted that He must be lifted up. In verse 14 Jesus says,

"And as Moses lifted up the serpent in the wilderness, even so must the Son of Man be lifted up, that whoever believes in Him should not perish but have eternal life."

Jesus was alluding to an episode during the wanderings of the Children of Israel in the wilderness after they had been brought out of Egypt, related in Numbers Chapter 21. The people were complaining about the lack of food and water—despite the fact that God had miraculously provided manna for them, and had brought forth water from the rock. As punishment for their complaining and their ingratitude, God sent among the people fiery serpents that had a lethal bite, so many of them died.

When the people confessed to Moses that they had sinned, Moses prayed for the people. In response, God did *not* take away the fiery serpents. Rather, He instructed Moses to make a bronze serpent and lift it up on a pole, so that all who looked on it would live.

I believe Christ's message is clear: All of us in this imperfect world have been bitten by the serpent of sin. To save us, God did not make the world sinless; rather he sent his Son, lifted up on the cross so that all who believe in Him, who look to him, will be saved.

PRAYER: Thank you, Lord, for providing the way, for as we look to and believe in Your Son Jesus, we receive eternal life. AMEN.

APRIL 12

THIS IS THE WEEK THAT WAS

(Scripture to ponder: John Chapter 12)

There used to be a television program entitled "This Is the Week That Was," that recounted various exciting weeks in history, usually with vivid newsreel clips. I don't recall that they ever did a segment on Holy Week, but if they did, wouldn't it be exciting?

Each of the Four Gospels relates the final week of Jesus' life, and each records the increasing tension as the final events fall into place. Taken together they describe:

- The triumphal entry into Jerusalem to fulfill prophesy, Christ riding on a colt, the crowd crying blessings and "Hosanna!" and spreading palm branches and clothing before him on the path;
- His pausing to weep over the holy city and its fate, perceiving with divine foreknowledge its destruction by the Romans in just a few decades;
- His wrath in driving out the merchants and money changers from the temple, incurring the enmity of the authorities;
- His teaching in the Temple and his skilful parrying of the verbal thrusts of the Scribes when they try to trap him into not paying taxes to Caesar;
- His predictions about the end times and his warning to the disciples to be always ready for his return;
- The last supper with his closest friends, serving them, washing their feet, sharing with them his final, intimate discourse;
- His agony praying in the garden and his betrayal by Judas;
- The mock trial and the screaming crowd, the condemnation and the shameful chastisement culminating in the crucifixion.

Wouldn't it be something to have been there for that week? It excites me, yet makes me sad, for though I believe I would have been among those who welcomed Jesus to the Holy City with palms, I suspect I might also have shouted out for releasing

Barabbas. For I don't consider myself as strong as Peter, and even he denied his Lord that night.

PRAYER: As we ponder the events of this Holy Week, O Lord, may we appreciate your love and understand your sacrifice for us. Forgive our sins. We pray in Jesus' name. AMEN.

APRIL 13

DON'T JUST DO SOMETHING! STAND THERE!

(Scripture to ponder: Psalm 46:10–11)

We're all familiar with the admonition, "**Don't just stand there! Do something!**" It's often used as a spur to action when folks are immobilized by fear or uncertainty. But during my career as a surgeon, I've learned that turning that expression on its head can be important in some situations.

If you've ever watched a medical resuscitation on T.V. a program like *E.D.* or *Emergency,* you know how fast moving and even chaotic such scenes can be. Actually, the real thing is an everyday occurrence in most hospitals, and is even more hectic than on T.V. When the call of "Code 99" or "Code Blue" comes over the P.A. system, interns, residents, nurses and technicians come running to the bedside of the cardiac arrest victim.

From my experience in many such situations, although there's always plenty to do—intubate the patient, do external cardiac massage, start an I.V., and prepare for defibrillation—there are usually lots of respondents. So I make my motto, "**Don't just do something! Stand there!**" Instead of getting involved in the fray, I'll take the nurse taking care of the patient aside and ask her questions: What the diagnosis was, what medications are being given, etc. I try to get some idea why the cardiac arrest occurred. Often by asking the right questions and by stepping back, out of the busy situation, I get an insight into how to care for the patient, once the heart rhythm is re-started.

I've found the same approach helpful in life itself. Often when we're super busy—too busy—with our time taken up with the hectic, myriad activities of our lives, we need to stop doing things and just stand back, to wait and listen for God's direction. As the old Anglican evening prayer goes, "**When the shadows lengthen and evening comes, and the busy world is hushed, and the fever of life is over, and our work is done,**" we do well to step aside and listen to the Lord.

PRAYER: **O Lord, help us to be still and to know that you are God, exalted over all the earth, and worthy of our worship and praise. Help us step aside in our hectic lives to commune with You. AMEN.**

APRIL 14

PREPARING GOOD SOIL

(Scripture to ponder: Matthew 13:3–9)

In the parable of the sower, Christ relates a story that was especially relevant to the Jews, people who lived in an agrarian economy. Farmers have always known the value of good soil to produce fruitful harvests. We in America have been blessed with excellent soil in our Midwest, such that the region has been called the breadbasket of the world, because of its great productivity.

In Biblical times, seed was sown by *broadcasting*—that is, by strewing it by hand as the sower walked. Unlike with modern, mechanized methods of planting seeds in neat rows, some broadcast seeds landed on good soil, others on inhospitable soil. Jesus makes use of that phenomenon as the parable unfolds.

In our selection from Matthew's Gospel, Jesus teaches about the importance of good soil to nurture the seeds of God's word. As I understand the parable, good soil is a receptive mind and spirit on the part of those who hear the Gospel. Christ explains to his disciples three things that will prevent or stunt the growth of the Gospel seed in those who hear it: *First* is a lack of understanding; *second*, a lack of perseverance in the face of tribulation or persecution; *third* are the cares of the world and the delight in riches which can choke out God's Word. But in good soil—in a tender, receptive, single-minded heart—the Word of God can germinate, grow and produce much fruit.

God has great promises for those who believe, but the way is not easy. Through study and discipline we must prepare the soil of our hearts to receive His Word.

PRAYER: Dear Lord, make us sensitive and receptive as we hear Your Word, so we may understand it. Let it grow in our hearts so it will produce much fruit for your Kingdom. AMEN.

APRIL 15

LOOPHOLES

(Scripture to ponder: Luke 18:18–27)

I've always enjoyed watching the old movies of that colorful curmudgeon, W.C. Fields. The story is told of a doctor being summoned to see the actor. He found the old reprobate on his death-bed, intently leafing through a large Bible. "**What are you looking for?**" asked the physician.

"**Loopholes**," replied Fields.

As April comes around each year, many of us hire tax accountants to make use of the loopholes in the Internal Revenue Code. The Pharisees in Jesus' time were fastidious people who gave great attention to the Law, who ascribed to themselves a special righteousness because of it. They spent their entire life trying to get it right. They made use of all the loopholes.

But Jesus said that unless our righteousness exceeds that of the Pharisees, we would not see the Kingdom of God. If you appreciate what careful, meticulous lives the Pharisees lived, you realize the impossibility of living up to the letter of the Law. Such attempts eventually lead to despair, and prompt the question posed by Tolstoy: "**What then shall we do?**" or lead to the anguished cry of the disciples in today's passage, "*Who then can be saved?*"

Jesus gave this simple answer: "*What is impossible with men is possible with God.*" His formula for salvation is likewise a simple one:

Love God and love your neighbor.

PRAYER: Help us know, that through the vertical relationship of Worship and the horizontal response of Service we will have no need of loopholes. AMEN.

APRIL 16

CLOSER THAN A BROTHER

(Scripture to ponder: Proverbs 18:24)

I have three sisters but no brothers. It wasn't until mid-career that I learned through experience what it was like to have a brother.

After my surgical residency I became chief of a busy emergency service at a large metropolitan hospital in the Pacific Northwest. In the department I directed the work of five emergency physicians, all competent and well trained. They were on salary to the hospital, so they received the same pay regardless of the volume of patients seen.

The five doctors got together, did some calculations, and decided that if they went to a fee-for-service billing system, they'd receive more money. They came to me as the department head to support them when they approached the hospital administration. I said I would be glad to, if I reviewed the figures and they were accurate.

Unfortunately, the figures were wrong, and the new salaries were inflated. I came back and told the doctors I could not support them. They in turn submitted a mass resignation, causing a crisis in coverage for the department. To reach a solution, the issue was submitted to a medical staff committee for arbitration.

At this time, as head of the department, I worked one day a week as an emergency physician, but put in over eight hours a day with administration and teaching duties. I was board certified in surgery and also had a small private surgical practice. For that I rotated night call with another surgeon who was a friend. When the committee's solution was known—*which involved my working more shifts, plus taking a pay cut, while the other doctors worked less, yet got a pay increase*—I was pretty discouraged and depressed.

I discussed it with my friend. He said, "**You don't need that! Come join me in practice. We'll split it down the middle!**" His was an offer such as a brother would make, and it touched me deeply. Although eventually, I decided to stay on as director, his offer was a bright spot for me during a bleak period of my career. I was reminded of today's scripture:

"There are friends who pretend to be friends, but there is a friend who sticks closer than a brother."

PRAYER: We praise you, O Lord, for giving us a friend closer than a brother. Help us to be so to others. In Jesus' name we pray. AMEN.

APRIL 17

STILL MIRACLES IN THE DESERT

(Scripture to ponder: Exodus Chapters 16 & 17)

In our scripture passage for today, God provides for the Children of Israel in the barren desert as they journeyed out of bondage in Egypt toward the Promised Land. The night before the Exodus, at the Passover meal, the Jews ate unleavened bread and cold lamb, and it's pretty sure they did not take many provisions with them.

In the desert of the Sinai Peninsula, God provided manna for them. It appeared in the morning like a fine powder or hoarfrost, and after gathering it up, they were able to make bread. Later He provided quail for meat, and to quench their thirst, He made water miraculously gush forth from a rock.

I think we moderns tend to believe that the day of miracles has past. But during the Gulf War in 1991, another miracle occurred in the desert. This time it was in Kuwait, as reported by Major Michael Halt in the November 2002 issue of *Guideposts*. On a clear morning his armored battalion received orders to move out toward the Kuwaiti border. As they progressed, it began to rain, a drenching downpour that lasted several days, thoroughly soaking the troops. The night before they were to cross the border, the rains stopped.

The morning of the invasion they awoke to clear skies and sunshine. As they moved across the border into Kuwait where Iraqi forces were waiting, they saw the glimmer of scores of metal discs scattered across the desert, right in their proposed path. The rains had uncovered a huge minefield they would have traversed, had it not been for the storm. God does indeed work in mysterious ways!

PRAYER: We praise You, O Lord, and thank You, that You provide for us and protect us today, just as You did for Your people in Biblical times. AMEN.

APRIL 18

SILENCE AND SOLITUDE

(Scripture to ponder: Genesis 1:2)

If we would see a moving of the Spirit in our lives, we do well to make preparation. Allowing time for silence and solitude is a means to that end, recalling how Our Lord often withdrew into quietness and communion with his Father.

Some of the most moving times in my own spiritual life have been times of silence and solitude, particularly the midnight vigils held in our dark, silent church at the end of Holy Week. The Spirit of God has moved in mysterious ways at those times. Reflecting on the silence and darkness of those experiences, I'm reminded of the opening sentences of the Creation as recorded in our selection from Genesis:

The earth was without form and void, and darkness was upon the face of the deep; and the Spirit of God was moving over the face of the waters.

If we allow silence and solitude to come into our lives, we enable God's Spirit to move. To do so often requires a conscious act on our part, a withdrawal from the hustle and bustle and tintinnabulation of the everyday world into the inner sanctuary of our souls where we can be alone with God.

Such times occur rarely nowadays, but can come as often as we will, if we but make the effort to call them forth. Usually this means late at night or early in the morning, when the busy world is hushed. It is easiest, perhaps, in the dark church, in the silence of the veiled cross, pondering the sacrifice or our Lord for our sins, when we allow the still, small voice of His Spirit speak to us.

PRAYER: Help us, Dear Lord, to set aside times of Silence and Solitude when we can commune with You. Fill us with Your Spirit and show us Your Way. In Jesus' name we pray. AMEN.

APRIL 19

THE SEVEN LAST WORDS

(Scriptures to ponder: Proverbs 18:15; Revelation 21:3–5)

You are probably familiar with what are called "The Seven Last Words of Christ," (as recorded in the four Gospels), the series of short sentences he spoke from the cross at the end of his life, words such as, *"Father forgive them; for they know not what they do,"* and *"I thirst,"* and *"It is finished."* The seven last words of our Lord have formed a focus of meditation for Christians down through the ages.

I recall once hearing a sermon entitled "The Seven Last Words of the Church," in which the pastor was poking fun at his congregation. He said the seven last words weren't those spoken by the Lord Jesus as he faced death. Rather, the seven last words are the response of many members of the modern church to any change of procedure. He said, they are: **"We never did it that way before!"** We all chuckled and got his point.

But one of the striking characteristics of the Church throughout history has been its adaptability to varying cultures and circumstances as the Gospel has spread across the globe, yet still preserving the essence of the Faith.

In the *Living Bible* our first selection reads:

"The intelligent man is always open to new ideas; in fact, he looks for them."

Continual renewal has distinguished the Church from its beginning. That's how it's been, how it is, and how it should be. From our second Scripture selection, hear the words of St. John's Revelation from our second selection:

I heard a great voice out of heaven saying, "Behold the tabernacle of God is with men, and he will dwell with them, and they shall be His people, and God Himself will be with them and be their God.

And God shall wipe away every tear from their eyes; and there shall be no more death; neither sorrow, nor crying, neither shall there be any more pain: for the former things are passed away."

And He who sits on the throne said, "Behold, I make all things new."

PRAYER: We praise and thank You, O Lord, that you continually renew all things. Help us be able to change and adapt and renew, to bring the freshness of the Gospel to all in this world. AMEN.

APRIL 20

NEW MERCIES EVERY MORNING

(Scripture to ponder: Lamentations 3:22–25)

What do you suppose would be different in this world, if we were to arise each morning to see something new to be grateful for? If, in the words of the hymn, we were to exclaim on arising,

Great is Thy faithfulness, Great is Thy faithfulness! Morning by morning new mercies I see!

Over the past decade there have been several "end-of-the-world" type movies depicting situations in which the world will be destroyed by colliding with a huge asteroid, or a similar cataclysmic event. Most of the time in these movies such a scenario results in the nations of the world uniting together to face the common danger—a marked contrast to the usual competition and warfare we read about in the daily news.

Astronomers emphasize the huge distances in space and the extent of the universe, which is billions and billions of light years across. Although our earth is 24,000 miles in diameter, we are situated 93 *million* miles from the sun, and our own solar system is many times that far from the nearest star. So based on size alone, it's unlikely that earth will be hit by an asteroid, even though such impacts actually did occur thousands of years ago.

I believe it's by God's grace that such things don't happen. He who created the universe to run by his eternal, inexorable laws spares us through His mercy. Unfortunately, I think it's far more likely that we humans will end up destroying ourselves in nuclear war, or make our planet uninhabitable through global warming. That of course would not be God's doing, but our own.

What a boon it would be if we all—all mankind—could put away our chauvinistic rivalries and recognize all the things we have to be thankful for! How blessed—how happy—could we be if we appreciated God's creation and were grateful. What if each morning we awoke, saw anew God's great mercies, and set out to share one another's burdens!

PRAYER: **Thank you O Lord for the magnificence of Your creation. Help us see new mercies each morning. AMEN.**

APRIL 21

HISTORY AND THE CHRISTIAN

(Scriptures to ponder: John 1:14; Mark 9: 2–8)

George Santayana, the onetime Harvard professor of philosophy who said, **"Those who cannot remember the past are condemned to repeat it,"** also wrote this about history:

> **"History is a pack of lies about events that never happened, told by people who weren't there."**

Those are the words of a cynic, of a man who was steeped in history and philosophy but who withdrew from the world in later life. He spent his last few years in a convent in Italy. His disenchantment is obvious.

How are we to regard history? Certainly we can learn from the past—even though the chronicle of mankind and of nations often shows the same follies are repeated. I believe the Christian sees history through the prism of Eternity. The source of our strength is *God.* In contrast to Santayana's view of history as a pack of lies, we believe the *Bible* contains eternal truths. The events surrounding the life of Jesus happened and were recorded by men who were there.

In our first selection, the Apostle John writes of Jesus:

"We have beheld his Glory, glory as of the only Son from the Father."

John was party to the startling event that he and James and Peter witnessed when Jesus was transfigured on the mountaintop, related in our second Scripture passage for today.

The life of Christ is the pivotal event of history. And it's also the focal point of Eternity: as the writer of the Letter to the Hebrews asserted,

"Jesus Christ is the same yesterday and today and forever."

[Hebrews 13:8]

PRAYER: **You are the Lord of Life and of History, the same yesterday, today and forever. We bless You for your unchanging nature and for the gift of Eternal Life we have through Your Son, Jesus Christ, our Savior. AMEN.**

APRIL 22

THE SERMON ON THE ROAD

(Scripture to ponder: Luke 24:13–24)

All Christians are familiar with the *Sermon the Mount*, the wonderful account of Jesus' teachings recorded in St. Matthew's Gospel. It begins with the Beatitudes and continues with many of the memorable and terse teachings of our Lord. What a privilege and joy it would have been to have heard that sermon!

There's another discourse of Jesus that I'd be just as eager to witness, one that I call the *Sermon on the Road*. It occurred after the Resurrection when Jesus appeared to Cleopas and another disciple as they walked along the road from Jerusalem to Emmaus. It's our scripture selection for today. St. Luke records the disciples did not recognize Jesus at first, as they related the events of the past week to Him.

But then, as they walk on along the road, Jesus begins to teach them. Luke relates it:

And beginning at Moses and all the Prophets, He expounded to them in all the Scriptures the things concerning Himself.

[*Luke 24:27*]

What a sermon that must have been, straight from the Risen Lord!

When they reached the town, the disciples urged Him to tarry and eat with them. They recognized Him as He blessed and broke bread with them at supper. Then he was gone, taken back to heaven. How I would have loved to share that meal!

PRAYER: **We thank you, Lord, that You are revealed to us through Your Word, and that in breaking bread together, our eyes are opened to behold you in our midst. AMEN.**

APRIL 23

NO OTHER GODS

(Scripture to ponder: Exodus 20: 2–3)

This devotion begins a series of ten that deal with the Decalogue. God gave the Ten Commandments to Moses during the time the Children of Israel were encamped at the foot of Mt. Sinai, after they had been led out of Egypt, miraculously through the Red Sea. The first commandment He gave was:

"Thou shalt have no other gods before me."

The Children of Israel had just come out of slavery in the polytheistic society of Egypt, where many gods were worshiped. Indeed, Pharaoh himself was worshiped as a god. Moses knew that there was only one God, and that He was the God of his forefathers, Abraham, Isaac and Jacob. He was the God of the twelve sons of Jacob, which—as God had promised—had become a great people.

As in ancient Egypt, in modern American society there are likewise many gods. Four of them in particular we bow down before: Prosperity, Pleasure, Possessions and Power.

All about us we see the worship of these false gods. But God speaks to us as he did to those in Moses' time:

"THOU SHALT HAVE NO OTHER GODS BEFORE ME!"

Again, in the sixth chapter of Deuteronomy, the commandment is repeated in slightly different form, one that later was used by Jesus in the parable of the Good Samaritan:

You shall love the Lord your God with all your heart, and with all your soul, and with all your might.

[Luke 10:25]

It's been said that in a Christian's life, relationships are governed by the cross: a vertical relationship with God and a horizontal relationship with one another. The first commandment establishes the vertical one, and it's the relationship that influences all others.

PRAYER: Help us, God, to always put you first in our lives, to love You above the false gods in our world, to live according to your word and in obedience to your son, Our Lord Jesus Christ. AMEN.

APRIL 24

NO GRAVEN IMAGES

(Scripture to ponder: Exodus 20: 4–6)

When I was a teenager I became an Eagle Scout. It was at that time my greatest accomplishment, and one of which I was proud. Two years later, I went away to boarding school a long way from home. I was insecure and fearful because of the new, strange environment into which I was thrust.

Before I left home for the new school, I took apart my Eagle Scout medal and mounted the small, silver eagle on a sterling silver chain to wear around my neck. At the school it bolstered my self-confidence during a shaky period in my life.

I was raised in a Christian home by faithful parents. But each of us must establish our own relationship with the Lord. During my college years, after I took Jesus as my Savior, I began closely observing the people around me. I was struck by the fact that although a necklace can appear to be a harmless piece of jewelry, what people wear around their necks often indicates what they believe or worship. I came to see that my wearing of the Scout Eagle was a form of idol worship that I had embraced during a period of my own insecurity. I took the necklace apart and put the eagle back on its original ribbon.

The Second Commandment is quite clear:

"Thou shalt not make unto thee any graven image"

Our symbols often indicate where our hearts are. No external image can substitute for God's majesty and His power. We must not bow down or serve any other master, and we must not—as I did with the silver eagle as the children of Israel did with the golden calf *[Exodus 32]*—worship any other object or any other image. We worship only the Lord.

PRAYER: Show us, Dear Lord, the idols and graven images that we hold up before us in our lives. Help us see that you are the one true God and that we must not erect any other images to worship. AMEN.

APRIL 25

GOD'S NAME IN VAIN

(Scripture to ponder: Exodus 20:7)

I have always had trouble with folks who use expressions like "Oh, My God!" or "Oh God!" It grates on my ear like fingernails across a blackboard. I think it's because my parents never swore, nor did they use God's name that way. It wasn't part of my life.

Did you know that among the Jews in Biblical times, the name of God was so sacred that it was not spoken? Even today, the solemn use of God's name is preserved when witnesses testifying in court take an oath. They swear to tell "the truth, the whole truth, and nothing but the truth, *so help me God.*"

The third commandment God gave his people was,

"Thou shalt not take the name of the Lord thy God in vain."

What do the words *in vain* mean? An analogy may help. If you were to set out with a screwdriver to do a home repair job, but discovered what you needed was a wrench to loosen a frozen nut, you would use the screwdriver *in vain*—in a way not intended and in a way that would not work.

Similarly, the name of God is sacred and intended for certain hallowed purposes only: for praise, for adoration, for reverence. It is not to be used in vain—as profanity, or for cursing, condemnation or exclamation.

PRAYER: **Dear Lord, show us Your majesty and teach us to properly reverence Your holy name, that we may be your faithful witnesses in the world. AMEN.**

APRIL 26

BREAKING THE SABBATH

(Scripture to ponder: Exodus 20:8–11; Mark 3:1–5)

Ordained by God, given to Moses, the Sabbath was of prime importance in the life of the Jew. Keeping the Sabbath was one way the people of Israel kept themselves apart from the pagan cultures that surrounded them for generations. It was a defining characteristic.

Was it ever right to break the Sabbath? We get some insight into these questions as we read in chapter three of Mark's Gospel about Jesus healing the man with the withered hand. It was the Sabbath, and according to strict Jewish law—following the fourth commandment—no work was to be done on that day, including **healing**.

Jesus knew He was being watched. He asked whether it was lawful to do good or to do evil, to save life or to kill on the Sabbath. The answer was obvious—one should do good, one should save life—but because of the hardness of their hearts, the Pharisees remained silent and would not answer Him.

Jesus did not denigrate the importance of the Sabbath, but rather put it in perspective: He asserted there was something greater than the Sabbath, and that was *human need*. People are more important than rules.

In our own lives we need to keep the same perspective. While we honor the seventh day as a day of worship, rest and renewal, we must always put human needs in perspective. Jesus declared:

"The Sabbath was made for man and not man for the Sabbath."

[Mark 2:27]

Saving a life, doing good for our fellow man is always honored by God.

PRAYER: Dear Lord, help us keep the seventh day Holy. Yet give us the insight always to see and serve the needs of those around us, whatever day of the week it may be. AMEN.

APRIL 27

HONORING OUR PARENTS

(Scripture to ponder: Exodus 20: 12)

Honor thy father and thy mother that your days may be long in the land which the Lord has given you.

[Exodus 20:12]

This is the fifth commandment given by God to Moses on the mountain for the guidance of the Children of Israel. It is the first commandment with a promise.

American society, unlike ancient Israel, is not based on extended families. Many of our families are plagued by divorce, or have only a single parent. Moreover, American families are mobile, moving on an average every five years. All these characteristics of modern life militate against living with, or even near our parents, making it harder for us to honor them.

And there's another factor: how we treat our aged. Visiting an old folks home or a retirement, life-care facility can be a depressing experience. Nowadays we live, on the average, several years beyond the Biblical norm of three score years and ten; the sight of many lonely and demented older folks in such a facility can be saddening. Moreover, even a cursory glance at TV, shows that our society celebrates youth and vigor, not infirmity and old age.

What's to be done? We should—as in so many areas of life—rely on the counsel of God's word. We need to consciously honor our parents. To honor means to respect, to love, to revere them for their gifts of nurturing and love. Whatever they have been to us, God instructs us to honor them, simply because they are our parents. To do so allows us to reap the blessing God has for us and for all who honor his commandments.

PRAYER: Help us to cherish and respect our parents, O Lord, honoring them as we do You, that we may do your will. AMEN.

APRIL 28

THOU SHALT NOT KILL

(Scripture to ponder: Exodus 20: 13; Matthew 5:22)

This commandment is often given as *"Thou shalt not kill,"* but that is not strictly a correct translation. The Hebrew is probably best translated, *"Thou shalt not murder."*

Why is this important? In Mosaic Law—and in English and American law—a distinction is made between premeditated (so-called first degree murder) and accidental killing. Although one should never condone killing, there is a difference between, say, a planned killing by a mobster and someone who gets killed by a drunk driver. The distinction is crucial and involves *motive*. The first instance involves planning and forethought; in the second case death may be due to irresponsible or negligent behavior, but it was not intended.

Jesus speaks to these issues and carries them further. In our second Scripture selection, he goes beyond the letter of the law to its spirit: Christ counsels us to not to be angry with our brother, for passion and premeditation are the precursors of murder. Expressions like, "I'd like to kill him!" indicate an inner attitude of the heart that is the genesis of an outward act of violence.

Christ expands further the issues surrounding murder, beyond just curtailing anger. He says,

"And whoever says Raca to his brother will be liable to the council and if you curse him you will be subject to the hell of fire."

[Matthew 5:22]

Raca is an Aramaic term of contempt. Jesus is saying that attitudes of contempt and cursing people precede acts of murder. If we have right attitudes, right actions will follow.

PRAYER: **Help us know our hearts the way You know them, Lord. Make them pure so our attitudes always lead us to right action. AMEN.**

APRIL 29

ADULERY: THE OVERLOOKED COMMANDMENT

(Scriptures to ponder: Exodus 20:4; Psalm 51)

The scripture selections for today—the seventh commandment and the psalm that King David wrote repenting of his sin with Bathsheba—have great meaning for me, for my adultery destroyed my first marriage. Although the actual divorce occurred several years later, the breaking of the bond of trust from an affair sowed the seeds that later led to a bitter harvest.

"Against thee, thee only, have I sinned," [Psalm 51:4] writes King David, emphasizing the sin against God and His law. But the sin of adultery always involves more than God; it involves a man and a woman, and is often damaging to children as well. Al-

though it's a sin against God's law, in the secular world, adultery often does not mean breaking a state or federal law, though it *is* grounds for divorce in most states.

"Having an affair" is viewed quite casually in our gossip-hungry society. The fact that its never called adultery in the media says less that it's taboo, than that it's taken lightly and tacitly accepted.

When I was pondering this devotional—which has been one of the hardest for me to write—I happened to attend a new church one Sunday. It was a congregation that was evangelical and conservative. Printed in the Order of Worship, in addition to the hymns and prayers and the Apostles' Creed, were the Ten Commandments (based on *Exodus 20:2–17*), but the seventh (verse 14) was given as "Thou shalt not lie." (Bearing false witness was included.) There was no mention of adultery.

When I asked one of the pastors about it after the service, he told me it either had been overlooked, or maybe it was done for effect. He wasn't sure, he said. *How ironic*, I thought, for the commandment against adultery is indeed the one that's perhaps most overlooked in our society. It's acknowledged as damaging to the relationship of marriage, true, but not seen as damaging to our relationship with God, at least not by the secular world.

PRAYER: O Lord, lead us not into temptation, but deliver us from the sin of adultery. AMEN.

APRIL 30

CANCER OF THE INTEGRITY

(Scripture to ponder: Exodus 20:15; Luke 16:10)

During the Enron investment scandal of 2002, did you ever wonder if those who stole millions also pilfered paper clips?

The eighth commandment is the shortest of all: *"Thou shalt not steal."* [Exodus 20:15] I suggest that petty larceny precedes grand larceny: people who end up stealing big amounts began by stealing little things. Jesus hinted at that phenomenon in the parable of the dishonest steward. It's our second scripture selection, quoted here from the *NEV*:

"Whoever is dishonest with very little will also be dishonest with much."

How does it happen? There may be an instructive analogy from the world of medicine as it relates to cancer of the tongue.

When watch companies first began to manufacture glow-in-the-dark dials for wristwatches, the workers who applied the luminescent paint with tiny brushes used to lick them to produce a fine point. The paint was mildly radioactive, though not enough to cause a problem on your wrist. But those occasional little licks over many months of work gave most of the workers cancer of the tongue.

So it is with pilfering and dishonesty: a little lick here, a little lick there, and pretty soon we have cancer of our integrity. If we steal little things, we'll benumb our conscience so we're not troubled stealing bigger things.

PRAYER: Keep us faithful and true in things little and large, O Lord, so we never stray from your path. Help us keep all the Commandments. AMEN.

MAY 1

DO NOT BEAR FALSE WITNESS

(Scripture to ponder: Exodus 20:16; Ephesians 4:15)

I thought of this commandment as I watched the workings of the congressional committee as the impeachment hearings of President Clinton proceeded. He artfully parsed questions put to him about his relationship with Monica Lewinsky, obviously navigating through the perilous shoals of perjury.

I once was involved in a medical malpractice suit in which I learned a lot about perjury. In a high-risk situation, a very obese woman had suffered a respiratory complication and died under anesthesia when I was doing a tracheostomy. I had not expected the outcome, and had not adequately prepared the family. When I broke the news they were very angry.

In a two-hour conference with the husband and son the next day, they at first agreed to my suggestion of a post mortem examination by an impartial pathologist to prove the cause of death. But then, just after I'd made the special arrangements for it (bypassing the hospital pathologist), the two men abruptly changed their mind, shook my hand, saying an autopsy would not be needed, and left the hospital. I dictated a detailed summary of the conference discussion after they left.

A month later I was served papers in a suit for wrongful death. During the four years it took to come to trial all of the major parties and several experts had their depositions taken under oath.

I had a sharp lawyer with a good memory. In the course of the trial he cross-examined the patient's husband, who was the plaintiff. Under oath, he asked the witness about the conference I'd had with him and his son the day after she died. Since the man's recall was quite good (and his story differed from mine), he asked if he'd kept any notes.

The witness responded, "**Yes, I recall very what was said, because I kept extensive notes.**" My attorney then turned to the judge and asked, benignly, "**Your honor, it's just after noon. Do you suppose it would be a good time to break for lunch?**" The judge agreed and court was adjourned to reconvene two hours later.

When we were alone in the elevator, my lawyer turned to me and exclaimed, "**We have him! That man just perjured himself.**" He went on to explain that two years earlier he'd asked the exact same question of the witness under oath in his deposition, and the man replied that he'd kept *no* notes or record of my conference with him and his son. So over the lunch hour my attorney had six copies of the deposition transcribed and he brought them back to court.

When the witness took the stand again, my attorney reminded him he was still under oath. He then confronted him with the two different answers he'd given, and pointedly asked,

"**Now, Sir, which of those two answers you gave is the *truth?***"

There were several other reasons why we won the lawsuit, but having a false witness lie about those notes impressed the jury and definitely worked in my favor.

PRAYER:　　　**Help us always speak the truth in love, O Lord. AMEN.**

MAY 2

DO NOT COVET

(Scripture to ponder: Exodus 20:17)

I wonder what Moses would say if he suddenly showed up in modern America. I think he'd be surprised and shocked, particularly as it relates to the Scripture for today, the Tenth Commandment:

> *Thou shalt not covet thy neighbor's house, thou shalt not covet thy neighbor's wife, nor his man-servant, nor his maid-servant, nor his ox, nor his ass, anything that is thy neighbor's.*

I think he'd be appalled by the advertising all around us, which is really the foundation of capitalist America. Our consumer-oriented society thrives by making us want more and buy more. It almost seems predicated on our being discontented with our lot. Advertising's purpose is to sell goods and services and it does so by subtly creating covetousness.

What's the cure? I think it's found in *contentment,* in being satisfied with what we have, grateful for our many blessings, neither considering ourselves entitled to more, nor wishing for someone else's property or possessions.

Along this line, one of my favorite sonnets is Shakespeare's # 29:

When in disgrace with fortune and men's eyes,
I all alone beweep my outcast state,
And trouble deaf heaven with my bootless cries,
And look upon myself and curse my fate,
Wishing me like to one more rich in hope,
Featur'd like him, like him with friends posess'd,
Desiring this man's art, and that man's scope,
With what I most enjoy contented least;
Yet in these thoughts myself almost despising,
Haply I think on thee, and then my state,
Like to the lark at break of day arising

From sullen earth sings hymns at heaven's gate;
> For thy sweet love remember'd such wealth brings,
> That then I scorn to change my state with kings.

Related to this commandment, I'd make only one small change. I'd have line 12 read: "Haply I think on *Thee*"—that is, on *God,* who is the source of our contentment.

PRAYER: **Let us find our Joy and Contentment in Thee, O Lord. So shall we never be tempted to be covetous. AMEN.**

MAY 3

HUNGER, THIRST AND DESIRE

(Scripture to ponder: Matthew 5:6)

Our Scripture text is from the Sermon on the Mount, the section of that teaching that is known as The Beatitudes. As happens often in the great religions, there are parallel teachings. Here is one from Buddhism.

There is a story of the Buddha, which tells of a man who came to him to ask to know the path to deliverance, that is, to salvation. The Buddha took him down to a river where the man assumed he would be instructed in some form of ritual washing. But suddenly the Buddha grabbed the man and held his head forcibly under the water. The man struggled but was held down. With a mighty effort he fought loose and came to the surface with a great gasp.

"When you thought you were drowning, what did you desire most?" asked the Buddha.

"Air!" the man replied, with a heaving chest.

"When you desire salvation as much as you desired air, you will find it," said the Buddha.

In a similar manner, in our selection today Jesus says,

"Blessed—that is, happy or content—are those who hunger and thirst after righteousness, for they will be filled."

Now, hunger and thirst are two of our strongest desires. So I believe Jesus is saying that when we desire *righteousness* as much as we desire food, or to assuage our thirst on a hot day, then will we find fulfillment.

So if we desire contentment and happiness, we do well to hunger and thirst after the wisdom revealed in the Scriptures that shows us how to live rightly, how to love God and to love our neighbor.

Prayer: **Dear Lord, our souls are restless until they find their rest in Thee. Help us to hunger and thirst after your righteousness and your wisdom, so we may truly find fulfillment. AMEN.**

MAY 4

YOU'VE GOT TO BE CAREFULLY TAUGHT

(Scripture to ponder: Proverbs 22:6)

Remember the song from *South Pacific*? The lyrics go:

You've got to be taught to be afraid of people whose eyes are differently made.

It sings of how prejudices are formed, but it applies to many other aspects of life as well. Children don't seem to have inborn prejudice, but they certainly do seem to be born *selfish*. They've got to be taught to share and to be kind to others. Our Scripture selection teaches:

Train up a child in the way he should go and when he is older he will not depart from it.

Probably the two most common ways we teach our children are through example and through repetition. If we set a good example for them, it often makes a lasting impression. Conversely, if we say one thing and do another, kids are quick to learn that lesson as well.

Repetition is important because things learned by repetition usually stay with us life-long. In my own life, the words of the Lord's Prayer, or the 23d Psalm or the Scout Oath—all learned when I was a boy—remain with me even now, in my seventh decade.

The Jews encouraged teaching the commandments to their children, memorizing them to become an intimate part of their store of knowledge. The Psalms speak of meditating on God's Word, another important way to learn right behavior and right responses.

PRAYER: Help us memorize Your Word, O Lord, so it enters our very marrow. Help us carefully teach our children Your ways. AMEN.

MAY 5

STEPPING OUT IN FAITH

(Scripture to ponder: Matthew 14:22–33)

What does it mean to "step out in faith?" I believe it means to embark on a venture—often perilous—with the faith that God will see us through. It's an important concept in the Christian life.

The expression comes from an episode St. Matthew relates in Chapter 14. After feeding the 5000, Jesus sent his disciples across the lake by boat, while He himself went up on the hillside alone to pray. As it grew late, he joined them by walking across the water to the boat, that was making its way with difficulty, due to the wind and waves. He must have looked like an apparition coming toward them. They were afraid, and Jesus called out to reassure them.

Then Peter exclaimed, *"Lord, if it's really you, tell me to come to you on the water!"* [Matthew 14:28]

"Come on then," said Jesus, and Peter stepped out and began to walk on the water toward the Master. But when he saw the fury of the wind, he panicked and began to sink.

He called out, *"Lord, save me!"* Jesus reached out His hand, caught Peter up. Then, when they had safely reached the boat, upbraided him for his lack of faith.

So "stepping out in faith" has two components: boldness and persistence or endurance. We must have bold faith to embark on a perilous venture, and we must have faith to persist despite what storms there are around us. *In faith* we need to begin, and we must follow through *in faith*. As St. James writes, *"Realize that trials come to test your faith and to produce in you the quality of endurance."* [James 1:3]

PRAYER: Grant us the faith, O Lord, to step out for You, and the faith to persist and endure in our Christian walk, for Jesus sake. AMEN.

MAY 6

AUTONOMY **VS** AUTHENTICITY

(Scripture to ponder: 2 Corinthians 12:9–10)

For several years I was on the Bioethics Committee of a large teaching hospital and dealt with many ethical problems. In medical ethics, the term *Autonomy* refers to the capacity of a patient to make independent decisions and their desire to do so. The concept has been a driving force in American medicine. Indeed it's a big issue in our society, as manifested in our attitudes toward personal freedom and independence, and in phrases like "I am Captain of my soul and master of my fate."

But as we get older and aging and disease take their toll, we become more dependent and vulnerable. In advanced, widespread cancer, for example, patients can become very dependent and vulnerable, a situation that many people fear. Most of us don't like to be dependent and vulnerable, even when we're in the best of health.

But if we can accept dependence and vulnerability, we can open the way to new insight and depth in relationships.

In our Scripture selection for today, St. Paul reveals one of the fundamental truths of the Christian Faith: it's *when we are weak that God's strength comes to us*. The irony is that few of us appreciate that truth, for when we are strong we are quite autonomous. We thereby rob ourselves of the greatest treasure life holds. For it's in being vulnerable, in acknowledging our dependence on God, or on another person, that we allow barriers to come down and let the healing waters of love wash over us.

Those who perceive that truth early in life are the most blessed, for they are loved, and can love, the most.

PRAYER: **Help us realize our dependence on You, Dear Lord, and open ourselves to Love. AMEN.**

MAY 7

COMPROMISE

(Scripture to ponder: 1 John 2: 15–17)

It's been said that politics is the art of compromise. I've never thought I'd make a very good politician, for I don't remember names very well and I decry the "Hail fellow, well met!" approach to others. I do, however, appreciate the role of compromise in a good marriage, and the need for flexibility as we love those close to us.

James Russell Lowell, the nineteenth century abolitionist poet and editor saw compromise as a temporary expedient. He said, "**Compromise makes a good umbrella but a poor roof.**" That's what I believe the Apostle John was getting at in today's scripture, given here in *The Living Bible*:

Stop loving this evil world and all that it offers you, for when you love these things you show that you do not really love God; for all these worldly things, these evil desires—the craze for sex, the ambition to buy everything that appeals to you, and the pride that comes from wealth and importance—these are not from God. They are from this evil world itself. And this world is fading away, and these evil, forbidden things will go with it, but whoever keeps doing the will of God will live forever.

I confess that although I'm a committed Christian, acknowledging Jesus as Lord, I do not always speak out when I see prejudice or injustice, and in that respect, I compromise with the world. I find I must continually come back to the intimacy of God's Love through prayer and meditation and reading His Word and ask for forgiveness and strength. Living in modern America, inundated by advertising and the media, one can be led to compromise one's values in many subtle ways.

In *Romans 12:2*, St. Paul puts it tersely:

"Do not be conformed to this world, but be transformed by the renewal of your spirit."

PRAYER: **We love You, Lord, and uphold Your Law and Your Values. Help us always do your will without compromise. AMEN.**

MAY 8

WRITING IN SAND—OR IN STONE

(Scripture to ponder: Matthew 18:21–22)

A friend recently shared the following story with me:

Two friends were hiking in the desert. At one point in their journey they had an argument, and one slapped the other in the face. The one who got slapped was hurt, but without saying anything, he wrote in the sand:

TODAY MY BEST FRIEND SLAPPED ME IN THE FACE.

They kept walking until they came to an oasis, where they went for a swim to cool off. The one who had been slapped got stuck in the mire and began to sink and drown. His friend threw him a line and saved him, pulling him to safety. When the friend had recovered, he took from his pack a chisel and hammer and inscribed on a nearby rock:

TODAY MY BEST FRIEND SAVED MY LIFE.

The one who had slapped and then had saved the other asked him, "After I hurt you, you wrote in the sand, and now you carve on a stone. Why?"

His friend replied, "When someone hurts us, we should write it down in sand, where the winds of forgiveness can erase it away, but when someone does us a good deed, we need to engrave it in stone, where no wind can erase it.

In today's scripture, Peter asked the Lord Jesus how many times he should forgive his brother: *"Seven times?"* Jesus replied, rather, *"Seventy times seven."* As followers of Christ, we are called to forgiveness. Indeed, in the Lord's Prayer, we ask God to forgive us in the measure that we forgive others.

PRAYER: **Help us, O Lord, to forgive one another, to write their sins in sand. And may we always write their good deeds in stone. Empower us through Your Spirit to do Your Will. AMEN.**

MAY 9

BEING YOUR UNIQUE SELF

(Scripture to ponder: Romans 12:2)

When I was an adolescent attending school in New England, I first got to know the writings of Henry David Thoreau. The man who introduced me to "the Bard of Concord" was a gruff-speaking master of English who used to put his feet up on his big desk in the front of the classroom, and whose constant refrain was, **"Read the books, boys, read the books!"** He was a nonconformist who ranked in my teen-aged mind with those two other New England prophets of self-reliance, Thoreau and Emerson.

I remember his quoting from one of Thoreau's works a statement to this effect: "**A monkey in Paris puts on a hat and all the monkeys in America put on the same hat.**" And it was Emerson who said, "**Imitation is suicide.**" In his teaching, our prep school master was urging us to find our own unique selves.

There's a marvelous story about the famous composer Irving Berlin. He could not read music, yet became America's most famous popular songwriter. Of the top ten all time great songs, five were his, including "God Bless America," and "White Christmas."

In the 1920s when Berlin was at the height of his fame, he was approached in New York's Tin Pan Alley by a young composer needing a job. Berlin offered to put him on at $35 a week as his musical secretary. But in offering him the job, he said,

"I advise you not to take this job, because if you do, you'll become a second-rate Irving Berlin. But if you say to yourself, I am unique, I'll be nobody else but myself, you can become immortal."

The young man didn't take the job and struggled on, on his own. But he became his own unique self, the immortal George Gershwin.

God calls us all in a similar way, and gives us the power to be great for Him.

PRAYER: **You have told us not to be conformed to this world, O Lord. Empower us by Your Holy Spirit to become our own unique selves and help us to do Your will in our lives. AMEN.**

MAY 10

BUMPER STICKER MESSAGES

(Scripture to ponder: Revelation 4:11)

Isn't it fascinating to see what people put on their bumper stickers? Usually it reveals what is in our hearts, what concerns us most, whether it's an award our child got in school, or something about the NRA or gun control. It often indicates where our loyalties lie.

Sometimes bumper stickers are humorous—like one I saw in tiny print that read, "If you can read this you're following too close!"

Occasionally bumper stickers have a hidden message. I recall one on a truck parked outside my home in Phoenix.

When I lived there, I periodically had need of a technician who helped me when my spa got into trouble. He was an excellent worker, reliable, honest and true. On his truck bumper I saw a sticker that read, "**My boss is a Jewish Carpenter.**" He was a Christian, and his bumper sticker was a subtle way to announce it. But he himself was an even greater witness than that slogan, because of the caliber of his work, which was of high quality and reasonably priced. He was, in short, *trustworthy*, a man who lived out his faith.

When I think of being worthy, I think of the chorus in Handel's *Messiah,* "**Worthy is the Lamb That Was Slain.**" The text of which comes from our selection for today. Jesus Christ, the Jewish carpenter who was slain, but whom God raised again from the dead, is indeed worthy of our trust, is worthy to receive blessing and honor, glory and power. He is indeed the Lamb that was slain to take away the sins of the world.

PRAYER: **Dear Lord, help us to show forth your praise and glory, both with our lips, and with our *lives*; not just with slogans, but with *service* to our neighbors. May we always be a blessing to You. AMEN.**

MAY 11

A MOTHER'S LOVE—AND GOD'S LOVE

(Scripture to ponder: Romans 5:8)

When I was a boy and went off to boarding school, I got into trouble with a group of classmates. We broke one of the school's cardinal rules by smoking. It occurred on a bus trip to a girls' school for a dance. Because the group was large—there were sixteen of us—the usual punishment of expulsion or suspension was not invoked. Rather, the faculty devised a severe curtailment of our freedoms and pleasures called *Special Discipline*.

Under *Special Discipline* we had no free class periods but instead had to attend study halls, and instead of participating in sports, we had to work afternoons on the "Wood Squad," chopping wood and repairing trails on the campus. We could not go into town, and while the rest of the school attended Saturday night movies in the auditorium, we had to sit in a study hall.

When we were given this "sentence" by the headmaster, we of course had to notify our parents. I called home and my mother answered the phone. When I told her I'd been put on **Special Discipline**, there was a pause, then she responded ecstatically. "**Why, that's wonderful!**"

I guess she thought it was something like the Dean's List in college, an academic honor. I of course had to set her straight . . . Good old Mother, upbeat, loving me in spite of myself, despite my errors and goofs. In great measure, it was through her love that I learned about God's love, as expressed in our text from St. Paul's Letter to the Romans:

But God shows his love for us in that while we were yet sinners, Christ died for us.

PRAYER: **We bless You, O Lord, for a mother's love that so often gives us a glimpse of the *Divine Love* that you have for us, in spite of ourselves and of our shortcomings. May we always love one another as you have loved us, and do Your Will. AMEN.**

MAY 12

SEEKING ADVICE

(Scripture to ponder: Matthew 6:34)

Do you read the advice columns in the daily paper? I do and often get a kick out of what they recommend. I suspect that if more people read the Bible regularly and sought to put its principles into practice, fewer folks would be writing to the papers to get advice for living their lives.

One of first advice columnists was Elizabeth Meriwether Gilmer, who wrote under the pen name of *Dorothy Dix*. At the time of her death in 1951, she was the highest paid and most widely read female journalist in the world, with an estimated audience of 60 million readers.

I recently read over some of her columns and was struck by how down-home, simple and wise her counsel was. Much of it seemed to come straight out of the Good Book. I suppose that many readers of her syndicated columns never darkened the doorway of a church or cracked open a Bible. But by design or not, she often displayed echoes of scripture, rendered in memorable phrases. Here's one of her maxims:

"Enjoy today and let tomorrow take care of itself. There is no sounder adage than that which bids us not to trouble trouble until trouble troubles us."

In a cute and memorable way, she was simply paraphrasing Jesus in the Sermon on the Mount, when he said:

"Do not worry about tomorrow; for tomorrow will care for itself. Each day has enough trouble of its own."

[Matthew 6:34]

Christians who read the Scriptures regularly are indeed blessed, for the Bible is full of pure, spiritual food that nourishes us and gives us all the advice we need for this life. It is God's *Handbook for Living!*

PRAYER: **Help us, O Lord, to always desire the pure, spiritual nourishment of Your Word. We thank You for sending us your Holy Spirit, who can be our Counselor for life. AMEN.**

MAY 13

LISTENING TO INNER MUSIC

(Scripture to ponder: 1 Kings 19:9–12)

I was amused recently while on a transcontinental flight to read an advertisement for a set of earphones manufactured by Bose. They looked like shooter's earmuffs and had some sort of electronic neutralizer for the noise from the engines. What first amused me was the price—over $250, payable in installments.

I was also amused by the contrast between those expensive earmuffs and the simple rubber earplugs that I use to block out the noise. Mine are cheaper by far, and they have an added advantage: they make hearing my own humming quite easy. I often enjoy singing softly to myself, hymns or spirituals or other tunes as the airplane roars along.

It's true that the noise of the modern world can be harsh and blatant. We don't, however, need an elaborate or expensive device to shut out the tintinnabulation of the world. Rather we need simply to be able to hear the soft voice that is within.

Jesus taught his disciples: don't look here or there; rather, *the Kingdom of God is within.* [LUKE 17:21] It calls softly with a still, small voice, if we will but listen. It comes to us like the one heard by Elijah (recorded in today's Scripture selection). It is the voice of God's spirit, calling out to our spirit within.

PRAYER: Teach us, O Lord, to listen to the inner voice of Your Love as it whispers to us, telling us of Your Kingdom. AMEN.

MAY 14

SENSITIVITY TO OUR SURROUNDINGS

(Scripture to ponder: Mark 5:24–34)

Recently my wife and I had an interesting experience at the Phoenix Zoo. We went with about twenty other folks on a bird walk with several members of the Arizona Audubon Society and saw over 25 different species of birds, not birds in cages, but birds in the wild. The leader was especially impressive as he shared his knowledge about the various characteristics of the birds we encountered. It was marvelous how he could spot birds and identify them so fast.

His knack for finding different birds, impressive as it was, was surpassed by another attribute: his sensitivity to the calls and songs of various birds. He'd hear subtle songs of birds that I didn't hear at all, and he was aware of bird calls that went right by me. It was uncanny.

This sensitivity to something I wasn't aware of reminded me of our Scripture passage for today from Mark's fifth chapter. Jesus is with his disciples in the midst of a throng of people who press around them, when he suddenly exclaims, *"Who touched my garment?"* I'm sure his disciples were surprised. Perhaps they even laughed, for verse 31 records they said, *"You see the crowd pressing in on you and you say, 'Who touched me?'"* They were like me at the Zoo, who couldn't hear the calls of the birds amid all the other noise of everyday life.

But Jesus was immediately sensitive to the need of the woman who had approached him with the faith that she would be healed if she but touched the fringe of his garment. And indeed, she was.

We too are surrounded by a hurting world that needs God's healing touch. Through His Holy Spirit, we too can become sensitive to the needs of those around us.

PRAYER: **We thank You, our God, for the Sensitivity of Christ, which we too can acquire through Your Holy Spirit. Help us see, hear and feel the needs of others and serve them. We pray in Jesus' name. AMEN.**

MAY 15

HOW DO YOU SEE IT?

(Scripture to ponder: Matthew 25: 31–46)

At the beginning of his book *The Little Prince,* the famous French author and aviator Antoine De Saint-Exupery tells an interesting story to explain why he became a pilot and not a painter. At the age of six he made his first drawing. He showed it to the grown-ups and asked if it frightened them.

"Frighten? Why should any one be frightened by a hat?" they replied, for the drawing did look like the silhouette of a black hat with a wide brim. But then the child explained what it really represented, by making a second drawing, one that showed a small elephant being digested inside a boa constrictor. The adults were amused, but encouraged him to attend to his studies rather than draw.

Perhaps there's more to this story than just childhood droodles. It reminds me of Christ's words, *"Anyone who will not receive the Kingdom of God like a little child, will never enter it." [Luke 18:17, NIV]* I believe that many people's conception of Jesus is like the grown-ups who saw only a hat, for they only see Jesus as the sweet little Christ child in the manger, a Jesus meek and mild, powerless and effete.

But there's another Jesus, just as there was another interpretation of the drawing of Saint-Exupery. That's Jesus as Judge of the world, related in the parable of the Last Judgment (our Scripture selection for today). He will appear in his glory before all the nations, to separate the sheep from the goats. He will judge the living and the dead, based on how they have treated him—or how we've treated the least of those he calls his brethren: we will be judged for all eternity by how we've treated one another.

It's a humbling thought.

PRAYER: Help us realize, O Lord, that the manger baby at Bethlehem is also he who will judge all the earth. May we listen and learn from him, and seek to do your will. AMEN.

MAY 16

GETTING AWAY TO SOLITUDE

(Scripture to ponder: Matthew 14:23)

There is no question that God created us to be in community. Jesus said, *"A new commandment I give unto you, that you love one another."* *[John 13:34]* Too often in the modern world we feel a sense of alienation and isolation, which is the opposite of community. We need to be reconciled to one another, and we can be, through Christ.

Within the human spirit there's also the seed of solitude—of getting away from the tintinnabulation of the world. That seed is within each of us—it was the Walden Pond of Henry David Thoreau and the "Lake Isle of Innisfree" of William Butler Yeats. But just getting away does not solve the alienation and isolation of this life. Solitude is a means of drawing closer to God.

Jesus often drew away into solitude to commune with his father. (One instance is recorded in our Scripture for today.) In solitude we too can speak to God and hear His voice. The great Christian mystics have always known and practiced the discipline of solitude. Men such as St. John of the Cross and St. Francis in ages gone by, Thomas Kelly and Thomas Merton in our own time, show us the way to the heart of God through meditation and prayer.

Pulling back to the Center of all Being restores our soul and calms our spirit and prepares us once again to go out into the world to serve our Lord.

PRAYER: Dear Heavenly Father, help us seek to find times of solitude and communion with You, so we can better find community with and serve our fellow man. In Jesus name we pray. AMEN.

MAY 17

WHAT WOULD CHRIST DO?

(Scripture to ponder: Matthew 26: 47–57)

"Once to every man and nation comes the moment to decide."

So reads the text of James Russell Lowell's famous hymn, which goes on to assert that a choice must be made between the good or the evil side. In his address to the nation after the September 11 terrorist attack on our country, President Bush implied that a similar, momentous decision must now be made by many countries in the struggle against terrorism.

I am a patriotic American. I am willing to die for my country and for the cause of liberty. But I am also a Christian, and the devotion and loyalty I give to God is even greater than that I owe my country. In the midst of all the confusion, chaos, destruction and anger of that week, as the toll of dead and missing in New York and Washington neared seven thousand, I as an American resolved that those who plotted and took innocent lives must be brought to justice and punished. We are right to go after them. But I also prayerfully ask myself "What would Christ do?"

We know from St. Matthew's account that when Jesus and his followers were threatened, Christ said, *"Do you think that I cannot appeal to My Father and He will at once put at my disposal more than twelve legions of angels?"* Yet he did not choose the path of violence.

Christ changed the world by changing lives. Although he had all the power of God, He humbled himself and became a servant. And He teaches us to do likewise. As St. Paul tells us, *We can do all things through Christ, who strengthens us. [Philippians 4:13]* I believe that love and not violence will rule the world only when the mind of Christ rules in the hearts of men, when the Spirit of God controls them.

PRAYER: Empower us, O Lord, to do your will. Give us the Mind of Christ, and by Your Spirit, show us each day how to respond. AMEN.

MAY 18

GOD'S MIGHTY POWER

(Scripture to ponder: Psalm 18: 7–15)

For twenty years I lived in the Pacific Northwest. During that time the awesome and destructive eruption of Mount St. Helens occurred. For several weeks starting in March, 1980, there was subtle, increased seismic activity. It continued for two months, during which most of the nearby residents were evacuated.

With a mighty roar on the morning of May 18, the entire upper side of the mountain blew away. With the twelve-mile blast, an earthquake of Richter magnitude 5.1 occurred and hundred foot tall Douglas fir trees—ten million of them in all—were mowed down like grass. The nearby Toutle River became mud, an ashen silt, from which jumbled, shorn trees stuck out like match sticks. For two days the sky turned dark and it rained ash, choking people in the cities downwind and plugging the carburetors of cars and trucks. All told, 1600 feet came off the top of the mountain, and sixty people died.

Recently, when reading Psalm 18 aloud, I was struck by the parallel to Mt. St. Helens:

Then the earth reeled and rocked; the foundations also of the Mountains trembled and quaked, because he was angry. Smoke went up from his nostrils and devouring fire from his mouth; glowing coals flamed forth from him. He bowed the heavens and came down; thick darkness was under his feet. He rode on a cherub and flew; he came swiftly upon the wings of the wind. He made darkness his covering around him, his canopy thick clouds dark with water. Out of the darkness before him there broke through his clouds hailstones and coals of fire. The Lord also thundered in the heavens, and the Most High uttered his voice. And he sent out his arrows, and scattered them; he flashed forth lightnings and routed them. Then the channels of the sea were seen, the foundations of the world were laid bare at your rebuke, O Lord, at the blast of the breath of your nostrils.

Isn't it phenomenal that our God, who spoke to Elijah in a still, small voice *[1 Kings 19:12]*, who speaks in the thunder, the earthquake and the volcano, can speak to each of us through His Word?

PRAYER: **We praise You for your power and might, O Lord; but most of all, for your gift of Eternal Life through Jesus. AMEN.**

MAY 19

A COMPANY OF SINNERS

(Scripture to ponder: Luke 5:30–32)

The young man had been raised in a Christian home, and when he got to college, remained active in one of the local churches, where he assisted in work projects that did home repairs for poor people throughout their city.

One of his college roommates, a boy from a large East coast city, made fun of him because he continued to believe in Christ when most of their classmates—whatever their upbringing—had become either atheist or agnostic. One time during a discussion, the roommate exclaimed, **"How can you go to church with all those hypocrites?"** And he continued, quoting Henry David Thoreau, **"Most of the folks in church today show the whites of their eyes on Sunday and the blacks the rest of the week."**

That attitude was not rare among college students when I was in school, and it is not uncommon today. But it's wrong. Harry Emerson Fosdick, the famous pastor of Riverside Church in New York City, once wrote,

"The church is the only organization in the world that advertises itself as a company of sinners."

In our Scripture selection for today, Jesus himself was criticized by the Pharisees and scribes regarding the type of folks he was associating with—namely sinners and other "low-life types." Christ responded,

"Those who are well have no need of a physician, but those who are sick. I have not come to call the righteous, but sinners to repentance."

We who confess Jesus as Lord do indeed consider ourselves sinners.

PRAYER: It is because we see our own weakness and sinfulness, O Lord, that we look to the Lord Jesus as our Savior. May we always help and associate with others, no matter what their station in life, and may we always do Your Will. AMEN.

MAY 20

FAITH THAT HEALS

(Scripture to ponder: Matthew 9:20–22)

The scripture passage cited today is perhaps the shortest account of Christ's healing a person in all of the Gospels. It occurs in three verses, sandwiched, as it were, in the midst of an account of another healing, the healing of the daughter of Jairus, a ruler of a synagogue, related in the ninth chapter of Matthew. This short account is of the woman who had an issue of blood for twelve years. It is a brief story, related in each of the synoptic Gospels, that is, in Matthew 9, Mark 5 and in Luke Chapter 8. In the latter account, Luke, a physician himself, is rather hard on us doctors, for he said she *"had spent all her living upon physicians, neither could she be healed of any."* [Luke 8:43] Granted, medical care was primitive at the time, but this was no psychosomatic complaint, for sure.

I am convinced that this woman had a particular kind of faith, one that I'll call *"Faith that Heals."* She had suffered greatly, not just from a chronic anemia, which she doubtless had, for she had been bleeding for over a decade. She did suffer physically; but she suffered psychologically, too: it was as though she was chronically "on her period" for twelve years. So by Jewish law, she was unclean, and therefore sort of a pariah. Yet her faith in Jesus was so great that, as the scriptures relate, *"She said within herself, If I may but touch his garment, I shall be whole."* Despite her outcast state, she ventured into the crowd to be near the Master.

Luke embellishes Matthew's stark account. In Luke, Jesus asks, seemingly out of the blue, *"Who touched me?"* The disciples were surprised, for the press of the crowd around them was great. But Jesus perceived that power had gone out of him—the power that healed the woman—and he stopped and singled her out. The woman was healed already, by touching the fringe of his garment. And Jesus confirms it by declaring to her, *"Daughter, thy faith hath made thee whole. Go in peace."*

PRAYER: **We marvel, O Lord, at the faith of this woman. Help us to have such faith in your power, the Faith that Heals. AMEN.**

MAY 21

WHAT DOES THE CHURCH DO?

(Scripture to ponder: Matthew 18:20)

Ernest Gordon, was a Scotsman who was prisoner of the Japanese for over three years during WWII. After the war he went to seminary and later became Dean of the Chapel at Princeton University. In his book, Through the Valley of the Kwai, [21] he tells of the transforming power of the church to change both lives and the environment in which those lives are lived. Here he writes of the prison camp before the transformation:

As conditions steadily worsened, as starvation, exhaustion, and disease took an ever-growing toll, the atmosphere in which we lived was increasingly poisoned by selfishness, hatred and fear. We were slipping rapidly down the scale of degradation.

[p. 74]

But God's Spirit was active in the camp. A few faithful men began to meet together, read Scripture and pray. It was a church. He describes what happened as the spirit began to change the hearts and lives of other prisoners in the camp:

Ours was the church of the spirit. It was the throbbing heart which gave life to the camp and transformed it in considerable measure from a mass of frightened individuals into a community. From it we received the inspiration that made life possible. Such inspiration was not merely a rosy glow in the abdomen, but the literal inbreathing of the Holy Spirit that enabled men to live nobler lives, to become kind neighbors, to create improvements for the good of others, including such mundane matters as learning to cook better rice. The fruits of the Holy Spirit were clearly in evidence—"love, joy, long-suffering, gentleness, peace, goodness and faith."

[p.174]

What does the Church do? I think Gordon described it well. The Church—whether in a prisoner-of-war camp, in the heart of a city, or in the suburbs—enables us to live nobler lives, to become kind neighbors and to create improvements for the good of others.

PRAYER: **Open our hearts, Dear Lord, to the transforming Power of Your Spirit, that our lives may show forth Your Love. AMEN**

MAY 22

THE PEACEABLE KINGDOM

(Scripture to ponder: Isaiah 11:6–9)

A few years ago the Philadelphia Museum of Art had a display of the works of Edward Hicks, the eighteenth century American painter who painted many pictures based on Isaiah's prophesy. In the collection of paintings were several dozen renderings of the theme that has come to be known as the *Peaceable Kingdom,* that have been called Hicks' "painted sermons."

Hicks became a Quaker minister in 1812 at age 32, and about 1820 he began to paint his renderings of Isaiah's Prophesy. In the foreground benign animals and trusting infants play together, while in the background William Penn is shown making his famous treaty with the Indians. Hicks started in his twenties as a sign painter, and his later work was characterized by its simplicity and serenity.

The prophesy of Isaiah about animals lying down together, being led by a child, follows in the scripture just after Isaiah has foretold the coming of Christ, the shoot that would spring from the stem of Jesse.

It's been 20 centuries since Christ came, and two hundred years since Edward Hicks painted the *Peaceable Kingdom*—and we Christians are still hoping for that time of peace on earth. We do not know when it will come; perhaps not until after Jesus has returned to this war-weary world to take back his own. But we do know that when it comes, it will be God's doing.

PRAYER: **We long for peace on earth, O Lord—not just the absence of war, but for the time we can all be led by you, in love. Help us do your will, to bring peace among men. AMEN.**

MAY 23

THE VALUE OF A SECOND OPINION

(Scripture to ponder: Proverbs 15:33)

As a surgeon, I'm convinced of the value of a second opinion, and I have often given them in consultation for patients or other doctors. I first learned the value of second opinions when I was a surgical resident, but it was not in a medical context. It happened this way.

I was in training at the University of Oregon Hospital, set on a hill overlooking the city of Portland. I drove in each day from my home about eight miles away. One foggy fall morning I left my lights on in the parking lot and at the end of the day the battery was dead. I was able to start the car by rolling it down the hill, and I presumed the battery would recharge as I drove home. But the next morning I couldn't start the car and needed a jump for the battery.

I stopped at the gas station at the bottom of the hill near the hospital and told my story to the mechanic on duty. He lifted the hood and took a look at the motor. "**Your** alternator's gone bad," he said. "A new one'll run about $200. But I can getcha a re-built one for $90, installed."

WOW! $90 on my resident's salary was more than a week's pay. I thanked him and innocently said I'd get back to him, and went on to work. That afternoon I called the service manager at the place where I'd bought the car a year earlier, for a second opin-ion. **"Why don't you bring it in and let me take a look,"** he said. **"It could be just a loose fan belt."**

Well, I did, and it *was* a loose fan belt, that wasn't engaging the alternator. He tight-ened the belt for no charge, and that solved the problem. It was an instructive lesson that made me think of the Scripture selection for today:

"Where there is no counsel purposes are frustrated, but with many counselors they are accomplished."

Second opinions can indeed be quite worthwhile.

PRAYER: **Give us Your wisdom, Lord, that we may seek safety in second opinions as we seek to follow Your way and do Your will. AMEN.**

MAY 24

SEEK AND HIDE

(Scripture to ponder: Psalm 119:11)

We're all familiar with the game of "Hide and Seek," which is great fun for children. I'd like to suggest another game, one for adults, that I call "Seek and Hide." It's not so much a game as it is an exercise or a habit.

It involves seeking out Bible verses and hiding them in one's memory. By a habit of regular reading of the Scriptures, one often encounters wise or pithy sayings that are worth committing to memory, verses such as the sayings of Jesus, quotes from the Psalms, or wisdom from the Proverbs. Such as:

Do unto others as you would have others do unto you.
[Matthew 7:12]

or:

Consider the lilies of the field, how they grow: they toil not, neither do they spin; yet Solomon in all his glory was not arrayed like one of these.
[Matthew 6:28]

Or from the Psalms:

The heavens are showing the Glory of God and the firmament proclaims his handiwork.
[Psalm 19:1]

or:

When I consider thy heavens, the work of thy fingers, the moon and the stars which thou hast ordained; what is man, that thou art mindful of him? And the son of man, that thou visitest him?
[Psalm 8:4–5]

Or from the Book of Proverbs:

Go to the ant, thou sluggard and be wise
[Prov.6:6]

and:

A good name is rather to be chosen than great riches
[Prov.22:1]

The best reason for seeking and hiding Bible verses is summed up in the 11th verse of Psalm 119: *"Thy word have I hid in my heart, that I might not sin against thee."* From the wise counsel of the Scriptures we can learn right living so we do not sin against God, nor trespass against our fellow man.

PRAYER: Help us seek your wisdom as we read the Bible, O Lord, so we may hide it in our hearts and lead righteous lives. AMEN.

MAY 25

SCRIPTURAL XANAX

(Scripture to ponder: 1 Peter 5:7)

Anxiety is one of the most common maladies of modern American life. This is evident in the sale of prescription drugs, where anti-anxiety medications have topped the list for decades. Twenty years ago it was Valium, and more recently it's been Xanax and Prozac.

The Bible speaks of how to handle anxiety, but doesn't mention medication. Both Jesus and St. Peter tell us how to deal with anxiety. Jesus said in the Sermon on the Mount,

"Do not be anxious about tomorrow! Tomorrow can take care of itself! One day's trouble is enough for one day."

[Matthew 6:34]

In a similar vein, a famous doctor once put it memorably: "**Live your life in day-tight compartments.**" He meant, of course, to take 'em one day at a time.

A second approach is given in St. Peter's First Letter, our Scripture selection for today. He writes,

"Cast your anxiety on God, for He cares for you."

A famous clergyman once asked one of his parishioners—a man who was a captain of industry, charged with great responsibility—how he handled the tension and anxiety that came with his job.

"I couldn't do it," replied the man, "if I did not, every night, hand over my worries to God. It not only gets rid of the tension that's built up over the day; it lets me have restful sleep."

It was *his* scriptural Xanax, and it's scripturally sound advice.

PRAYER: Help us to let go of our worries and anxiety by casting our cares on You, knowing we are secure in Your Love. AMEN.

MAY 26

THE CHURCH INCANDESCENT

(Scripture to ponder: Matthew 5:14–16)

Harry Emerson Fosdick, pastor for many years of the large Riverside Church in New York City, was once asked if he had ever formulated a doctrine of the Church. He replied:

"I have been too busy working in the church to ever construct a doctrine of it . . . The Church should be the point of incandescence where, regardless of denominationalism or theology, the Christian life of the community bursts into flame."

As I read the words of Jesus in the New Testament, Fosdick's comments strike a responsive chord. In the Sermon on the Mount (today's Scripture selection) Jesus said:

You are the light of the world. A city set on a hill cannot be hid. Nor do you light a lamp and then put it under a bushel basket. You put it on a stand so it gives light to all in the house. Let your light shine before men so they may see your good works and give glory to your Father who is in heaven.

Fosdick spoke of incandescence—of a bursting into flame—such as when coals in a fire coalesce to burn brightly.

In a sense, each of us is a coal in a fire. Single coals go out, but coals gathered together will generate a heat beyond what any single one could.

In the same way, we Christians need the church, to gather together, both to worship God and to stoke the fires of our faith so that, like Jesus' city set on a hill, we can burn brightly in a dark world. Filled with God's spirit, we can indeed be the light of the world.

PRAYER: Bring us together, Lord, as coals glowing with Your love, so we burst into flame, to become the light of the world. AMEN.

MAY 27

EXPOSE YOURSELF TO JESUS

(Scripture to ponder: Colossians 2:9)

When I lived in Portland, Oregon, there was a colorful and crusty old chap who frequented one of the local pubs. He got on well with folks, and by dint of his personality, ended up becoming mayor of that great city. He was a nonconformist and a bit of a wit. I recall him best from a bronze statue in front of the Portland Art Museum. It shows him from the rear, dressed in a raincoat that he's holding open like a "flasher." (You can't see the exposed front of his body.) The pedestal is inscribed, "**Expose Yourself to Art.**"

That somewhat bawdy message came to mind as I was reading the 14th chapter of the Gospel of John, in which Jesus remarks to the disciple Philip,

"He who has seen me has seen the Father."

[John 14:9]

In a similar vein, in our Scripture selection for today, St. Paul writes to the Church at Colossi,

"In Christ all the fullness of the Godhead dwells bodily."

I am convinced that many people today would like to know God, to believe in Him. They'd like to be aware of Him as a force in their lives and in the world. They can, through knowing the Lord Jesus Christ. To get to know God, we need only to expose ourselves to Jesus as we encounter Him in the New Testament. In him the fullness of God is manifest *incarnate*, for God became a man and dwelt among us.

It is God's way of saying:

I love you; I will walk among you, so you can know me.

PRAYER: **Grant us the desire and the discipline to know you, Dear Lord, through reading Your Word each day. AMEN.**

MAY 28

WHOM DO YOU FOLLOW?

(Scripture to ponder: Matthew 16:24)

During my practice years I was often responsible for supervising many physicians, some who were residents and some who were colleagues in departments or sections in which I was in charge. On several occasions I had to deal with situations in which a physician who was on call failed in his duties or responsibilities.

Sometimes this was due to laziness, a significant deficiency in a physician, particularly one in training. But often it was due to a conflict of priorities. A physician who was paged when he was on call would place a greater priority on what *he* wanted to do—say, get more sleep or stay at a ball game—than on the needs of the patients he was responsible for.

While it's true that many times clinical problems can be handled over the phone, the thing that got me involved in these situations, and that got these doctors into hot water, was that he was needed at the bedside of a patient (when called by a nurse, for example), but he didn't respond. What's true in the field of medicine is true in life itself.

The willingness to subordinate one's own desires to the needs of others is what Christ is talking about in Matthew's Gospel, when he asserts,

"If any one would come after me, he must deny himself and take up his cross and follow me."

[Matthew 16:24]

The self-denial that makes a physician get out of bed when called by a worried nurse is the same self-denial we see in a Christian who chooses to follow Christ, even though the way may be steep and narrow.

PRAYER: Help us, Dear Lord, to put you first in our lives, serving the needs of others; for in you is our trust and our security. AMEN.

MAY 29

THE VALUE OF CHRISTIAN SUFFERING

(Scripture to ponder: 2 Corinthians 1:3–4)

The question of why suffering occurs is one of the most challenging in all history. One answer, given by the famous Protestant preacher Harry Emerson Fosdick was what he wrote about himself to a troubled young woman:

I went through a nervous breakdown once, during which my despair was so great that I went to get a razor to cut my throat. Now as I look back on that hideous experience, I count it one of the most valuable of my life. There are multitudes of people I never could have helped if I had not gone through that. It was a more important part of my education than a whole lot of my scholastic training.[22]

As a surgeon, I can echo Fosdick's words from my own experience. As important and as valuable as were my years of residency training in surgery, almost as valuable—though in a different way, perhaps—was my own experience of having the agonizing pain of a herniated lumber disc, and having to go through surgery for it. That suffering, that experience, taught me what my patients go through. It made me far more understanding and empathetic than I otherwise would have been.

St. Paul, in his Second Letter to the Church at Corinth (our Scripture selection for today) asserts that the suffering we endure has a purpose: so we can comfort others who suffer. It's an important part of the Christian life, for becoming a Christian does not mean we'll be granted a pain-free existence. Rather, knowing Christ enables us, through sharing His suffering, to comfort others who themselves are suffering.

PRAYER: Help us, O Lord, to comfort others with the peace that we ourselves have received through Your Spirit. AMEN.

MAY 30

MEMORIAL DAY THOUGHTS

(Scripture to ponder: Ecclesiasticus 44:1–17)

Throughout our history there has been an understandable tendency for our military leaders to be singled out for praise and glory. We erect monuments to men like Grant and Lee, Pershing and Eisenhower. This is as it should be.

But one of the things I like best about Memorial Day is that it tends to honor and remember the average soldier, not the great and celebrated leader. There's a passage of the Bible that I am reminded of each Memorial Day. It's in the book of Ecclesiasticus, one of the books of the Apocrypha, a section of the Bible that is not often read. It's today's Scripture selection.

It begins by praising famous men, and then continues:

And some there be who have no memorial, who are perished as though they had never lived. But they were men of mercy, whose godly deeds have not failed. Their descendants are a holy inheritance: And their seed hath stood in the covenants. Their bodies are buried in peace, but their name liveth forever.

It is those unsung soldiers that we honor on Memorial Day, those who lie beneath the thousand crosses of Arlington, beneath the sod at Gettysburg, Normandy, Flanders Fields and Tarawa. These we honor on Memorial Day.

The wonderful thing about God's love is that He knows each of us and honors us individually.

PRAYER: Today we honor the many dead who gave their lives for their country. May we always remember them as you do, O Lord. AMEN.

MAY 31

SPIRITUAL COACHING

(Scripture to ponder: 2 Samuel 11:1–12:7)

St. Paul compares the Christian life to an athletic contest, and speaks of "running the race to win" *[1 Corinthians 9:24]* and "fighting the good fight." *[2 Timothy 4:7]* I've lately been watching the Olympic figure skating tryouts and I'm impressed with the value of good coaching to improve performance. What's valuable in sports is valuable in everyday living.

Historically, men and women who enlisted in full time Christian service as monks or nuns always had a "spiritual director," someone who counseled them and helped them to objectively evaluate their lives. Nowadays, we too can benefit from such "spiritual coaching," for left to our own devices, we may not improve, we can go astray in a world of temptations.

One of the most dramatic examples of "spiritual coaching" involves King David, related in our Scripture selection for today. Although he was "a man after God's own heart," David could also be a great sinner. The Scripture tells how, after he saw the beautiful Bathsheba at her bath, he lusted after her. He not only committed adultery with her, but he then had her husband murdered to cover his foul deed.

But David's spiritual "coach"—the prophet Nathan—brought him up short, telling the King a simple story. When David reacted strongly, condemning the rich man who took the poor man's ewe lamb, Nathan exclaimed, *"Thou art the man!"* King David recognized his own sin, repented of it, and wrote Psalm 51. David needed spiritual coaching, just as we do.

PRAYER: We need spiritual coaching from our pastors, from our fellow Christians and from our spouses, Dear Lord. Help us to open ourselves to others' opinions of our actions, and benefit from their counsel. AMEN.

JUNE 1

WAIT AND PRAY FOR THE DYNAMITE!

(Scripture to ponder: Acts 1:4–5; 14)

We Americans are impatient people, folks who don't like to wait. I suspect the early disciples—the apostles and those to whom Jesus showed himself after the resurrection—were equally impatient to get on with telling others that the Lord was risen, indeed. But they were told to wait, and during that waiting period, the scripture says that they devoted themselves to prayer.

Why did they wait? Because as our Scripture text says, they had been promised *dynamite:*

> "But you shall receive power when the Holy Spirit has come upon you; and you shall be my witnesses in Jerusalem and in all Judea and Samaria and to the end of the earth."
>
> [Acts 1:8]

The Greek word used here for power is *dunamis*—from which our word **dynamite** comes. What do you suppose the prayers of the disciples were like as they awaited the promise of the Holy Spirit. I imagine they were different from the lick-and-a-promise prayers that all too often characterize my hectic life. In contrast, hear what author Edward Day, in his book Existence Under God, calls true prayer:[23]

> "It is not merely a flash of Godward desire, but the passionate fervor of a whole self that pants to know God and His will above all other knowing. It is not a hurried visit to the window of a religious drive-in restaurant for a moral sandwich or a cup of spiritual stimulant, but an unhurried communion with God who is never in a hurry. It is not merely the expression of a transient mood of dependence or loneliness, but the consistent cry of one who seeks to perceive and express the Ultimate Beauty. It is the antithesis of dilly-dally devotions, drowsy murmurs from a pillow where sleep lies in wait, the lazy lisping of familiar phrases that [rather] should shake one to the core of one's being. It is the find-or-die outreach of the soul for God."

True prayer is dynamic prayer. It's dynamite prayer!

PRAYER: Teach us true prayer, O Lord. Teach us to patiently wait for the promise of the Holy Spirit, the dynamite of the Christian life, to empower us to do your will and spread the Gospel. We pray in the Name of Jesus, our Savior. AMEN.

JUNE 2

SELECTIVE HEARING

(Scripture to ponder: Mark 4:11–12)

Have you ever noticed how some folks have selective hearing? I first encountered this phenomenon when I was a boy visiting my grandparents. I was twelve and went by train by myself from Pennsylvania to Iowa to stay with them. My 85-year-old grandfather could not hear my voice very well, and couldn't hear sirens or car horns either. One afternoon we had an exciting ride into town to visit my aunt. My grandfather was weaving along the road and we began to be followed by a police car. I could hear the frenetic siren and could see the flashing lights through the rear widow. We finally lurched into the driveway of my aunt's place. Fortunately Aunt Leone, who was the wife of the town's chief attorney, interceded for granddad.

Yet my grandfather could hear the voice of grandmother quiet well, maybe because they spent over sixty years together.

It got me thinking about what we selectively tune in or tune out. I for example often press the mute button on the TV when the commercials come on, to tune them out, whereas my wife is able to work on a crossword puzzle and not be at all distracted by a TV commercial blaring in the background. She can tune them out quite easily.

Maybe the same idea of selective hearing applies to listening to God. I suspect folks who regularly read the scriptures and pray get "tuned in" to God, so they are able to hear His voice, and are able to "tune out" the noise of the world about them. In our Scripture selection for today, Christ indicates that some folks who hear the Gospel hear but do not understand. For spiritual lessons, they seem to hear selectively.

PRAYER: Help us through close association, to stay tuned in to you, Dear Lord, hearing Your message for us and not the world around us. AMEN.

JUNE 3

CARING FOR ONE ANOTHER

(Scripture to ponder: John 13:34–35)

Someone once asked the famous anthropologist Margaret Meade her opinion as to when human civilization began. I was surprised by her answer. I thought as an anthropologist her reply would be based on some ancient shard or evidence of a primitive tool. Instead, she said the first evidence of human civilization was a crooked bone, a healed fracture of a human femur. It was evidence that one individual was concerned enough about another to provide enough attention and care to let the fracture heal.

It is, of course, the opposite of what we often see in the animal kingdom, where wounded or maimed individuals get left behind, to be set upon by predators. Unfortunately some human social systems have been similar. Nietzsche's concept of the *Ubermensch* and Hitler's Master Race both extolled might and strength, urging survival of the fittest. They advocated leaving the infirm and weak to die, or would actually even kill them. Callousness, not compassion was seen as a virtue.

But that is not what the Lord Jesus taught. *"A new commandment I give unto you, that you love one another,"* records St. John in today's Scripture verse, words from Christ's last discourse to his disciples. They must have heeded his words, for of the early Christians, it was exclaimed, *"Behold how they loved one another!"*

Caring for the sick, the wounded, the outcast and the lame has always been the mark of the true follower of Christ. The saintly life of Mother Theresa is just one example of that kind of love. Such love should characterize all Christians.

PRAYER: Help us, Dear Lord, to love one another as you have loved us, with caring, sacrificial love. AMEN.

JUNE 4

CHRIST HIDDEN AMONG US

(Scripture to ponder: Luke 24: 13–35)

George Fox, the seventeenth century founder of the Society of Friends asserted, "**There is that of God in every man.**" Fox believed we minister unto God Himself when we reach out to those around us. But often we can fail to recognize Him when we are face to face with him. Consider Christ's life.

Three times during our Lord's ministry, the Bible describes his being among us without our recognizing Him. The first was at the outset of His ministry, when Christ's forerunner John the Baptist proclaimed, *"Among you stands one you do not know."* *[John 1:26]* Christ was in the crowd, unrecognized.

At the very end of Jesus' ministry, after His resurrection, as recorded in our scripture for today, two disciples walked the road to Emmaus with a stranger, a man they invited to supp with them. As he broke bread with them, their eyes were opened and they recognized the Lord. After he was gone, they exclaimed, *"Did not our hearts burn within us as he taught us on the way!"* [Luke 24: 32]

The third allusion to the unrecognized Christ among us comes from His teaching in Matthew's gospel concerning the last judgment. In that parable, the righteous ask him, *"When did we see thee hungry, or thirsty, or a stranger, or sick, or in prison?"* [Matthew 25:37] To which Christ replies,

"If you did it unto the least of these my brethren, you did it unto me."

[Matthew 25:40]

What an amazing, holy mystery—that as we minister to our needy brothers and sisters, we minister unto Christ himself! It's one of God's richest blessings.

PRAYER: Dear Lord, help us to see your face in those around us, so we may minister to their needs, each day and every day. AMEN.

JUNE 5

SAVANT OR SERVANT?

(Scripture to ponder: 1 Corinthians 3:18; 1:25&27)

A *savant* is defined as a person of exceptional knowledge or brilliance. Occasionally in the church we encounter persons—usually preachers—of great knowledge and brilliance, and I like to hear them expound God's Word. Through their great learning they often weave strands of wisdom from the Scriptures into a variegated and lovely cord to bind us to the Lord.

But savants are rare in the church and in the world. Indeed, as Christians we worship God as the font of all wisdom and knowledge and don't need to look anywhere else for guidance in life. In today's Scripture, St. Paul puts it succinctly:

Let no man deceive himself. If any man seems to be wise in this world, let him become a fool that he may be wise . . . For the foolishness of God is wiser than men, and the weakness of God is stronger than men . . . God has chosen the foolish things of the world to put to shame the wise, and God has chosen the weak things of the world to put to shame the things which are mighty.

How does this happen? It can occur because although not all Christians can be savants, all can be *servants*. Indeed, Christ calls us to be servants. For it is loving, neighborly service that will reach the hearts of persons who do not know the Lord—more than all the sophisticated preaching from all the pulpits of the world.

PRAYER: Not all of us have eloquence, Dear Lord; but through your Spirit, all of us can serve our neighbor to do Your will. AMEN.

JUNE 6

OVERLOOKING THE SCRATCHES

(Scripture op ponder: Ephesians 4:32)

I wear glasses and have several pairs. When I do outside jobs like trimming trees, I wear one of my old pairs. Recently, while trimming some limbs in the yard, I took a break to chat with a neighbor. As we were talking, she looked right at me, smiled and exclaimed, **"Did you know you've got a big scratch on your glasses?"**

I did indeed have a scratch, a fairly large one—that's why I wear my *old* glasses for handyman jobs. But the interesting thing is, I was unaware of the scratch—although I knew it was there, I looked right by it, I overlooked it.

A similar situation occurs when we are close to someone and love them: we overlook their faults. We look right by the blemishes and scratches and overlook the imperfections. St. Paul, in his letter to the church at Ephesus (today's Scripture selection), urges us in love to overlook the scratches. He writes:

"Be kind to one another, tenderhearted, forgiving one another, even as God for Christ's sake has forgiven you."

Overlooking the faults of others, accepting them as they are, is part of loving them. As the famous American philosopher William James put it, **"the art of being wise is the art of knowing what to overlook."**

PRAYER: **Give us that divine wisdom, O Lord, that lets us overlook imperfections, so we can love others as You love us. AMEN.**

JUNE 7

SEEING BUT NOT SEEING

(Scripture to ponder: Matthew 13:13)

In the medical school I attended there was a sign over the entrance to the radiology department. It stated, **"We see what we look for, we recognize what we know."** It was referring to patterns of shadows on X-Rays, but could refer to medical diagnosis as well.

The same pertains to spiritual matters. Jesus was the Messiah of the Jews, but almost all who saw and heard him did not recognize him as such. They were looking for another sort of deliverer and did not recognize the Son of God. The Jews sought a leader who would cast off the yoke of Roman rule, and were looking for a military leader, not the suffering servant of God.

Christ Himself understood that he would be recognized through *spiritual discernment*, and he wanted it that way. It's the reason he used parables so often in his teaching. In our Scripture selection for today, Jesus quotes the Prophet Isaiah, saying:

Therefore I speak to them in parables: because seeing they see not; and hearing they hear not, neither do they understand.

Spiritual discernment is a gift from the Holy Spirit. Those who seek it must earnestly desire it. But God has assured us,

If with all your heart you truly seek me, you shall surely find me

[Deut.4:29]

The key is to ask with single-minded, earnest desire.

PRAYER: We know, Dear Lord, that You reveal Yourself to those who truly seek You. Help us through Your Holy Spirit to earnestly seek You. AMEN.

JUNE 8

AN EASY YOKE

(Scripture to ponder: Matthew 11:28–30)

As a boy I learned to paddle a canoe because we had a summer place on a lake in New Jersey, and as a young man I greatly enjoyed canoeing. When I was fourteen I improved my skills when I attended a camp in Maine. There we had to pass a test by singly lifting an 85 lb Old Town canoe up on to our shoulders and carry it 100 yards.

We got it up by balancing it on our knees, rocking it three times, and heaving it up and over our head. We'd slide underneath as the middle thwart came down on our shoulders. Then we carried it the distance. The heavy canoe was quite uncomfortable, for it dug into the back of my neck. That summer during a four-week canoe trip in Northern Maine, I carried one of those heavy canoes on several portages.

Years later, when canoeing in Minnesota, I discovered there was an easier way, by using a canoe yoke. It's a specially shaped and padded device that fits around one's shoulders, over the thwart. It's a much more comfortable way to carry the canoe.

In our Scripture selection for today, Jesus says of Himself,

"My yoke is easy and my burden is light."

We know Jesus was a carpenter who often fitted yokes and knew the importance of a yoke that was comfortable and did not chafe. He spoke metaphorically, of course, urging us to come live our lives by his example and his precepts.

PRAYER: Help us, O Lord to take your yoke upon us and learn from you, so we may do your will and so we may have rest unto our souls. AMEN.

JUNE 9

TO RUN AND NOT BE WEARY

(Scripture to Ponder: Isaiah 40)

Recently on television I watched the Triathlon from Hawaii. To see the weariness on the faces, the utter fatigue of the participants as they neared the end of that grueling course, some fainting, some stumbling, reminded me of today's Scripture passage:

Have you not known? Have you not heard? The Lord is the everlasting God, the creator of the ends of the earth. He does not faint or grow weary, his understanding is unsearchable. He gives power to the faint, and to him who has no might he increases strength. Even youths shall faint and be weary, and young men shall fall exhausted; But they that wait on the Lord shall renew their strength, they shall mount up with wings as eagles, they shall run and not be weary, they shall walk and not faint.

Not many of us are triatheletes. But all of us grow weary, with fatigue of body, mind, or spirit. The marvelous thing, to which Isaiah alludes, is that if we wait upon God, H e will renew our strength. If you are weary—from any cause—call upon Him.

PRAYER: Dear Lord, when we are weary, renew our strength, so that with renewed vigor, we may do thy will. AMEN.

JUNE 10

CONSIDER THE HEAVENS

(Scripture to ponder: Psalm 8)

Whenever I read today's selection, which speaks of *the heavens, the work of God's fingers, the moon and the stars which He's ordained*, I'm reminded of the summer before I went to medical school when I spent three weeks backpacking in the Sierra Nevada mountains of California.

My cousin Vic and I hiked the John Muir Trail and ended up climbing Mt. Whitney, at over 14,000 feet, the highest point in the contiguous 48 states. After that we went to Sequoia National Park where we camped out. We slept out without a tent, in a meadow out under the stars. Because we were many miles from the nearest city and there was no moon, the night was radiant, with the firmament overhead fretted with twinkling stars.

After the sun had set and the afterglow was fading and the stars came out, we noticed a bright object—brighter than the planet Venus—that slowly began to cross the night sky. At first we thought it might be an airplane, but through binoculars it looked spherical, and we could see no contrail such as an aircraft might make. This luminous object took about three minutes to pass from one horizon to the other. As we watched in the clear stillness of the night, its long, silent trajectory was impressive.

A few days later, after we returned to civilization and caught up on the news, we discovered what the mysterious object was: one of the first earth-orbiting satellites. Since then over 2000 have been launched and they've become commonplace. But back then—almost 50 years ago—seeing a satellite for the first time was a reminder, not just of God's heavens, but also that he's *crowned man with honor and glory, and put all things under his feet.* And I ask myself, as I see what's happened since: have we been faithful stewards of all that God has committed to us?

PRAYER: We are grateful, O Lord, for the advances made in science. May we always use wisely what You've entrusted to us. Help us live by your Spirit and do Your will. AMEN.

JUNE 11

JUST ASK ME!

(Scripture to ponder: Matthew 7:7)

I usually carry around a small packet of 3 x 5 cards in my breast pocket, on which I jot down things to do, calls to make, and so forth. Occasionally I misplace it and when that happens, I get thrown off stride and have to retrace my steps to find it.

This morning I couldn't find that little packet. I got increasingly vexed as I looked in all the usual places—in coat and shirt pockets, in the bedroom and in the den, on the desk and by the computer—but I still couldn't locate it. Finally, exasperated, I asked my wife if she remembered seeing it recently. She smiled and said, "Just ask me!" She went to her purse and pulled it out, reminding me that yesterday when we'd gone shopping at a nearby department store that had suits on sale, I'd given my shirt pocket contents to her as I tried on several suit coats. We laughed about it.

"**Just ask me!**" Those words triggered in my memory what Jesus says to us in the Sermon on the Mount (our Scripture selection for today) *"Ask and it shall be given you."*

Again, in his last discourse, Jesus said,

"If you ask anything in my name, I will do it."

[John 16:23–24]

God knows us better than anyone else. He is closer than a brother, closer than a spouse. He knows our needs, and we need but ask.

PRAYER: So often, Lord, we miss out on richness and joys in life because we don't come to You and ask. Help us to always ask for Your wisdom and Your peace. AMEN.

JUNE 12

MAKING GODS

(Scripture to ponder: Acts 17:22–31)

When the XVIII Century philosopher Voltaire said, **"If man had no god, he would make himself one,"** he was stating a truth that's been repeated through the ages, from the time of the Golden Calf that the Israelites cast while Moses was on the mountain, up to the present time, when British author J.B. Philips wrote a book entitled *Your God Is Too Small*.

Today's Scripture tells how St. Paul, when he arrived in Athens, seized upon this tendency of man to create deities, in his famous sermon on Mars Hill. He'd seen a peculiar shrine on his way into the city, so he used this as a point of departure. As related in Acts 17, Paul opens with this statement:

"Men of Athens! I perceive you are very religious, for as I have beheld your devotions, I found an altar with the inspiration, "To the Unknown God."

Paul then proceeds to explain that this God, which they worshiped in ignorance, was the creator of all the universe, yet is near to all of us. Paul then uttered the memorable lines,

"For in Him we live and move and have our being."

[Acts 17:28]

He went on to explain and proclaim Jesus and His Resurrection to his Greek listeners.

Today in our affluent country, we too have many gods, worshiped by many persons: Success, Money, Power, or Possessions. But ever the Gospel proclaims with St. Paul that there is but one true God, and only He is worthy of our worship and our devotion. In Him we truly live and move and have our being.

PRAYER: Through your spirit, O Lord, help us perceive and worship You, the one true God, serving you all our days. AMEN.

JUNE 13

TRUST, DELIGHT, COMMIT AND WAIT

(Scripture to ponder: Psalm 37)

Have you ever gotten discouraged, really down—particularly when things have not gone well—and then looked around and seen the prosperity of those who have no qualms?

The Psalmist knew those feelings well, and what he wrote in Psalm 37 can be a great source of comfort in such times. It's a Psalm you can read and repeatedly return to, for it is God's comfort and consolation for all those who seek to do His will. It gives a formula: Trust, Delight, Commit and Wait: (I've capitalized those words.)

Fret not yourself because of the wicked; be not envious of wrongdoers!
For they will soon fade like the grass and wither like the green herb.
TRUST in the Lord, and do good; so you will dwell in the land and enjoy security.
Take DELIGHT in the Lord, and He will give you the desires of your heart.
COMMIT your way to the Lord; trust in Him and He will act.
He will bring forth your vindication as the light, and your right as the noonday.
Be still before the Lord and wait patiently for Him;
Fret not yourself over him who prospers in his way, over the man who carries out evil devices!
Refrain from anger and forsake wrath! Fret not yourself; it tends only to evil.
For the wicked shall be cut off; but those who WAIT for the Lord
Shall possess the land.

PRAYER: Thank You, Lord, for the comfort and wisdom of Your Word. Help us always to *Trust* in You, to take *Delight* in You, to *Commit* to You, and to *Wait* upon You in love. AMEN.

JUNE 14

THE BOTTOM OF THE BARREL

(Scripture to ponder: John 1:43–51)

You've doubtless heard the expression "the bottom of the barrel," which means the dregs or the leftovers. Usually it has a negative connotation, but in the case of our sixteenth president, it was the way he got started in the law.

As a young man, Abe Lincoln owned a dry goods store in Illinois. One day a man who was loading a wagon with household goods to move west brought in a barrelful of sundry items he could not carry along and Lincoln bought it from him for a modest sum. He put the barrel away in the back of the store, intending some day to empty it.

Later that summer when business was slow, Lincoln dumped the barrel out on the floor. There, at the bottom of the barrel, was a copy of *Blackstone's Commentaries* on the law, that Lincoln proceeded to read during his spare time, of which there was a lot, for most of the townsfolk were farmers occupied with their crops. Out of that summer of reading—out of the bottom of the barrel, if you will—came Lincoln's interest in the law, which became his chosen profession.

Similarly, in Biblical times, the town of Nazareth, away from the trade routes and off the beaten path, was considered the bottom of the barrel. When he hears where Jesus hails from, the future disciple Nathaniel cynically exclaims,

"Can anything good come out of Nazareth?"

[John 1:46]

But that's how God often works, and out of a humble carpenter shop in that small village emerged the savior of the world. God does indeed work in mysterious ways!

PRAYER: Show us through Your Word, Dear Lord, that the humble way, the bottom of the barrel, is often the way You would have us grow to serve You. AMEN.

JUNE 15

CAMPING IN A WASH

(Scripture to ponder: Matthew 7:24–27)

I enjoy camping. For years I lived in Oregon, which is a lovely state, but there camping is curtailed by a lot of rain. Arizona is ideal for camping, since it rarely rains, and the nighttime heavens are clear and studded with stars.

But finding a place to pitch a tent in desert camping can be problematic, for you rarely encounter a clear area without cacti or other spiny vegetation. To the novice, a dry streambed—called a wash or arroyo—can seem ideal: it's flat, often sandy, and usually devoid of vegetation. But camping in a wash is a dangerous trap for the unwary.

It rarely rains in the desert, but when it does, it often comes as a cloudburst, as a torrential thunderstorm. If the topography is hilly or mountainous, the water from such a deluge runs off fast, rapidly filling the washes, causing flash floods. Dry stream beds suddenly spring to life as water roars down them, picking up rocks, debris and even small trees in a headlong rush that can even lift cars and tumble them—hence the signs you see posted where roads cross washes that warn, **"Do not cross when flooded!"** Someone asleep in a tent pitched in a wash may have no time to escape if a sudden thunderstorm occurs at night.

In our scripture selection for today, Jesus likened someone who hears his words and doesn't do them to a foolish man who built his house on the sand. If Jesus were teaching today, do you suppose he would use as an example the man who pitches his tent in a wash?

PRAYER: Help us heed as well as hear your words, O Lord, that we not perish in the thunderstorms that come our way in life. AMEN.

JUNE 16

SCRITPURAL SAUNTERING

(Scripture to ponder: Ephesians 4:1)

In his essay entitled "Walking," Henry David Thoreau writes:

> I have met with but one or two persons in the course of my life who understood the art of walking, that is, of taking walks—who had a genius, so to speak, for *sauntering:* which word is beautifully derived from idle people who roved about the country in the Middle Ages, and asked charity under pretense of going *a la Sainte Terrer,* to the Holy Land, 'til the children exclaimed "There goes a *Saunterer*"
>
> —a Holy Lander.

The Bible speaks in several places of walking. If you were to look up *walking* in a concordance, you could have a rewarding time *sauntering through Scripture.* Here's but a small sampling:

The 23d Psalm says that *even though we walk through the valley of the shadow of death,* God is with us.

The Prophet Micah declares what is required of us: *"To do justly, to love mercy and to walk humbly with God." [Micah 6:8]*

Jesus said *I am the Light of the world; whoever follows me will never walk in darkness, but will have the light of life. [John 8:12, NIV]*

It was to a small group of men walking on the road to Emmaus that the risen Christ showed himself after his Resurrection. *[Luke 24:13]*

And St. Paul bids us to *"walk worthy of the calling to which we have been called, in humility and gentleness, bearing with one another with patience and love." [Ephesians 4:1]*

PRAYER: Grant that we may always walk with you beside us, Dear Lord, whether it be through the valley, or on mountain paths, to do Your will, serving one another in love. AMEN.

JUNE 17

LET GO AND LET GOD

(Scripture to ponder: Psalm 3:5 and Psalm 127:1–2)

As one who loves to climb mountains, I got a kick out of a story about a skeptic who was climbing alone on an open face of a mountain where vegetation was sparse. He slipped and as he tumbled headlong down the mountainside, he arrested his fall by grabbing on to a branch of one of those craggy bushes that have roots growing into the rock. As he hung there, he cried out for help:

"Help! Help! Is there anyone there who can save me?"

A deep, booming voice answered from above, **"Yes, I am here."**
"Oh, thank goodness!" called the mountaineer. **"Help me!"** The deep voice came down a second time, saying,

"Let go of the branch, my son. Trust me. Let go of the branch."

There was a long pause. Then the mountain climber looked up and called,

"Is there anyone else up there?"

It's a silly story, but part of why it's amusing is it has a measure of truth in it. Sometimes the solution of a problem involves letting go of it, allowing God to work. But we can hold on so tight!

Norman Vincent Peale tells of a captain of industry responsible for one of America's mightiest corporations who had weighty and important decisions to make almost daily. Peale asked him how he could take the constant strain and worry. The leader replied that each night before retiring, he got down on his knees and turned over all his worries and decisions to the Lord. He said every night he let go and let God work on them. And he added, as a result, he was given a marvelous rest every night, and often awoke in the morning with an answer to what yesterday had been a vexing problem.

Each of us, with God's help, can do likewise.

PRAYER: When we lay down to sleep, Dear Lord, help us let go of the cares of the world, knowing you give to your beloved even in their sleep. AMEN.

JUNE 18

BUMPED ON THE BUMPER

(Scripture to ponder: Proverbs 15:1)

I was in New York City visiting a new friend, a physician I'd met at a medical meeting in Kansas City a month earlier, who was President of the New York Academy of Medicine. He invited me for lunch to see that venerable institution and to take me through its library of old medical books, one of the finest in the country. I drove up from Philadelphia.

The traffic was terrific. It took me half an hour just to get across the Lincoln Tunnel from New Jersey. It seemed like every other car in the city was a yellow cab. Although the avenues were broad and one way—most of them like Fifth Avenue or Madison Avenue had five lanes—things moved agonizingly slow, for trucks and cars were double parked on both sides of the curb lanes, which in turn were lined with tightly parked cars. The flow of traffic was often reduced to one or two lanes. And none of the traffic lights was timed.

My little white Nissan Sentra tends to creep when it's halted in traffic. At one red light I was behind a yellow cab that had no fare in it. The weather was hot and muggy, and drivers' tempers were flaring. Only about a foot separated me from the cab ahead, and as I paused to look at the map, my car crept up and bumped his bumper.

Well, he jumped out and came back and started cursing and yelling at me. No damage had been done, but he got really cranked up, gesticulating and shaking his fist. What to do? I sat tight, knowing if I got out to reply to his ranting, things would just get worse. So I waited. He approached my door, but the light changed, and cars around us began to honk. He gave me one last angry look, got in his cab and roared off.

PRAYER: Thank You, O Lord, for the wisdom to know when to use a soft answer, and when to refrain from responding. AMEN.

JUNE 19

BUT WHAT HAVE YOU DONE FOR ME LATELY?

(Scripture to ponder: Philippians 4:6)

You've perhaps heard the story about the person who prayed to the Lord that God might be revealed to him. God is said to have responded—much as He did to Job—by relating all the mighty deeds He had done for His people, such as leading them through the Red Sea and sustaining them in the desert during the Exodus, etc. To which the petitioner responded,

"But what have you done for me lately?"

It's a simple and silly story, but it does make a point. In our selfish sinfulness we often focus on a current problem or loss, and overlook the many blessings that God has showered upon us. Taking time to count our blessings helps restore that attitude of gratitude that sets us right with God. Hear the words of Psalm 103:

Bless the Lord, O my soul, and all that is within me
Bless his Holy Name.
Bless the Lord, O my soul, and forget not all his benefits:
Who pardons all your iniquities, who heals all your diseases;
Who redeems your life from the pit;
Who crowns you with loving kindness and compassion;
Who satisfies your years with good things,
So that your youth is renewed like the eagle.

In our Scripture selection for today, St. Paul urges us to let our prayer requests be made known to God with *thanksgiving!*

PRAYER: We praise and thank You, Lord, for Your mighty acts in history, and for the many blessings you bestow on us in this life. Help us always to do Your will. AMEN.

JUNE 20

RESTLESS HEARTS

(Scripture to ponder: Isaiah 26:3)

In the field of medicine there is a peculiar group of symptoms called "the restless leg syndrome." It refers to a twitching that occurs in the muscles of the leg. Patients who have it have much grief and don't have much peace, for it's quite distracting and keeps them awake at night.

But I sense a restlessness of the spirit nowadays, a dissatisfaction with life as it is, a yearning for something more that possessions cannot give. Despite all our material wealth, there's an unrest in the souls of many in our land.

I'm reminded of a well-known quote from St. Augustine:

"You have made us for Yourself, O Lord, and our hearts are restless until they find their rest in You."

As a part of our human condition, we have hearts that are restless, that long for the peace which passes understanding, the peace that comes only from God. We long for it, but how can we find this peace?

In today's Scripture selection, the Prophet Isaiah writes,

Thou wilt keep him in perfect peace, whose mind is stayed on Thee.

The secret to overcoming the anxiety and restlessness that so infects the modern world is to seek God's perfect peace by staying our mind on Him, through reflection, meditation, prayer, and contemplation of God's Word.

PRAYER: We are indeed restless until we find our rest in You, O Lord. Help us set aside time to pray and read Your Word, that we may have your peace. AMEN.

JUNE 21

HOW DO YOU PLAN?

(Scripture to ponder: Jeremiah 29:11)

Summer is often the time for vacations and taking trips. How do you go about planning for a vacation or a trip—how, for that matter, do you go about planning your life? Do you do it prayerfully?

As Christians, we believe life has purpose. We believe God has a plan for our lives. As our Scripture selection for today states:

Surely I know the plans I have for you, says the Lord, plans for your welfare and not for harm, to give you a future with hope.

How do we know the Will of God? How do we tap into His knowledge, to perceive the plans He has for us? I believe there are two keys to understanding God's Will for us.

First, we need to stay immersed in God's Word, through regular reading and study of the Bible. Second, we need to set aside specific times of prayer.

Prayer has been called the bridge between our conscious and unconscious lives. If we are steeped in God's Word, and if we pray regularly, we will begin to perceive the Mind of God, and know His Will in our activities and plans.

PRAYER: **Keep us faithful, O Lord, to set aside times to be nourished by Your Word and to pray regularly. In Jesus' Name we ask it. AMEN.**

JUNE 22

ANN THE JUDGE

(Scripture To ponder: Luke 12:13–15)

The famous columnist Ann Landers died on this day in 2002. Over a long life she dispensed advice to millions of people through her syndicated Newspaper columns. Reading her obituary in our local paper, I was surprised to see no mention of her religion, and I did not remember any mention of it in her writings during her life.

In talking about Ann Landers and her twin sister, who also published an advice column called *Dear Abby*, my wife and I imagined a humorous scenario, as follows.

A husband and wife cannot agree on the need for a certain new appliance, so she decides behind his back to write to Ann Landers or her sister, under an assumed name. The letter is chosen for publication, so when it appears in print (with an opinion favoring the wife) she cuts it out and pastes it to the bathroom mirror where her husband will be sure not to miss seeing it. What do you think the outcome will be? How many people, do you suppose, resort to that approach to solve their differences?

Jesus had a similar experience, related in Luke 12, our Scripture selection for today. When someone in the crowd asked him to arbitrate the division of their father's estate, Jesus replied,

"Who made me a judge or divider over you?"

Christ went on to say, as recorded in the *Living Bible*,

"Don't always be wishing for what you don't have."

He then told his disciples the parable about the man who tore down his barns to build bigger ones, the man who died that very night, before he could enjoy any of his bounty. Christ concludes:

"Everyone is a fool who gets rich on earth but not in heaven."

The words ring true today, twenty centuries later.

PRAYER: Give us right values and attitudes toward material things, O Lord, to live as you would have us live. AMEN.

JUNE 23

ON EAGLE'S WINGS

(Scripture to ponder: Isaiah 40:29–31)

When I was a teenager I took a four-week canoe trip in the North Woods of Maine. On that trip we saw all sorts of wild life—beaver, moose, muskrats and many varieties of bird life. It was then that I first appreciated the power of an eagle's wings.

One sunny afternoon we were paddling down a long, calm lake. We could see several large lake trout were up near the surface, feeding and sunning themselves. All of a sudden an osprey—a large fish hawk with a five-foot wingspan—swooped down and grabbed one of the trout. It was a big fish and a heavy load, even though the bird was large. The fish was about two feet long and must have weighed over five pounds, and as it struggled in the claws of the osprey, the bird flapped hard and circled to gain altitude. We watched, fascinated. It circled slowly, gaining about twenty feet with each gyration, until it was about one hundred feet above us.

Suddenly, seemingly out of nowhere, there was an explosion of feathers, as the osprey was struck from above by an eagle. The smaller bird dropped the fish and scurried away. The eagle folded its wings and fell like a rock until it was just alongside of the fish, then reached out with its massive talons and grabbed it. With a few flaps of its huge wings, it headed up and away from the lake. The contrast between the power of the osprey—by no means a small bird—and that of the eagle was dramatic and memorable.

I'm reminded of that incident whenever I encounter today's Scripture passage from the book of Isaiah:

They that wait upon the Lord shall renew their strength; they shall mount up with wings as eagles; they shall run and not be weary; and they shall walk and not faint.

I think of it also when I myself am tired or weary. I praise God that He can indeed renew our strength. In Him is refreshment and rest.

PRAYER: **We bless you, O Lord, that when we are weary we can wait on you, who renews our strength like the eagle. AMEN.**

JUNE 24

ANSWERING JOHN'S QUESTION

(Scripture to ponder: Matthew 11:2–6)

Our Scripture selection from St. Matthew's Gospel records a question sent to Jesus from prison by John the Baptist. John inquires,

"Are you he who is to come, or are we to look for another?"

I often ask myself that when I see such a dramatic difference between the peaceable kingdom that Isaiah foresaw, and the wars, destruction and hatred that dominate our world.

Much of what we see occurring in the world today does indeed resemble the signs of the End Times that Jesus described. If he is coming again, **"surely the second coming is at hand!"** as the poet Yeats wrote. What should we be looking for in his return?

I suspect that one side of our being, in the light of terrorist attacks on our cities, longs for justice, for a rooting out of the awful evil we have seen. Should we be expecting a powerful, mighty leader who will even the score? There's a part of our nature that longs for retribution, for power as manifest by the Jehovah-God of the Old Testament. But is that the right answer?

Christ answers John with a different response from what the Jews expected, and from what we long for, too. The leader Christ described is Isaiah's Suffering Servant. When I meditate on His Suffering and on His Servanthood, when I consider who and what has touched me most deeply in my own life, I realize I have indeed encountered Christ in those who have *suffered* for me and in those who have *served* me. And Christ calls me to do likewise to others for His sake, to further His kingdom.

PRAYER: In a world so full of sin and violence and destruction, help us, Dear Lord, to respond as You would, serving others, even when it means suffering. AMEN

JUNE 25

COMING TO THE LIGHT

(Scripture to ponder: Matthew 10:39)

While I was camping recently, I made use of a small candle lantern. As it sat on the table, a small flame in the darkness of a moonless night, a moth fluttered to it and was consumed. It brought to mind two verses, one from a poem, the other our Scripture selection.

The first was from a poem by the great German poet, Johann Wolfgang von Goethe entitled "Selige Sehnsucht" ("Trance and Transfiguration"). In it he uses the metaphor of the moth and the candle, relating it to human life. Here's how one stanza reads in German:

Und so lang du das nicht hast, Dieses: Stirb und werde! Bist du nur ein truber Gast Auf der dunklen Erde.

Which translates:

And until you have grasped this—'Die and be transformed!' You will be nothing but a sorry guest On the somber earth.

In today's Scripture selection the Lord Jesus says that to find *life*, we must lose our life:

"He who finds his life will lose it, and he who loses his life for my sake will find it."

The transformation that occurs when we give up our lives in love for another is the portal to eternal life. We are drawn to the Light of the world, to the Eternal Christ, as a moth is to a candle, and in dying to ourselves we receive life eternal from the Master.

PRAYER: **We are drawn to You, O Lord, because we perceive you are the only enduring light. Through you we have eternal life. AMEN.**

JUNE 26

WHEN THE SAINTS GO MARCHING IN

(Scripture to ponder: Matthew 11:7–15)

"O Lord, I want to be in that number, when the saints go marching in!"

So go the words of the Negro Spiritual that became a New Orleans jazz hit. Are you among the Saints?

It's often thought that Saints are those who have been canonized by the Roman Catholic Church. But it is clear from New Testament teaching that the saints in the early church were actually the fellow believers like you and me. The saints, according to Paul, were ordinary Christian believers who were trained and equipped in the church to minister to each other and to those outside the church, being taught by the teachers and evangelists, pastors and prophets in the Church. If you have given your life to Christ, accept his teaching and seek to do God's will, you're a Saint!

John the Baptist was a great prophet, and Jesus said of him that among those born of women, no one was greater than John. Yet Christ went on to say that someone who is *least* in the Kingdom of God is greater than John! *[Matthew 11:11]*

We can rejoice that we are indeed Saints!

PRAYER: We are grateful, O Lord, to be a part of Your Kingdom and counted among the Saints. Help us always to do Your will. AMEN

JUNE 27

INSPIRATION

(Scripture to ponder: Genesis 2:7)

I always like an inspiring sermon, don't you? When I think of inspiration, I think of my days as a Boy Scout, when I earned merit badges in First Aid and Life Saving. The method of resuscitation we learned was called the Shafer Prone Pressure Method. The rescuer straddled the body of the victim who was lying face down, head turned to one side. The rescuer pushed on the back ribs in a rhythmical fashion, as he repeated, "**Out goes the bad air, in comes the good! Out goes the bad air, in comes the good**" The method was not very effective.

By the time I got to medical school ten years later, a new method, called mouth-to-mouth breathing, had replaced the old Shafer method. It was much more efficient and effective. It involved "inspiration" in the literal sense of that word, which comes from Latin and means *to blow into*. The victim's lungs were actually inflated with air from the rescuer.

Inspiration! It's the same word the Bible uses when it speaks of how God created mankind. The Spirit of God, which moved across the face of the waters in the creation of the world, is the same Spirit with which God *in-spired* the clay that became man.

And God's Holy Spirit is able to give us Eternal Life, through *inspiration*, as we receive Jesus into our hearts. That's **inspiration** indeed!

PRAYER: **Inspire us with your Spirit, O Lord, that we may be an inspiration to others as we work toward Your Kingdom. AMEN.**

JUNE 28

MUTUAL SELF-REVELATION

(Scripture to ponder: Philippians 2:5–11)

"He's pretty hard to get to know," a friend remarked about a mutual acquaintance. I had to agree, for I too had found the person hard to know.

How *do* we get to know another person? And how do we get to know God? Jesuit scholar William Barry has written, "**Intimacy between two persons develops through mutual self-revelation.**" It is only as we reveal ourselves to others that they can really get to know us. It's our choice.

We can get to know God by reading his Word because God has revealed Himself through the scriptures. Christianity is unique in that our God, the creator of the universe, became incarnate in Jesus and lived among us. He became human and suffered all the natural shocks that flesh is heir to (to use Hamlet's phrase) so we might come to know Him. Our Scripture selection captures the essence of it.

We can let God get to know us by revealing ourselves to Him—through prayer and confession. If you protest that God is omniscient—that is, He is all-knowing—so He knows all about us already, I would respond that knowing God occurs in the context of *a relationship.* And just as a relationship between two people—husband and wife, or mother and child, for example—is based on honesty and openness, so we must truly share from our heart if we are to know God. And He will do the same for us.

PRAYER: Help us honestly share our hearts—our dreams and our hopes, our short-comings and our sins—that we may come to know you as we share ourselves with You. AMEN.

JUNE 29

SPONTANEOUS CHRISTIAN COMBUSTIION

(Scripture to ponder: Isaiah 64:6)

I was painting the edge of some flagstones on our patio. The root of a nearby tree had lifted up part of the flagstone walkway about an inch, and my wife had stumbled over it. After considering several things we could do, we agreed on the simplest and least disruptive solution: paint the edge with luminescent paint so it would stand out and folks would not trip on the edge.

As I read the label on the small jar of paint, I had to chuckle:

"Danger—rags soaked with UGL Nite-Brite luminous paint may spontaneously catch fire if improperly discarded. Immediately after use place rags in a sealed, water-filled container."

As I finished the painting and cleaned up with some old rags, I was reminded of Isaiah's verse (our scripture selection for today):

We have all become unclean and all our righteous deeds are like filthy rags.

I thought also of the words of St. Paul, who asserted we have **all** *sinned and fallen shout of the Glory of God. [Romans 3:23]* All our righteous deeds are like filthy rags.

John the Baptist said that *Christ will baptize with the Holy Spirit and with fire. [Luke 3:16]*

Isn't it amazing that we, who are as filthy rags, can catch fire? When Christ baptizes us with the Holy Spirit, we become aflame with energy to do God's will. We can, as did the early apostles, set the world on fire!

PRAYER: Thank you, Lord, for sending your Son to us. And thank you, Jesus, that you have baptized us with the fire of the Holy Spirit, so we may further your Kingdom. AMEN.

JUNE 30

BEING ALONE

(Scripture to ponder: Luke 6:12)

The wife of the celebrated aviator Charles Lindberg was famous in her own right as author of the best seller *A Gift from the Sea*. As a writer, she knew the value of solitude, yet understood how strange it was to many in our society. Here is Ann Morrow Lindberg on being alone:

If one sets aside time for a business appointment, a trip to the hairdresser, a social engagement, or a shopping expedition, that time is accepted as inviolable. But if one says: I cannot come because that is my hour to be alone, one is considered rude, egotistical or strange. What a commentary on our civilization, when being alone is considered suspect; when one has to apologize for it, make excuses, hide the fact that one practices it—like a secret vice.

Our Lord chose often to be alone, as in our Scripture selection for today. Repeatedly we see in the Gospels, that He went away to a lonely place to pray. It is apparent as one reads in the New Testament that that these times set apart were His times of communion and renewal with God.

I believe that those who choose to give spiritually and emotionally to others must do as the Lord Jesus did, and set aside time to commune with God, times for recharging our spiritual batteries. It's true that we can get energized in church, but it also means times alone.

This came home to me vividly when I was a third year medical student when I first began to work on the wards with patients. I not only was working long hours, but was giving to my patients emotionally and spiritually. I found when I got home at night I had little left over to give to my family and to support my wife. I found I needed to set aside times—despite a busy schedule—to be alone, to recharge my spiritual batteries and receive sustenance from God so I could fully do His will.

PRAYER: **Help us, Dear Lord, to set aside regular times when we can commune with You. Fill us with Your Spirit that we may be empowered to love others and do Your Will.**

JULY 1

NARCISSUS IN MODERN DRESS

(Scriptures to ponder: Romans 12:3; Philippians 2:5–7)

Do you recall the ancient myth of Narcissus? He was a handsome youth who shunned the proffered love of several nymphs. One of them prayed that he might feel just what it was like to love and not be loved in return. Soon afterward Narcissus saw his own reflection in the still, calm, clear waters of a pool. Bullfinch [25] records the scene:

"He stood gazing with admiration at those bright eyes, those locks curled like the locks of Bacchus or Apollo, the rounded cheeks, the ivory neck, the parted lips and the glow of health and exercise over all. He fell in love with himself."

I thought of the myth of Narcissus—from which the psychiatrists have coined the term *Narcissism*, which means being in love with one's self—when our pastor alluded to his days playing college football, contrasting them with the pro-ball games nowadays. He said when he was playing, the coach said, **"When you score a touchdown, just drop the ball and go back to the huddle."**

What a contrast with what we see on television nowadays, the little narcissistic dances in the end zone, with the ball thrown to some adoring fans! In a sense, it's the same contrast we see between the values of the world and those of our savior. The world would have us say, like a two-year old, "Look at me! I'm the greatest!"

But St. Paul, in our Scripture passage from Romans, writes, *"I say to every man among you not to think more highly of himself than he ought to think."* Our model is the Lord Jesus, of whom Paul wrote to the Church at Philippi: *"Though he was God, he emptied himself and took the form of a servant." [Philippians 2:6]* For the follower of Christ, the world's lust for recognition, fame and power is replaced, through the power of the Holy Spirit, by humility and a desire to serve others. For we have Christ's example.

PRAYER: **All around us, O Lord, we see worldly examples of Narcissism, of self-love and exaltation. Help us love you and exalt *YOU*, and love our neighbor, so that we may do you will. AMEN.**

JULY 2

PETER'S ANAMNESTIC RESPONSE

(Scripture to ponder: Luke 5:1–9; John 21:3–7)

As a physician I'm continually impressed with God's marvelous design. For example He made possible our immune system's *anamnestic* response. This refers to the greatly increased production of antibodies that occurs with a second exposure to certain antigens. For example, when you get tetanus shots, the first shot produces a certain low level of antibodies. The second shot, coming after the immune system has been sensitized, produces not a double, not a four-fold increase in antibodies, but a manifold increase, a far greater response than one might otherwise expect.

I like to think Simon Peter experienced that same phenomenon. You recall (as our first selection in Luke relates) that he initially encountered Jesus as a fisherman. Jesus preached from Peter's boat to the crowd on the banks of Lake Gennesaret. Peter knew his business. He'd not caught any fish during the previous night, and I think he was sure there were no fish nearby. But at Jesus' command he lowered his nets—and hauled in a catch so great it began to tear the nets. Peter responded by confessing his own sinfulness, and he followed Jesus. Peter the fisherman became Peter the fisher of men.

Flash forward now to just after the Resurrection as John records it in our selection. Peter decides to go fishing once again. It's an instant replay of the account in Luke. Once again he'd fishes all night without catching anything. *"Cast your net on the right side of the boat,"* a man calls out from the shore. Peter does, and, beholding the huge catch, realizes it is the risen Lord. Peter's *anamnestic* response to this second, personal encounter with Christ energized him to do God's will for life.

PRAYER: **Stimulate us repeatedly, O Lord. Through Your Holy Spirit, give us an anamnestic response, energizing us to do your will. AMEN.**

JULY 3

LIGHTING THE WORLD

(Scripture to ponder: John 3:19)

One time in my surgical practice, I got a subpoena to testify in court on behalf of one of my patients. He was bringing a lawsuit against a local bank. I pulled the chart and as I read, I recalled the case.

He owned his own business, and one Friday night went to deposit the week's proceeds at the night depository of this bank. The area of the building was dark, and as he got out of his truck to make the deposit, he was attacked, robbed and shot. I'd been on emergency call that night and treated him for his wounds.

In the courtroom I was asked to testify about the extent of his injuries. In his suit against the bank, he maintained that the lack of light at the depository made it an unsafe place—and he was right, and he won the suit.

Our Scripture selection for today states:

"And this is the condemnation, that light is come into the world, and men loved darkness rather than light, because their deeds were evil."

[John 3:19]

Many crimes are committed under cover of darkness. But studies have shown the effect of light upon darkness: it dispels evil and crime. Having light in supermarket or hospital parking lots, for example, has reduced the incidence of robberies occurring there.

Jesus said of his followers, *"You are the light of the world."* *[Matthew 5:14]* I believe he was speaking of light in the same way, the way that dispels evil. As his followers, we are to be beacons of light in a dark world.

PRAYER: **Help us, Dear Lord, to bring light into all the dark places of this earth and thus fulfill your will among all people. We pray in Jesus name, AMEN.**

JULY 4

PRIDE GETS IN THE WAY

(Scripture to ponder: 1 Kings 5:1–15)

You've doubtless heard the expression, **"Pride goes before a fall."** It's a paraphrase of one of the Biblical proverbs *[Proverbs 16:18]*. As related in our scripture selection for today, pride almost prevented the healing of Naaman. And in our own lives, pride often gets between us and God, when we think we deserve better out of life.

Naaman was a Captain in the Army of the King of Syria, the commander of his successful troops. The Scripture calls Naaman a mighty man of valor; but it also notes that he was a *leper*, a terrible scourge in those days.

Now Naaman's wife had a maid who had been brought captive out of Israel, a woman who knew of the Prophet Elisha. So because Naaman was valued by the King of Syria, the king wrote to his counterpart, the King of Israel, asking for healing for his soldier-captain. When he arrived in Israel with the letter, Naaman was "referred" to Elisha.

The prophet did not come out to meet Naaman, but simply sent word for him to wash in the Jordan River seven times.

Well, Naaman regarded himself as an important man. In his pride, he was upset: first that Elisha did not personally come out to meet him; and second, that the "prescription" Elisha gave was ridiculously simple. Naaman thought that the rivers of his own country were better than the Jordan, and spurned Elisha's suggestion.

But fortunately, one of his servants was wise and asked Naaman if he wouldn't have performed some great feat if he'd been asked to do so? Naaman understood, swallowed his pride, obeyed Elisha and washed in the Jordan. He was cleansed of his leprosy.

I find I often need to do the same—put aside my own importance and do Christ's bidding, if I am to receive his fullest blessing.

PRAYER: As we hear Your Word and hear Your Call, O Lord, Help us to humbly accept, obey and do Your will. AMEN.

JULY 5

LIFE-SAVING SCRIPTURE

(Scripture to ponder: 2 Tim 3:15)

Nowadays it's not especially common to have to memorize scripture in Sunday School, just as it's unusual for kids in school to have to memorize poetry. But the benefits of both are great.

We Christians believe the Scriptures hold the power of salvation. As St. Paul wrote in his letter to his fellow worker Timothy (our selection for today):

"From a child thou hast known the holy scriptures, which are able to make thee wise unto salvation through faith which is in Christ Jesus."

I have found it so in my own life, and I recently ran across another reason to memorize Bible verses.

The U.S. Department of Defense studied American servicemen who'd became prisoners of war. They found that soldiers who'd memorized Scripture in their youth were able to draw strength from it later during imprisonment when they were denied all reading materials, were being tortured, or were in solitary confinement. Those who had memorized God's Word and could recall it were not only consoled by it; the study showed their rate of survival was greater, and their chances of going crazy under interrogation or brainwashing were less.

That same power of the Word of God has been manifest countless times among Christians who've come under the stress of grief or persecution. Scripture is indeed life-preserving and life saving!

PRAYER: Help us, O Lord to so cherish your word that we not only read it, but we memorize it and hide it in our hearts. AMEN.

JULY 6

ENTHUSIASM!

(Scripture to ponder: Luke 17: 20–21)

I had the pleasure of hearing the St. Olaf College Orchestra recently. I was struck by their poise and musicianship. They performed a selection of symphonic music with a finesse that any major American city would be proud of.

I was especially impressed with one of the percussionists who played both a large bass drum and a gong during the final movement of Respighi's *The Pines of Rome,* which depicts a Roman Legion on the march down the Appian Way. This drummer was bent almost into a crescent as he leaned on the drum, pounding it with one hand, as his other hand swung an arc beneath him to sound the gong. It was a wonder to behold!

If I had to choose a single adjective to best describe the members of the orchestra, it would be *enthusiastic,* in the best sense of that word. For the word comes from the Greek: *en* = within, and *theos* = God. These young people were full of God within!

In today's Scripture passage, Jesus urges his followers not to look here or look there for the kingdom of God. Rather, he asserts: *"The kingdom of God is within you."[Luke 17:21]* Enthusiasm is the outward manifestation of God's Spirit within.

PRAYER: Come into our hearts, Lord Jesus, and impart your enthusiasm to our lives today, that we may do your will. AMEN.

JULY 7

MOBS, CROWDS, APOSTLES, AND DISCIPLES

(Scripture to ponder: Luke 6:12–16)

Have you ever thought about how you might have reacted if you'd been present when Jesus walked the earth? Would you have been drawn to him?

Mobs, crowds, disciples and apostles are all mentioned prominently in the New Testament related to the ministry of our Lord. It was a *mob* that cried for Barabbas to be released and for Jesus to be crucified. Far be it for us to be part of such a mob!

But could we be part of the *crowd*—one of those who came for healing, or to see Christ perform some other impressive miracle—but then melt away at the first sign of difficulty, discomfort or discontent? I'd like to have been more than that.

The *apostles* were chosen by Christ in a particular place, at a particular time, and there were only twelve of them, so we'd not likely have been an *apostle*. But we could have been one of his *disciples*.

And even today, we can become one of his *disciples*.

The word disciple comes from the same root as *discipline* and implies one who follows another at some cost to himself. To be a *disciple* of our Lord means more than simply to follow as one of a crowd or congregation. It means more than to be a listener, part of an audience.

To be a disciple means study, sacrifice and dedication. It means we willfully incorporate into our lives certain Christian *Disciplines*. In a valuable book [20] Emilie Griffin and Richard Foster have described twelve of them: *Meditation, Prayer, Fasting, Study, Simplic-*

ity, Solitude, Submission, Service, Confession, Worship, Guidance and Celebration. Their book is of great help in becoming a *disciple.*

PRAYER: Help us, O Lord, to become your faithful disciples. AMEN.

JULY 8

FEAR THIS!—OR—FEAR NOT!

(Scripture to ponder: Luke 12:4–5)

Have you ever pulled up behind one of those high-slung pickup trucks, the ones with waffle tires, a gun rack in the back window and a bumper sticker proclaiming *"FEAR THIS!"* Whenever I encounter that type of vehicle, I'm reminded of a tragic incident in my surgical career.

For seven years I was director of a large hospital's emergency department in one of our Western states, where that kind of vehicle is common. One afternoon I was on duty when one of them came to a screeching halt outside our doors. A woman jumped out holding in her arms a small child wrapped in a bloody bath towel.

The little girl was just under two. She'd been playing on the drive in front of their garage. Her father, a macho-man type, was inside watching a football game on T.V. when he'd run out of beer. He jumped in his pickup during a commercial to rush to the nearby convenience store to grab another six-pack. He ran right over his own daughter, crushing her head with the truck's huge, waffle-treaded tires. I examined the child, who was beyond saving. It was a horrible, preventable death.

Our scripture passage is one of some 365 in the Bible that speaks of fear—but not in the macho sense of *"Fear this!"* Rather, it's the assurance of the Lord Jesus that, trusting in him, and in God's spirit, we can *"Fear not!"* The world is indeed full of fears, but, thanks be to God, the Lord Jesus Christ has overcome the world *[John 16:33]* and we can be free of fear.

PRAYER: **You have said in your Word, O Lord, that it's not by power, nor by might, but by your Spirit that we are saved. Fill us with Love and Peace. AMEN.**

JULY 9

IDOLS AND BUFFER SOLUTIONS

(Scripture to ponder: Acts 17:22–28)

When I was a medical student I had the chance to visit India, where I lived with five different families on a program called The Experiment in International Living. For three months I was immersed in the Hindu culture. I was impressed with the number of gods and idols that were worshiped in the homes and in the temples.

I read through the New Testament that summer as part of my daily devotions. Not long after reading about St. Paul's experience with idols in Athens recorded in Acts Chapter 17 (our selection for today), I spoke with a Christian missionary and asked him about the many gods and idols in Hinduism. I wondered if they impeded his efforts to introduce Indians to Jesus Christ.

He said the usual response of a Hindu was to put Jesus up on the shelf with all the other idols. Since I had just taken organic chemistry in medical school, I was struck by how much the vast Hindu society resembled what's called in chemistry a *buffer solution*.

(A buffer solution is one that has a great capacity to absorb hydrogen ions. Pouring an acid that ordinarily would be very dangerous—such as concentrated sulfuric acid—into a buffer solution produces a resultant solution that's almost harmless.)

I mentioned that chemical phenomenon to the missionary and he said, yes, that was indeed true: the cutting edge of the Gospel was often blunted by the vast buffering effect of Hindu society with its vast pantheon of gods.

When I got back to the United States, I reflected that it's also true here too: we often allow a collection of little gods and idols in our society—money, success, possessions—to dilute the Gospel, negating its transforming effect on our lives.

PRAYER: We worship you, dear Lord, as the one and only true God, and we praise you Holy Name. Remove from our lives all of the other little gods we tend to worship, that we may worship You alone. AMEN.

JULY 10

CUTTING STEPS

(Scripture to ponder: Hebrews 12:1–2)

When I was younger I did a lot of mountaineering. When climbing a snow-covered peak, particularly after a storm, the leader had the hardest job and took the greatest risk. He was out in front, first on the rope, cutting steps. In fresh snow you could often kick steps, but on glaciated peaks setting the route and leading the way often meant cutting steps on a steep, icy slope with an ice axe, a difficult and exhausting job. It was always easier to be second or third on the rope than to be first.

In the Christian life, our Lord and Savior Jesus Christ is always first on the rope, the one who goes before us, who does the hard work of cutting the steps for us. He has done the difficult work, and we walk in His footsteps.

Today's selection from the Book of Hebrews puts it aptly:

"Let us look to Jesus, the pioneer and perfecter of our faith."

How we rejoice that he's gone ahead of us! He's cut the steps and has shows us the way. Through Him we have more than an example; we have salvation and eternal life. As St. Peter proclaimed in his defense to the authorities, after being arrested for healing the lame man at the gate of the temple,

"There is salvation in no one else! Under all heaven there is no other name for men to call upon to save them."

[Acts 4:12 TLB]

PRAYER: We praise you Lord and thank you that you have shown us the way of salvation. Let us always follow in your footsteps. AMEN.

JULY 11

INSIDE THE GEODE

(Scripture to ponder: 1 Samuel 16:6–13)

We were father and son, together at the special science camp in the high plateau of Central Oregon. I was the camp doctor for a week, enjoying a relaxed schedule that allowed me to spend more time than usual with my ten-year-old son. My son was handicapped from a car accident, so we couldn't enjoy the usual outdoor activities of the camp such as hiking or digging for fossils. But this camp had a splendid set of machines for cutting and polishing rocks, and we had fun working with some of the things that others had found.

In a heap in the corner of a shed was a pile of snowball-sized rocks that were dug from a hillside near the camp. "Those are geodes," the camp director told us, and he showed us how to mount one of them on a special apparatus to cut it in half with a diamond saw.

The rock we selected to bisect was rough and gray, not especially remarkable. In fact, it looked like a snowball packed out of mud. But what a treasure awaited us on the inside! The central cavity was studded with bright purple and blue crystals and looked like a fairyland cavern!

I was reminded of the Bible verse for today which describes the selection of David. It asserts that man looks on the outward appearance, but God looks on the heart. It seems to me that people are often a lot like geodes. If we just take time to chat and get to know a stranger, we find a treasure beneath a rough exterior. Praise God!

PRAYER: As we encounter others, Dear Lord, help us perceive the inner beauty that exists beneath the surface. In Jesus' name we pray. AMEN.

JULY 12

FORGIVENESS

(Scriptures to ponder: Isaiah 1:18; Ephesians 4:32)

Our first Scripture selection for today tells of God's forgiveness: Though our sins be as scarlet, they will be forgiven and will be as white as snow.

Our pastor told an interesting personal story about forgiveness. When she and her husband had a son about to go to college, they took out a loan to pay for the tuition. It happened that in their son's final year at the school, his father died. After graduation, she made inquiry about paying off the loan. When she got no reply to her letter of inquiry, she called the school and asked about information to pay off the loan. She was told that there was no loan to pay off. On further inquiry, she found the loan had been forgiven.

It was a policy of the school to forgive student loans if the father of the student died. She was surprised and pleased. Our pastor said it was quite a lesson in forgiveness for her.

When we give our lives to God, asking forgiveness for our sins, He readily forgives us. And as the apostle Paul affirms in our second Scripture selection, so ought we to forgive one another, for we have been forgiven by God. Jesus was quite specific on this point, not only dealing with it in the parable of the unforgiving servant *[Matthew 18:23–35]*, but he also incorporated it into the Lord's Prayer:

"For if you forgive men their trespasses, your heavenly Father will also forgive you; but if you do not forgive men their trespasses, neither will your Father forgive your trespasses.

[Matthew 6:14–15]

PRAYER: As You have forgiven us our many debts, so help us to forgive others. We pray in Jesus' name. AMEN.

JULY 13

SILENCE—OR STATIC?

(Scripture to ponder: Psalm 46:10)

If you ever get your hearing checked, you may experience a testing method called "masking." In this test, the audiologist has you wear a special headset. Through one ear you will be asked to listen to a series of pure musical tones, while in the other ear you will be listening to a static, background noise which is confusing and can mask the notes to be heard in the other ear.

People who have trouble hearing during testing with masking are often those who have difficulty at a noisy reception, or in a restaurant where there is constant background noise.

In a similar manner, when our lives have too much background noise, we can have difficulty hearing God. The contemporary Christian author Paul Wilkes has written about this phenomenon:

It is true that God seems closest to us when we are silent.

It is not so much that God is speaking more clearly; it is rather that, having turned off the static of our lives, we are just listening better.[26]

There is definite value in silence, in being still, to allow us to hear God's voice. In our Scripture selection for today we are urged to *"Be still and know that I am God."* It is in quietness and in confidence that we most often come to the knowledge of the Lord.

PRAYER: Help us set aside time each day, O Lord, when we can be still, tuning out the static that so often masks your voice. Help us listen when you speak to us. AMEN.

JULY 14

THROUGH GATES OF SPLENDOR

(Scripture to ponder: Mark 16:15)

Today's scripture has been called "The Great Commission." It occurs at the end of Mark's Gospel, after Jesus' resurrection, just before he ascended into heaven. It is among his last words to his disciples:

"Go into all the world and preach the gospel to every living creature."

Jim Elliot was a young man from Portland, OR, who took those words seriously. The part of the world where he and four other missionaries chose to go was the jungle of South America. They reached out to a tribe called the Aucas, who lived in a remote, forested region of Ecuador, in an area accessible only by river or floatplane. Previous responses of these tribesmen to outsiders had been to attack. They had never heard the Gospel, had never experienced the love of Jesus.

Perhaps you know the outcome. The missionaries were not well received. When the anxious wives of the five men got back no radio report, a second plane was sent out. On a sandbar in the river lay the bodies of the five, pierced with spears. Some folks called Jim Elliot a fool for venturing into such a remote and dangerous situation.

But in the mysterious ways the Lord works, triumph came out of tragedy. Elisabeth Eliot's account of the martyrdom of her husband, in a book entitled *Through Gates of Splendor,* has been the inspiration to hundreds of thousands of people.[27]

Jim Elliot had grown up in a small Plymouth Brethren assembly. On a college term paper, he made this statement:

"He is no fool who gives up what he cannot keep to gain what he cannot lose." [28]

Well did he personify Christ's injunction to go into the world and preach the Gospel. He also personified another of Christ's teachings also found in Mark's Gospel

"For whoever would save his life will lose it; and whoever loses his life for my sake and the Gospel's will save it."

[Mark 8:35]

PRAYER: You have promised abundant life and Life Eternal to those who follow you, O Lord. Help us through Your Spirit to give up that which we cannot keep, to gain what we can never lose. Help us do Your will, to follow You through gates of splendor. AMEN.

JULY 15

DEALING WITH EVIL

(Scripture to ponder: Romans 12:21)

Mankind has always struggled with evil. In 1954 British author William Golding wrote a novel entitled *Lord of the Flies* about a group of English schoolboys stranded on a Pacific island during a global atomic war. It relates their descent from average adolescents to teenagers controlled by their dark side who cease to care for one another and become cruel and malicious.

The book is both scary and symbolic, a chronicle of the struggle between good and evil written by a man who had witnessed first hand the ravages of the spirit as a naval officer in World War Two. Of that war, Golding writes:

"Anyone who moved through those years without understanding that man produces evil as a bee produces honey must have been blind or wrong in the head." [29]

In this life, all of us are constantly faced with choices between good and evil. As a friend of mine once put it, "Good and evil have been dating for a very long time." For the struggle, so evident today in the world around us—and as Golding also witnessed in the Second World War—is also being carried out within each us.

I like to think of it this way. We humans have a body and a mind, and over them, a spirit that acts as a judge and mediator between them. Although it's designed to function in harmony, it's a sort of democracy, and the body and mind can team up against the spirit and overrule it, so we can succumb to urges from within and without. If unchecked, if uncontrolled by the spirit, the body and mind of man are capable of great evil.

But if we align our spirit with God's Holy Spirit and let it rule our mind and our body, we begin to live as we were created to live. Controlled by His Spirit we reach out in love to others, becoming people who build up, not destroy, workers for good in this world, against evil and darkness, to further God's kingdom.

In our Scripture selection for today, St. Paul urges us to overcome evil with good:

"Do not be overcome by evil, but overcome evil with good."

PRAYER: **As we pray in the prayer you taught us, O Lord, Deliver us from evil. Make us instruments of your peace, that we may overcome evil with good. AMEN.**

JULY 16

THE ARTESIAN WELL OF THE SPIRIT

(Scriptures to ponder: John 4:14; John 7:38–39)

I suspect that most of us nowadays get our household water from a municipal water supply and not from a well. In many rural areas, however, wells are still drilled. Such wells are usually of one or two types. Most commonly, a well is drilled into the water table, the porous underground layer into which rainwater seeps and from which it is pumped out into a storage tank.

A second, more rare type of well is called an Artesian well, named after the area in France where its principle was first discovered. In that type of well, the water beneath the surface is under pressure, so when the drillers hit water, it gushes up and flows freely without need for a pump.

I think it was the Artesian type of well that Jesus spoke of in our scriptures for today. In his encounter with the Samaritan woman at Jacob's well, (our first selection), he tells her:

"Whoever drinks of this water [that is, the water she was drawing from Jacob's well] *will become thirsty again. But whoever drinks of the water that I will give him will never thirst again. For my gift will become a spring in the man himself, welling up to Eternal Life."*

[John 4:14]

This is a puzzling statement, but it's clarified a few chapters later in John's Gospel, in our second selection (here in J.B. Phillips translation), when Christ elaborates further, by saying:

"The man who believes in me, as the scriptures said, will have rivers of living water flowing from his inmost heart. (Here he was speaking about the Spirit which those who believe in him would receive.)"

Christ's disciples received the Holy Spirit at Pentecost. We too can receive it, if we but ask. It's the ultimate thirst quencher, the source of life and power for the Christian Church and for our life in Christ.

PRAYER: We do pray, O Lord, that you give us the living water that only you can give, your Holy Spirit, to empower us to do your will and work for the Kingdom to come. We pray in Jesus' name. AMEN.

JULY 17

HAVING A MIND

(Scripture to ponder: Romans 12:2)

When I was in residency training to become a surgeon, I had to decide if I wanted to sub-specialize. Heart surgery interested me a lot—my father was a cardiologist so I knew the field well—and I wrestled with a decision about going for special training as a cardiac surgeon. I was challenged and fascinated by congenital heart disease and its surgical repair, and I enjoyed the technical aspects of valve-replacement surgery.

At our university program the Chief of Cardiac Surgery was a superb clinician and a masterful technician. He was one of the pioneers of heart surgery. He wanted me to take further training in his program. But over the first two years in my general surgical residency, I made an observation: most of the men who trained under him adopted his values. He was quite worldly and dapper. He wore tailor-made clothes, Italian shoes and drove a Ferrari.

It was not my style, yet I saw those who worked under him gradually and subtly came to take on his mind-set. Whatever they were before they entered the training program, they seemed to get transformed over the two years they spent with him. They began to wear expensive suits and drive fancy cars. It was as though they got transformed.

I was reminded of St. Paul's counsel in today's Scripture selection:

"Do not be conformed to tis world but be transformed by the renewal of your mind, that you may prove what is the will of God, what is good and acceptable and perfect."

I don't know if I would have turned out the same way, but I decided to remain a general surgeon, and I've never regretted it.

PRAYER: As we make decisions about our lives, Dear Lord, may we be always guided by Your Spirit. AMEN.

JULY 18

GET A LIFE !

(Scripture to ponder: Luke 12:16–21)

You've doubtless heard the expression, "**Get a Life!**" I find most often it means "Do something meaningful!" or "Get serious!"

Jesus said, *"Many are called but few are chosen."* [Matthew 22:14] As I look about our society I see many folks who are making a living but few who are making a life. Dr.

Peter Gomes, Professor of Christian Morals at Harvard and a Baptist Minister at the Memorial Church at that University has remarked:

> "The object of an education is to make a life and not a living. What troubles me more and more about great research universities is that we are far more interested in teaching how to make a living." [30]

It's not hard to make a living, that is, to take a job to make money to live off of. Unfortunately, we in America often wish to live in great affluence, and to do so requires husband and wife, father and mother to work to make an income to support our chosen life style.

Making a life, though, is different from making money.

I believe much of the dishonesty and corruption of our society—witness Enron and other corporate deceptions—is directly due to the desire for money and for things. But life, (as Jesus asserts in the parable that forms our Scripture selection for today) does not consist in the abundance of our possessions, in our houses or our SUVs. Its richness is in relationships, especially in knowing God and seeking to do His will, and through relationships with our fellows. The key to making a life, and to Eternal Life, is to *love God and love our neighbor.* It's why Jesus called those the two great commandments.

PRAYER: We get so caught up with *things,* with our *possessions,* that we leave you and others out. Help us, O Lord, to first love you and love our neighbor, and thereby find your abundant life. AMEN.

JULY 19

THE CUT-FLOWER CIVILIZATION

(Scripture to ponder: Matthew 4:1–11)

The Quaker Philosopher, Elton Trueblood, has called ours the "cut-flower civilization." He goes on to say, "Beautiful as cut flowers may be, and much as we may use our ingenuity to keep them looking fresh for a while, they will eventually die, and they die because they are severed from their sustaining roots."

We hear much nowadays about *roots*, about efforts to determine our genealogy, to know who our forebears are.

For Christians, our roots are firmly planted in the rich soil of the Christian past, of the innumerable saints who have transmitted the faith down the generations from Christ Himself. We are sustained by the nourishment of God's word, believing, as the scripture says in our selection for today, that *we do not live by bread alone, but by every word that comes from God.* In the midst of a cut-flower civilization, we can stand tall and firm and strong, because our taproots are deep in the soil of Faith.

Such sustenance comes from reading the Bible and from studying the lives and writings of the saints and martyrs of the church, both Catholic and Protestant, whose lives have so enriched the soil in which we have been planted.

PRAYER: Nourish us, Lord, from your word and from the lives and teachings of those who have faithfully followed you throughout the generations. AMEN.

JULY 20

SIR, WE WOULD SEE JESUS

(Scripture to ponder: John 12:20–26)

When I was a medical student in Rochester, NY, I sang in the choir at Central Presbyterian Church. In that sanctuary the choir sat in the front of the church behind the pulpit. Our seats were in tiers, from which we could look out on the assembled congregation. We saw the preacher's back when he was in the pulpit.

On the back of the pulpit—where we (and the pastors) could see it, but the congregation couldn't—were carved the words spoken by the two Greeks who came to the apostle Philip (included in our Scripture for today):

"Sir, we would see Jesus."

As our Scripture selection for today relates, the apostles Philip and Andrew went and told Jesus.

I believe that just as the two apostles in this account brought the two Greeks to Jesus, it's we Christians who are to bring others to Jesus today. How do we do that?

I think Jesus gives us a clue in the parable of the last Judgment as told near the end of Matthew's Gospel *[Matthew 25: 31–46]*.

Christ said,

"If you do it unto the least of these my brethren, you do it unto me,"

He referred to the actions of those who feed the hungry, visit the sick and those in prison.

He calls us to do likewise for him today.

PRAYER: **Dear Lord, help us to show you to others, by our lives and with our lips. In Jesus' name we pray, AMEN.**

JULY 21

RESPONDING TO GOD'S CALL

(Scripture to ponder: Jeremiah 1:4–8; John 14:26)

Ex-President Jimmy Carter in his book, *Sources of Strength*, tells a story that he says his Daddy used to tell his Sunday School students. It's about a boy who worked from dawn to dusk on the family farm. He got it into his head that he was destined to receive a call from God. Sure enough, one morning as he worked the fields, he looked up and saw the clouds in the sky forming the letters "G O P."

"That's my call from God!" he said. "It's telling me that I need to **Go Out & Preach.**" So he left the farm and began to preach, but no one wanted to listen to his sermons. He was just no good at it. Only then did he come to figure out what the message in the clouds had really meant: GO ON PLOWING.

It's not always easy to discern God's call in our lives. But based on Scripture, such as today's text from Jeremiah, I believe we can conclude some things about a divine call. Many who were called by God faced doubts, people like Jeremiah or Moses or Mary, the Mother of Jesus. But if God calls us into His service, He will provide the strength and the means to meet it. He will not call us to impossible tasks.

Perhaps the best way we have to check on a Call from God is the reaffirmation that comes through prayer and through the Holy Spirit. In his last discourse with his disciples, Jesus tells us God will send the Spirit, the Counselor, in his name, and the Spirit will teach us all things, and remind us of Christ's teachings. God's Holy Spirit will confirm our call.

The Key—and one lesson of Jimmy Carter's story—is that God most often uses us right where we are, with our present skills and talents. We need but be willing to serve Him.

PRAYER: **We love You, Lord, and seek to respond to Your Call and do Your will, right where we are, right now. Strengthen us to respond. AMEN.**

JULY 22

TO DESTROY OR TO FULFILL?

(Scripture to ponder: Matthew 5:21–30)

The Christian Faith has strong roots in Judaism. To me, that leaves no room for anti-Semitism. Jesus said he came not to destroy but to fulfill the Law of Moses. St. Augustine made the comment concerning the Old and New Testaments that

"What is concealed in the Old is revealed in the New."

Jesus accepted the Law and the Prophets but was not bound by them. Many of his teachings can be found in the Old Testament, but often He goes beyond the letter of the law to the spirit that lies beneath. For example, the sixth commandment says "Thou shalt not murder," but Christ goes beyond the law, asserting that we must curb our anger, which leads to murder. Likewise, going beyond commandment seven, if we would not look lustfully, we would not commit adultery. Christ does not destroy the law; rather in going beyond the law; he fulfills it.

As I write this, the headlines of the paper blare out the news of another suicide explosion in Israel that killed 19 people in a restaurant. I am sure there will be a retributive strike against someone within a day or two.

What do you suppose would happen among Jews and Arabs in the Middle East, if the attitude of *"an eye for an eye" [Deuteronomy 19:21]* was replaced with *"You shall love your neighbor as yourself?" [Matthew 19:19]* What if the old retributive law of vengeance was replaced by love? Then we would indeed get a glimpse of the Kingdom to come.

PRAYER: Help us live our lives by the fulfilled Law of Love, as You've have taught us through Your Son, Jesus Christ. AMEN.

JULY 23

THE MARVELS OF MYSTERY

(Scripture to ponder: 1 Corinthians 15:51–57)

A Princeton Seminary theologian has written about mysteries:

"We do not solve mysteries; we enter into them. The deeper we enter into them, the more illumination we get. Still greater depths are revealed to us the further we go."

"Behold I tell you a mystery," wrote St. Paul about the resurrection in his Letter to the Corinthians in today's Scripture selection. Nowadays our scientific approach to the unknown treats such matters as problems to be solved, not as mysteries. But the great imponderables such as life and death, good and evil are perhaps best treated as mysteries.

Consider of how great mystery writers such as Agatha Christie and A. Conan Coyle approach mystery. Their detectives are reflective, patient, and imaginative, individuals like Hercule Poirot or Sherlock Holmes. The resist solutions that are easy and obvious. They *enter into* and so ultimately solve their mysteries.

In life—and faith—easy answers aren't always the right answers.

So must we, through belief, *enter into* the great mysteries of the Christian Life: that God became incarnate, that there was indeed a virgin birth, and that through Christ's resurrection we ourselves may obtain Eternal Life. Such mysteries must be *entered into,* must be experienced, to begin to understand them. We enter through commitment and faith.

PRAYER: **Grant us faith to enter into the great mysteries of the Christian Life, so we may partake of Christ's Resurrection. AMEN.**

JULY 24

POPPING THE BUBBLES OF PRIDE

(Scripture to ponder: Luke 14:7–11)

Peter Gomes, the Minister of the Memorial Church at Harvard University, in his book entitled *The Good Book,* tells an amusing story. He happened to be in the office one Saturday when the phone rang. He picked up the phone. It was someone inquiring who would be preaching the next day. Gomes was slated to preach, so without identifying himself, he said warmly,

"The preacher is the minister of the Memorial Church and Plummer Professor of Christian Morals."

The caller paused, then asked, **"Is that that short, fat, little black man?"**
With some annoyance, Gomes says, he replied, **"Yes,"** and slammed down the phone.
In the book, Gomes goes on to say the caller had in reality given a true description of him. He was insulted because the description popped the bubble of his pride, pointing out the difference between how Gomes saw himself and how others viewed him.
It may be natural for us to want to be seen in the best light possible. But it's not what the Scripture teaches. In our selection for today, Christ said those who want to be first will be last. He gave the example of someone attending a wedding feast who comes in

and sits down at the head table, only to be moved to the back of the hall to make room for a more honored guest.

Instead, Jesus says we should take a more humble seat. Then we may be honored by the host, who will welcome us and move us to the head table.

PRAYER: We want so much to be special, to be respected, Dear Lord. Help us know our worth comes because we are Your children. Help us do Your will and show us Your way. AMEN.

JULY 25

THE TWO GOLDEN RULES

(Scripture to ponder: Matthew 7:11; Philippians 2:4)

Most of us are familiar with the Golden Rule: *"Do unto others as you would have them do unto you."* That's the Golden Rule of Christ as recorded in our selection from Matthew's Gospel.

Many people are unaware, however, of another version of the Golden Rule, as set forth by Confucius, which is, "Do not do unto others as you would not have them do unto you." It resembles the Golden Rule of Christ, but there's an important difference: the Golden Rule of Confucius is *negative*, whereas Christ's is *positive*.

I recall more than once getting into discussions in college bull sessions when friends would argue that the "do-goodism" of Christians was meddlesome. They resented folks poking into other people's business. It's "risky business," messing around with other people's lives, they maintained. I saw their point, but remained unconvinced. For in a sense, the Christian life *is* risky business. Reaching out to someone in live often means taking a risk.

St. Paul echoed Christ's words when he wrote the following counsel to the Church at Philippi (it's our second selection):

"Let each of you look not to your own interests, but to the interests of others."

A key distinguishing attribute of Christians ought to be their concern for others' needs.

In the parable of the Good Samaritan *[Luke 10:30–37],* it's obvious that the priest and the Levite were looking to their own interests, when each passed by on the other side of the road when they saw the man who'd been beaten and robbed. Perhaps they even justified their actions by suspecting the thief might be hiding, waiting for someone to stop so that he could rob that person, too. The Samaritan, in stopping to care for the man, was being meddlesome. But he was following Christ's Golden Rule, doing God's will. By doing so, he was taking a risk, the risk of Love.

PRAYER: Help us to actively love others, O Lord, as you have loved us. In Jesus Name we pray. AMEN.

JULY 26

GOD REACHING OUT TO US

(Scriptures to ponder: Psalm 51; Isaiah 57:15)

As Christians, we know and believe that God reached out to us in the Incarnation, when the Word became flesh and dwelt among us as His son Jesus Christ.

But in addition to that historic event, God reaches out to us today as we reach out to Him. Countless Christians—through the ages and today as well—have attested to God's working in their lives. The scripture tells the conditions under which God will act:

"A humble and a contrite heart Thou wilt not despise."

[Ps. 51:17]

"The Lord lifts up those who are bowed down."

[Ps. 146:8]

"I dwell in the high and holy place, and also with him who is of a contrite and humble spirit."

[Isaiah 57:15]

In this life we are always dependent on God, but usually we don't realize or recognize it. Rather, in our sinfulness, it's only when we feel helpless, at the end of our rope, that we turn to God. We cry out to God in our anguish, and He rescues us. As Scripture asserts, God acts to save the weak and the vulnerable and the humble who call upon Him in truth.

So if we live our life in utter dependence upon Him, in humility and vulnerability, we'll continually see God act in our lives. In that way we will live the life that Jesus lived, serving him in our lives, experiencing His power.

PRAYER: **Hear our prayer, O Lord, when we cry out to you. Keep us always humble and vulnerable, that we may realize our dependence upon you in all things and know Your Power in our lives. AMEN.**

JULY 27

REALLY HUMAN

(Scripture to ponder: John 1:14)

When I served in the Indian Health Service I knew a hard-driving physician who had high expectations of his staff. He served in a busy clinic. One winter during flu season when his partner was out of town at a medical meeting, this doctor himself got the flu. It was a hectic time, with about fifty patients needing care in the office that day. He was the only doctor.

He made it through the morning, but at noon was exhausted. He told his nurse that he had to lie down for a while if he was going to make it through the afternoon. During lunch he slept for an hour on the X-Ray table in the back of the office.

A few weeks later the staff of the clinic had a retreat. During an animated discussion, it came out that this episode showed a whole different side of that doctor to the nurses and clerks. One of the nurses remarked to the doctor, **"That was the first time that we realized you were *really human*, and it made it a lot easier to relate to you after that."**

You've probably guessed: I was that doctor.

In our Scripture selection St. John writes concerning God:

"The Word became flesh and dwelt among us."

God became *really human* when He came to us in human form as Jesus. Throughout the long history of Israel, God revealed Himself in His power, in His creation, and as He spoke through the prophets. But God perceived that in order for us to know Him—to *really know* Him and relate to him—He must become incarnate in a man. So He became flesh and lived with us, a suffering servant who died for our sins. The scripture says he was tempted in every way as we are, yet did not sin.

The German language has two verbs for to *know: wissen* and *kennen. Wissen* means to know a fact, to know about something, whereas *kennen* means to be familiar with, to know intimately. It's a distinction we usually don't make in English, but it's a useful one here. For in the Incarnation, we are able to know—kennen—God, to get to know him intimately, through Jesus.

Through Jesus—God as *really human*—we can know God as Father and Friend.

PRAYER: Thank you, dear Lord, for revealing Yourself to us as really human, so we can relate to You through your son Jesus Christ. AMEN.

JULY 28

KNOWN BY COMPUTER—OR BY GOD?

(Scripture to ponder: Psalm 139:1–12)

It seems like every few years we read in the newspapers about another scandal related to cheating in college. I recall it has happened at two of our great military schools, Annapolis and West Point. It's happened at other institutions as well. The most recent variation on the cheating theme is plagiarism by students writing their theses.

A solution proposed by one faculty member was to cross-index all the source materials for his course, putting them on the Internet, so any student's work could be quickly compared by computer against these source materials, to detect patterns of plagiarism.

Computers can indeed keep track of huge volumes of data, and are often used to check up on us, to establish credit ratings, for example.

Our scripture passage today tells of the knowledge God has of us—far greater than any computer program to detect plagiarism or check our credit rating. God knows not just what we do—how we act—but even knows our motivation and our desires.

I don't believe God wants to pounce on us when we step out of line. But He does want us to be honest, to admit our sins, and to allow Him to lead us in paths of righteousness. This He will do, and has done, for those who truly seek to do His will.

PRAYER: **You indeed know us and seek us, Lord. We love You and confess our sinfulness. Empower us through your Spirit to do Your will. AMEN.**

JULY 29

MARTHA'S CONFESSION

(Scripture to ponder: John 11:1–47)

In the New Testament there are two great confessions of Christ as Lord. One might be called public, the other private. The public one was made by the Apostle Simon, after Christ asked his disciples who they thought he was. His response *[Matthew 16:16]* was the exclamation,

"Thou art the Christ, the Son of the living God!"

It moved Christ to give Simon a new name, Peter, petros, the Greek word for rock, for his confession was the rock on which the Christian Church would be built.

Martha's confession was private, taking place in a solitary encounter between her and Jesus, when she went out to meet him after the death of her brother Lazarus. Recall that Martha was one of two sisters of Lazarus, the busy one, more prone to do the cooking and serving than was her sister Mary, who chose to sit at Jesus' feet and listen to him teach.

Yet it was Martha who made the confession of belief to Jesus. He asked if she believed he was the resurrection and the life. She said *[John 11:27]*,

"Yes, Lord; I believe that you are the Christ, the Son of God."

What was the result of her confession? It did not produce the same response from Christ as Peter's had. Rather, It led to a miraculous demonstration of Jesus' power, to the raising of Lazarus from the dead.

Many times in Christ's ministry, when Christ encountered persons of great faith— such as Jairus, whose daughter was ill *[Luke 8:41]* or the men who took apart the roof to lower their friend to Jesus for healing *[Mark 2:3]*—such miracles occurred.

PRAYER: **Dear Lord, we confess, as Peter and Martha did, that you are the Christ, the Savior of mankind. We pray for healing of our wounded world, through your miraculous power. AMEN.**

JULY 30

CUTTING OFF A BRANCH

(Scripture to ponder: John 15:4–6)

I recently returned from the Big Island of Hawaii where I saw much beautiful tropical vegetation. In the warmth and humidity of the lush rain forest, almost anything can grow, and gardeners there often start new plants by cutting off a branch and sticking it in the ground, where it takes root and grows.

The ability to grow and to flourish like a Hawaiian branch reminds me of folks who say they can be Christians without being part of a Church. I don't believe it's possible, for the soil and the environment of society do not promote Christian growth.

Indeed, Christ Himself in teaching his disciples uses the analogy of the vine and its branches (our Scripture selection for today). He said,

"The branch cannot bear fruit in itself, except as it abides in the vine . . . If one abide not in me he is cast forth as a branch and withers."

But if the branch remains attached to the vine it can bear much fruit.

We cannot, as Christians, be cut off from Christ or the Church and expect to grow and mature. We must remain connected to the source of nourishment and life—Jesus Christ—if we are to experience the power and productivity of the Christian Life.

PRAYER: Dear Lord, Keep us firmly bound to you and to your church that we may bear much fruit for your kingdom. Keep us in touch with your word and with fellow Christians that we may grow and mature and be fruitful. AMEN.

JULY 31

FEET THAT SLIP

(Scripture to ponder: Psalm 17:5)

The first ascent of the Matterhorn in Switzerland, which should have been a triumph, became a tragedy because one man's feet slipped.

For years the Matterhorn, a rugged promontory that tends to attract foul weather, remained unclimbed while other Swiss peaks, many of higher elevation, were conquered. Edward Whymper, a young English artist who sketched and climbed many Alpine peaks, had made six previous attempts to scale the Matterhorn before he finally succeeded in 1865.

At the time of that climb, Whymper was aware that an Italian group was also about to attempt the peak. In order to get the guides he needed, and to beat the Italians to the top, Whymper joined forces with another English party, one that included a younger and far more inexperienced climber named Charles Hadlow.

As is often the case, going up was less risky than coming down. On the ascent Hadlow needed some help, but on the descent he needed much more. He was unsure, and at one point required the Swiss guide to help place his feet. Just after the guide set aside his ice axe to do so, Hadlow slipped, crashing into the guide and initiating a fall that pulled two more in the party off the face of the mountain. As the four climbers tumbled backward, the rope between them and Whymper's party became taut and then broke. The lower four fell several thousand feet to the glacier below. Of the seven climbers who first conquered the Matterhorn, only Whymper and two others returned alive.

What's the relevance to today's scripture? The Psalmist says, *"My steps have held fast to thy paths, my feet have not slipped."* God's word guides and protects us so we do not slip.

PRAYER: **Lead us in your paths, O Lord, and keep us from slipping in this mortal life, which can be more perilous than any Alpine climb. Keep us in you love and help us always to do your will. AMEN.**

AUGUST 1

IMITATING CHRIST

(Scripture to ponder: Ephesians 5:1)

One of the most famous of all devotional Christian books was written by an XV century Augustinian monk who was born in Germany but spent his adult life in a convent in the Netherlands. The little volume by Thomas á Kempis, entitled *The Imitation of Christ,* has influenced countless Christians through the ensuing centuries.

"Imitation" nowadays has overtones of deception or pantomime. But the word as used by Kempis and as used in scripture is much more related to what we would call *role modeling.* Some sociologists and historians have attributed many of our current problems to a lack of good role models for our youth, and the influence of the media has certainly glorified some strange characters, it is true. In our formative years, we humans tend to imitate the behavior we see.

For Christians the role model was and remains God incarnate, Jesus Christ. In his letter to the church at Ephesus, St Paul writes in our selection for today,

"Therefore be imitators of God as beloved children imitate their father."

We who are parents have all seen that pattern of learning and of growth occur with our children. It is fundamental to human behavior, one of the main ways we all learn and grow. It's a method of learning not confined to children. We adults, too, can learn by imitation, as we study and model the life of our Lord.

PRAYER: Dear Lord, help us set aside time each day to study Your Word to learn about Your son Jesus, that we may imitate Him in our lives and grow into His likeness. AMEN.

AUGUST 2

THE WISDOM OF THE BODY

(Scripture to ponder: 12 Corinthians 12:14–26)

Recently I flew from Philadelphia to Phoenix in August. The high temperature on the day I left Philadelphia turned out to be lower than the low temperature in Phoenix on the day I arrived. The temperature was fifty-six the morning I left and one hundred and six the afternoon I arrived. The difference between the low in Philadelphia and the high in Phoenix was fifty degrees!

In spite of those environmental temperature changes, my body temperature stayed quite constant at about ninety-seven degrees. It did not vary more than one degree, in spite of the fact that the temperature around me changed by fifty degrees.

The process by which the body maintains its constant temperature is called *homeostasis*. It was so named by a prominent physiologist, Dr. Walter Cannon, who wrote a book called *The Wisdom of the Body*. In it he described many marvelous ways that our bodies regulate themselves to maintain their internal constancy.

As another example, you can rapidly drink several glasses of water, yet your blood does not become diluted. Or you could drink nothing for a day and although you'd get thirsty, your blood's concentration would remain the same. The wisdom of the body is an example of God's marvelous design. In today's Scripture selection, St. Paul describes how the various parts of the body work together harmoniously, and gives that as an example of how the members of the Body of Christ—the Church—ought also to work together.

PRAYER: We praise you, Lord, for the wonderful wisdom of our bodies. Help us always to work harmoniously together to accomplish Your will. AMEN.

AUGUST 3

SETTING PRIORITIES

(Scripture to ponder: John 10:10)

I once watched a telecast of a news conference in which Mayor Rudy Guliani of New York City bowed out of an upcoming Senate race with former First Lady Hillary Clinton. He had recently been diagnosed with prostate cancer, and in connection with pondering the treatment choices, Guliani said he'd reestablished his priorities. He indicated that it wasn't a bad thing. In fact he'd gained a new perspective in his life: politics was no longer as important as it had been, now that he faced his own mortality.

Once when he was asked why he went to spend time alone at Walden Pond, Henry David Thoreau replied that he **"did not want to come to the end of his life and find that he had not lived."** Mayor Guliani, when faced with a serious illness, also realized he did not want to come to the end of *his* life and find he'd missed out on what was really important: family and relationships were more important than politics.

As a surgeon who's cared for many patients with serious illness, I can testify how often this situation gets repeated: when there is limited time left, they rearrange their priorities. Sometimes, though it is too late.

What *is* important in life? When all's said and done, what really *is* important?

In our Scripture selection, Jesus said, *"I am come that you may have life, and have it more abundantly."* He wants us to establish—often to *re*-establish our priorities along God's lines. I believe that means to live a life of love, love for God and love for one another.

We are indeed wise if we establish your priorities—God's priorities—before we are faced with a serious illness.

PRAYER: Dear Lord, help us to examine our priorities to see what is important in life, to realize that following You is the most important thing we can do. We pray in Jesus' name. AMEN.

AUGUST 4

LISTENING WITH CARE

(Scripture to ponder: Isaiah 6:9; Matthew 13:13)

When I was a Boy Scout, I earned Bird Study Merit Badge. We learned to recognize many different species by their colorful markings. Many other birds—the songbirds—we learned recognize by their songs. To do it was satisfying, but took time to listen to and memorize their songs. We became keen listeners, hearing calls and songs that most folks were not even aware of.

But nowadays, in my daily life, I find bird songs often get drowned out by all the other noise of modern life around me. I don't hear them unless I specifically listen for them.

So it is with God, who speaks to us through his Word. Those who listen and study most attentively are the ones who hear His voice. But they must take time to study, and take time to listen attentively.

In our Scripture selection today from Matthew's Gospel, Jesus was quoting the prophet Isaiah. Jesus said of many listeners,

"They have ears but do not hear."

We all have ears, but do we hear? Do we hear the birds? Do we hear God?

To hear God speaking, we must study His Word to sensitize our mind and spirit to hear His voice, just as one who seeks to recognize bird songs must study to become familiar with them, then listen carefully for them.

PRAYER: Dear Lord, sensitize us so we read Your Word and hear Your Voice. Speak to us and show us the way we should walk. Help us do Your Will. AMEN.

AUGUST 5

THE CURE FOR RELATIVISM

(Scripture to ponder: Romans 3:23)

The existentialist writer Albert Camus was unable to accept Jesus Christ. The Christian acknowledges God is sovereign, that He alone is righteous, and that our strength lies in confessing our own sinfulness before his absolute righteousness.

Camus could not do this, namely confess that he was a sinner before God. He neither accepted Christ as his savior, nor did he accept the counsel of Jesus to *"Judge not that you not be judged" [Matthew 7:1]* But he recognized the tendency of man toward sinfulness and judgment, and he deals with that in one of his books.

In his short novel, *Le Chute* (in English, *The Fall*), we find the main character, Jean Baptiste Clement, sitting in a bar in Amsterdam. Soon another patron sits down and they begin to drink and talk. Jean shares his story with the listener, a tale describing the many bad things he has done in his life, things he is ashamed of.

Invariably the other person says, in effect, "Gee, that's not so bad. Listen to my story," and he goes on to relate a tale far more sordid that Jean Baptiste has told.

"Then," says Clement, "**I judge him.**" For you see, Camus recognized our need to judge, to compare ourselves with others so we emerge on top. It's a part of human nature and happens all the time.

So it is in the secular world. We cannot live without passing judgment, so we make relative judgments that we come out best.

But the Christian knows that God alone is judge; our Scripture selection sums it up:

"All have sinned and fallen short of God's glory."

As Christians we acknowledge our sinfulness before God and ask His forgiveness. He has promised to forgive us our sins—as we forgive others.

PRAYER: **Acknowledging our sin before You, O Lord, help us to not judge others, but commend them to Your care. AMEN.**

AUGUST 6

BURNING MY TONGUE

(Scripture to ponder: Isaiah 6:1–6)

Recently at lunch, my wife ladled out soup just as I like it—warm but not too hot. At the end of the meal she asked if I wanted the last little bit left in the pan. I did, and served myself; but I forgot the pan had been on the stove throughout the meal. My "seconds" were too hot and I burned my tongue and my lips.

Doing that reminded me of the memorable passage in chapter six of Isaiah, our Scripture selection for today:

"In the year that King Uzziah died I saw the Lord sitting upon a throne, high and lifted up, and his train filled the temple . . . And one seraphim called to another and said, 'Holy, Holy, Holy is the Lord of Hosts; the whole earth is full of his glory.'"

In response to this vision of God, Isaiah cries out:

"Woe is me! For I am lost; For I am a man of unclean lips and I dwell in the midst of a people of unclean lips, for mine eyes have seen the King, the Lord of Hosts."

But then a seraphim touches Isaiah's lips with a burning coal. It purges him of his sin and prepares him to for service to the Lord.

What is it that allows us to determine if something or someone is unclean? We are able to do that by seeing, understanding and accepting the unmatched glory of the Lord. For left to ourselves and immersed in our secular society, we can become complacent and prideful, comparing ourselves with others, making relative judgments.

But if instead we meditate on the purity and the glory of the Lord, we see ourselves as we truly are. By so doing, we prepare ourselves, as did Isaiah, to be sent by God to carry out His mission.

PRAYER: Make us always aware of your Glory, Dear Lord, so we may see ourselves in true perspective, to prepare our hearts for Your Service. AMEN.

AUGUST 7

CHRISTIAN LOVE AND DISABILITY

(Scripture to ponder: 1 Thessalonians 5:14)

I have a nurse friend whom I helped with her PhD thesis devoted to Christian Ethics and Disability. She did a study of several families in our metropolitan area who had a family member who was disabled. She found that Christian faith and love were important positive factors in producing joy and overcoming some of the trials of disability.

Her findings fit with my own observations of disabled persons I've encountered in my professional practice. Those who have a strong faith are often—despite their obvious handicaps—full of joy and appreciation. Those who do not, who become bitter or cynical, often are angry and can develop an attitude of entitlement. Some actually don't make it at all: they commit suicide or die of intercurrent disease. The support and love of fellow Christians is crucial to those who do well.

In our Scripture selection for today St. Paul reminds us:

"We exhort you, brethren, admonish the idle, encourage the fainthearted, help the weak, be patient with them all."

I'm reminded of research done about 75 years ago, first in monkeys and then in humans. An investigator in Boston named Harlow raised monkeys without maternal love and nurturing, and they all died. Thereafter Spitz, in a study done in a foundling home in South America, tried to raise babies without giving them any nurturing support such as holding or rocking or having nurses otherwise interact with them. The experiment was inconclusive, because none of the babies who were denied nurture and love survived.

So it is with all of us. We all need nurture and love, the disabled person especially so, if they are to grow and thrive in God's family. We need to love and help one another.

PRAYER: Help us, dear Lord, to reach out to the disabled, to love and nurture them in Jesus' name. AMEN.

AUGUST 8

THE GIFT OF GRATITUDE

(Scripture to ponder: Luke 14: 7–11)

I recall one visit to my mother in the life-care facility where she lives. She was 97 at the time. She loved me to read to her, and as I searched among the small volumes on her shelf I came across a plastic, compact-like object. It had a flip top like a compact, but when I opened it, instead of a mirror, there was a photograph of my oldest sister, and out of the compact came a recording of my sister's voice, saying

"I love you, Mother, and just want to thank you for the wonderful gift you gave me years ago, the *Gift of Gratitude*."

That attribute of Gratitude has been one of the distinguishing features of the life of both my mother and my sister, and I am convinced that it has been the secret of their happiness, for they are two of the happiest people I have known in my lifetime.

Is an *attitude of gratitude* a secret of happiness? I've thought a lot about it, and believe it is, indeed. One reason is that the person with an attitude of gratitude is appreciative and content. They seem to notice the little blessings of life and are grateful for them. It's almost the opposite of the attitude of entitlement that one encounters so often nowadays.

I think Christ was getting at the issue in today's Scripture selection, the parable of the wedding feast. Jesus counsels us to take a seat at the foot of the table, instead of at the head, where we perhaps are more inclined to want to sit. Christ says,

"Whoever exalts himself shall be abased; but he that humbles himself shall be exalted."

PRAYER: Give to us, Dear Lord, the gift of gratitude, that we may appreciate all the many blessings we have. Make us mindful not of ourselves, but of the needs of others, that we may serve them, and serving them, serve You. AMEN.

AUGUST 9

SERVING THE ELDERLY

(Scripture to ponder: Luke 6:38)

He who would pass the latter part of life with honor and decency, must when he is young, consider that he shall one day be old and remember when he is old that he once was young.

[Samuel Johnson in *The Rambler*]

When I was in college I switched out of pre-med to become an English major, which meant that when I finally decided to become a doctor, I had to take several more science courses to get into medical school. This I did by living at home and attending Bryn Mawr College for a year.

During that year I attended my home church, Bryn Mawr Presbyterian, and participated in a ministry they had to bring audiotapes of the Sunday services to shut-ins, folks who were unable to get to church. We would pick up the tapes at church on a weekday and play them for folks in their homes.

As a young man full of energy, this work of bringing tapes to older individuals in their homes required little effort on my part. But I could see what a big difference it made to those whom I visited. They were grateful and it was the high point of their week. A small investment on my part paid large dividends in their lives. It was an important lesson in my life. It reminded me of today's Scripture:

"The measure you give will be the measure you get."

PRAYER: Help us, dear Lord, to expend that little extra effort of someone else, that it may pay rich dividends in their lives for your kingdom. AMEN.

AUGUST 10

FIGHTING PREJUDICE

(Scripture to ponder: Luke 23:34)

Recently I attended an exhibition in our art museum of Norman Rockwell's work. One of his most famous and most dramatic works depicts a small Negro girl being escorted to school by four U.S. Marshals. Her white dress is a contrast with her black skin. The wall behind her is punctuated with bigoted graffiti and the splat-mark of a thrown tomato. Perhaps you recall that famous illustration.

That little girl's name was Ruby Bridges, and she walked to and from that school for an entire year accompanied by the Marshals. In class she was the only pupil, for all the white children boycotted the school. Each day she endured many taunts from those she passed.

One day her teacher watched her coming to school. It looked as though she was conversing with someone as she walked. In class, the teacher asked her with whom she had been speaking on the way to school. Ruby replied that she wasn't talking to anyone, she was praying, praying for them what Jesus prayed for his enemies:

"Father forgive them for they know not what they do."

It was that spirit of forgiveness, of loving your enemies, which enabled progress in integration to occur. It is the same spirit that will allow God's kingdom to come on earth.

PRAYER: **Through your indwelling Spirit, Dear Lord, help us to pray for those who persecute us, that Your will be done and Your kingdom come. AMEN.**

AUGUST 11

BELIEVING WITHOUT SEEING

(Scripture to ponder: John 20: 24–29)

I believe in the sun, even when it is not shining. I believe in God. I believe in love, even when God is silent.

[Anonymous verses in Cologne, Germany]

Those verses were found in the basement of a bombed-out house in Cologne at the end of World War II. They bespeak great faith in the midst of a civilization that was crumbling from the ravages of war. I try to imagine who lived there and inscribed them on the wall. Were they Christians? Were they Jews in hiding?

As Christians, we are called to believe in the Lord Jesus Christ, even though He walked the earth twenty centuries ago.

After the crucifixion, as related in our Scripture for today, Jesus returned and showed Himself to his disciples. Thomas was absent; and afterward told his brethren,

"Unless I see in His hands the mark made by the nails, and put my hand into His side, I will never believe."

Eight days later Jesus again appeared to his disciples and this time Thomas was with them. The Lord had Thomas put his hand into the wound in His side; so Thomas believed. Jesus then declared something of great relevance to us who follow:

"Blessed are those who have never seen me and yet believe."

We latter day Christians are those who believe and trust and rely on Jesus, even though we never knew the twelve, or felt the marks of the crucifixion in the living Lord.

PRAYER: **Although we have never seen you, or put our hand into your wounded side, Dear Lord, we love you and believe you are the savior of the world. Increase our faith and help us share that faith with others. AMEN.**

AUGUST 12

GET ENTHUSIASTIC!

(Scripture to ponder: Ephesians 4:23)

Norman Vincent Peale, the Pastor of New York's Marble Collegiate Church and author of the best seller, *The Power of Positive Thinking*, was big on *enthusiasm*. But it was not always so. As a young man, he was quite unsure of himself. One summer he tried to make money by selling aluminum cookware door-to-door. He tells of it in an article he wrote. [31]

He started out in a negative manner on a somewhat run-down street, thinking, *"These people won't buy any aluminumware."* Moving to another street he paused in front of a house that was spic-and-span, but he didn't ring the bell there, either, thinking, *"These people are so progressive they've already got aluminumware."* He of course made no sales and went home and told his father he was no good at selling. His father, who had been trained as a physician but who'd become a preacher, stirred him up:

"Get enthusiastic! Go to the door, look the lady of the house in the eye, love her in your heart, and tell her that you've come to render the greatest service that anyone has ever done for her."

"You want me to say that?" the son replied.

"Yes, Norman—and get enthusiastic about it."

So the fledgling salesman went out the next morning and banged on the first door he came to. It opened to reveal the littlest woman he ever saw. He looked her in the eye.

"Madam, I have something you've been waiting for all your life." She smiled, took him into the kitchen and had him dry the dishes as he told her of all the benefits of cooking with aluminumware.

"My, my, you're the most enthusiastic young man I've ever met," she said, and gave him a big order. Years later, she came to his church and listened to him preach. Afterward she shook his hand, and said he sold the Gospel as enthusiastically as he'd sold those pots and pans.

Peale went on in his article to quote our scriptures for today, and also Ralph Waldo Emerson, who said **"Nothing great was ever achieved without enthusiasm."**

PRAYER: Fill us with your Spirit, O Lord, so that with enthusiasm we are renewed in the spirit of our minds and walk in newness of life, to do your
will. AMEN.

AUGUST 13

RUSHING TO JUDGMENT, WRITING FOLKS OFF

(Scripture to ponder: Luke 7:31–35)

How easily we rush to judgment, how quickly we write folks off! It happened in Biblical times and it happens today. When John the Baptist came eating no bread and drinking no wine, they said of him, *"He has a demon!"* And when his cousin Jesus came,
eating and drinking, they said, *"Behold a glutton and a drunkard, a friend of tax collec-
tors and sinners!"* This takes place in our Scripture selection from Luke's Gospel. Christ
comments, *"Yet wisdom is justified by all her children."* By that, I believe he meant that
we write folks off when we don't like their behavior or what they have to say.

In modern times, a humorous example occurred in the family of Jimmy Carter. As
you may recall, Carter had a brother named Billy, the pot-bellied, beer-drinking owner
of a gas station in Plains, GA. Billy not only looked funny, he often made peculiar, memorable remarks, like Yoggi Berra, the oft-quoted catcher for the Brooklyn Dodgers used to
make. The press loved it and made the most of it.

About the time Jimmy Carter ran for President, Billy was approached by a reporter.
He asked Billy if he didn't admit that he was a bit peculiar. I suspect Billy saw the reporter's
comment as a rush to judgment, a desire to write him off, for Billy responded:

> "My mother went in the Peace Corps when she was 68; my younger sister is a Holy-
> Roller preacher; my other sister is eight years older than I am and spends half her
> time on a Harley Davidson motorcycle; and my brother thinks he's going to be Presi-
> dent of the United States! *I'm the only one in the family that's normal!"*

It all depends on our perspective, doesn't it? Those who don't want to heed Christ's
words, write him off as an idealist who cavorted with low life, or say that his message of

love and peace just isn't applicable in the real world today. But those who confess Him as Lord and Savior know that He indeed has the words of Eternal Life! In Him is fullness of life, forever.

PRAYER: At times your words are hard, O Lord; but may we never want to write them off. They can transform our lives, if we let them. Help us to love you and love our neighbor with our whole heart. AMEN.

AUGUST 14

FASHIONING FALSE GODS

(Scripture to ponder: Exodus 32:1–6)

Among the strongest urges of humanity is the desire to have someone or something to worship. A good example is the account of Aaron's fashioning of the Golden Calf from the adornments of the Children of Israel while Moses was on the mountaintop, today's Scripture selection. It seems, as members of the human race—in contrast to animals—we must have someone or something to worship, to look up to, to revere. Ancient Greece and Rome had their pantheon of gods, and Hindus today worship scores of gods.

Voltaire said, "**If God did not exist, we'd have to invent him.**" Indeed, throughout history, man has created many gods, and modern man, despite his seeming sophistication, worships many gods.

But all gods are not equal. When Augustine wrote, "**Our hearts are restless until they find their rest in Thee,**" he was referring to the one true God, the Creator of the Universe, the Father of our Lord Jesus Christ, who after the resurrection sent the Holy Spirit to be our Counselor and Comforter. If we acknowledge, recognize, and worship the one, true, Triune God, we are secure and free indeed. We need no other gods.

PRAYER: When we worship You, O Lord, we have no need of other, lesser gods to satisfy our souls, for You alone are Holy, you alone are the One, True God. AMEN.

AUGUST 15

POACHED FROGS AND ERODED INTEGRITY

(Scripture to ponder: Luke 16:10–14)

There's an Eastern Indian proverb that goes like this:

"If the water is boiling, the frog will naturally leap out; but put the frog in a pot of cold water and then turn on the stove, and you'll end up with a poached frog."

It's a catchy saying and it's true to life! It talks of frogs and heating water, but really it's talking about our integrity, about how we can be compromised little by little. If we give way in small things, over time we end up doing something easily that we once thought was quite wrong.

Most of us would never think of robbing a bank. But confidential surveys show that many people cheat on their taxes, in little subtle ways, and rationalize it to themselves. While they wouldn't jump into boiling water, by their little lapses they subtly turn up the temperature of the water. Little compromises poach the integrity of the soul.

In our Scripture selection from Luke's Gospel, Jesus speaks of integrity. He says if we are honest in small matters, we'll be honest in large ones too. But if we are dishonest in little things, we'll not be entrusted with the riches of the kingdom.

PRAYER: **Keep us ever mindful of little lapses, Dear Lord. Keep us faithful and true in small things, so we may receive the great riches of your kingdom. AMEN.**

AUGUST 16

SOARING ON THERMALS

(Scripture to ponder: Isaiah 40:31)

Several summers ago I visited a nephew in the Netherlands. He and three friends owned a sailplane. He was an avid soarer, and one day we drove to the eastern part of the country where the topography was not so flat, to the airfield where he kept his red sailplane. I watched him as he went up and then rode the thermals for almost an hour. I noticed that he was able to stay aloft longer than many of the others who were out soaring in gliders that were newer and more sleek than his glider. When he landed and we were dismantling the plane, I asked him how he could stay up so long. What was his secret?

He said "**The secret is you have to know how to catch the thermals, the updrafts. If you get into the downdrafts, you won't stay aloft very long.**" His advice to catch the thermals reminded me of our Scripture selection from Isaiah:

> *They that wait on the Lord shall renew their strength: They shall mount up with wings as eagles, they shall run and not be weary, they shall walk and not faint.*

In life, as in gliding, we can choose to ride the thermals or we can get caught in the downdrafts. God's word is full of thermals, of uplifting passages like those from Isaiah. Happy are those who commit such scriptures to memory and can be lifted up by them each day.

PRAYER: Uplift us daily by the inspiration of your word, O lord. May we do your will with joyful hearts. AMEN.

AUGUST 17

THAT WE ALL MAY BE ONE

(Scripture to ponder: John, Chapter 17)

Our Scripture selection today is from John's Gospel, Christ's last discourse with his disciples. It occurred on the night before he died. Jesus prayed to his Father that they—his Father, he and his followers—might all be one. Christ's prayer presaged the Unity of the Church Universal, the cohesive Body of Christ down through the ages.

What does it mean to be *ONE*? I do not believe it means—for the universal church, or for an individual congregation—that we should or must all be alike. It means rather that we should be united, one in Spirit, Hope and Love, as we seek to serve our Master.

I believe there is a useful analogy to a symphony orchestra. When each player plays his own line, or practices a certain passage, as when the orchestra is on stage, just before the arrival of the conductor, the result is a cacophony of sound, a jumbled mishmash that's hard on the ears. But when each player submits to the discipline of the conductor, and plays his part under the direction of the maestro, beautiful music results. Although the players are many, and are playing different parts, they become *one* together, and the result is a beautiful synthesis of sound.

So it is with the Church: though we are many, we are one. Our many talents intertwine to let us reach out in service to our Lord.

PRAYER: Although we are many in our talents and our diversity, Dear Lord, unite us, that we may be ONE in Your Spirit, to worship You and to serve others. AMEN.

AUGUST 18

BLESSINGS OF A GOOD WIFE

(Scripture to ponder: Proverbs 31:10–31)

Today is my wife's birthday. The final part of the last chapter of Proverbs (today's selection) fits her well. It extols the virtues of a good wife. I would submit that every married man who is of great achievement is deeply indebted to his wife. I haven't achieved all that much in my life, but I sure have a good wife.

There is a relevant story about the New England author Nathaniel Hawthorne. He was employed as a clerk at the Salem, MA Custom House when there was a change of party in the government. He went home and told his wife he'd lost his job. Her response was, **"Now you can write that book you've always wanted to."**

Hawthorne asked, **"And just what are we supposed to live on while I do?"**

His wife went to the desk and pulled open the drawer, revealing a stack of gold pieces she'd saved from her household allowance. It covered their expenses for the next several months, while Nathaniel Hawthorne wrote *The Scarlet Letter.*

Many Christian counselors have stressed the importance of the husband-wife relationship, emphasizing its shared nature. Christ himself asserted the distinctiveness of that union, when in his teaching he quoted the book of Genesis, saying,

> *For this reason a man leaves his father and mother and cleaves unto his wife. And the two become one flesh.*
>
> [Matthew 19:5; Genesis 2:24]

Ideally—and in Christ's view—they become a unique, new being, a blending of what each was before.

PRAYER: Help us husbands, O Lord, to cherish our wives, loving them like our own bodies, as Christ himself loved the church and gave himself up for her. AMEN.

AUGUST 19

CARRYING LIFE'S BURDENS

(Scripture to ponder: Matthew 11:28–30)

In our Scripture selection for today, Jesus says,

"Come unto me all you who labor and are heavy laden, and I will give you rest."

Hearing His words reminds me of a story from my youth.

After I graduated from college, before I began medical school, I spent three weeks backpacking in the High Sierras of California with a cousin. In preparation, before I left home in Philadelphia, I made myself a pack, hand-sewing material around the frame of an old army rucksack I'd bought at an Army surplus store. I was proud of the pack, for it was my own handiwork although it was not especially comfortable.

Each evening for two weeks I hiked the neighborhood carrying the pack, which I loaded with volumes of the encyclopedia, adding another one every other day until I was carrying about thirty-five pounds. (My dear Mother met me one night coming back into the house and exclaimed, "You're not going to take all those books with you out west, are you?")

I flew west to join my cousin in L.A. Before we set out, he said we should have a look at a new pack designed by a man named Dick Kelty from nearby Glendale, CA. It was one of the first with that particular design. It had a special frame that transferred the weight on to one's hips, securing it with a broad strap. I discovered it was far more comfortable than my own self-made pack, and I bought one for the trip. There was indeed a better way.

When we are burdened with the cares and worries of this world, Christ has a better way.

PRAYER: **So often we insist on carrying our own burdens in our own way. Help us, Lord, to share the load and take your yoke upon us. Give us Rest and Peace. We pray in Jesus' name. AMEN.**

AUGUST 20

REFLECTIONS ON SURVIVOR

(Scripture to ponder: Galatians 6:2)

I watched two segments of the popular CBS television show *Survivor* before I gave up. I found it superficial and tasteless; but it did stimulate me to reflect on its mass appeal to worldwide audiences, for it was at the top of the Nielson ratings.

Survivor is what is called "a reality show," that is, it's an unrehearsed, let fly, devil-take-the-hindmost format, one step removed from public brawls like *Geraldo.* Of such shows, best selling author Norman Mailer commented, "Out of the crucible of improvisation, great things can emerge. It just depends on who is in charge." Fair enough.

Of course on *Survivor,* everyone is in charge, in that, one by one, the contestants get eliminated until the sole survivor collects one million dollars. The food-for-thought question (to use Lincoln's words) is: Is such a format designed to bring out the "best or the worst angels of our nature?"

Saint Paul, in our selection for today, wrote to the Christians at Galatia:

"Bear one another's burdens and thus fulfill the Law of Christ."

So the question I asked myself as I watched the show was, "Were they indeed bearing one another's burdens?" Most of the time, it seemed to me, they were intent upon looking out for themselves, or scheming to vote someone out.

PRAYER: Dear Heavenly Father, help us to do the will of your Son and bear one another's burdens in this life. Help us to love our neighbor as we love ourselves. AMEN.

AUGUST 21

THE INSIGHT OF ILLNESS

(Scripture to ponder: 1 Peter 5:5)

Have you ever noticed that major illness is often associated with insight? I've made that observation, both professionally and personally: when one experiences a serious illness, one tends to reevaluate one's priorities and sometimes, even, reorient one's life. It is a pattern that has been repeated in human lives throughout history.

Why does this happen, and why is it so often life-changing? I think it's because so often major illness is a *humbling* experience, pointing out to us our weakness, showing us our mortality. When we get seriously ill we usually become weak and dependent. I recall once having a severe gastrointestinal infection that left me weak as a kitten, almost unable to go from bed to bathroom.

But it is often in weakness that we find God is responsive. Both St. James *[James 4:6]* and St. Peter (in our Scripture selection for today) assert that God gives grace to the humble.

Do you recall St. Paul's "thorn in the flesh? Most scholars think it was some sort of physical aliment. Paul says that three times he petitioned God to take it from him. But God did not; rather He answered Paul,

"My grace is sufficient for thee, for my strength is made perfect in weakness." [2 Corinthians 12:9]

Wisdom and insight come when we see our lives in true perspective and not through the distorting lenses so often provided to us by society or advertising. When faced with illness, cognizant of our own weakness and mortality, we recognize the strength of God and can call upon Him in Truth.

PRAYER: **Help us see ourselves in true perspective, for You are the source of our wisdom, our insight and our strength. AMEN.**

AUGUST 22

WHEN THE FOG LIFTS

(Scripture to ponder: 1 Corinthians 13: 8–13)

Diane and I once spent a weekend on Catalina Island, off the coast of California. The first two days were glorious, with brilliant sunshine. From where we stayed, at the Zane Grey Pueblo Hotel, high above Avalon Harbor, we could see the boats lying at moorings amid the shimmering, sparkling waves scattered like diamond dust across the bay.

But when we awoke on the third morning, a thick fog had settled over the whole island. All we could see as we looked downward was a vague, ground glass appearance that obscured the entire bay, while visible above was a brilliant, radiant spot, the sun.

Gradually, as we watched, the brightness and warmth of the sun burned off the fog and all the boats and moorings became clear again. There they sat, gently rocking amid the shimmering waves.

In his Hymn to Love in First Corinthians 13, St. Paul speaks of how we now see God as through a dark glass, and alludes to the time when we shall see Him face to face. When the veil of mist that is our earthly life gets dispersed by the white radiance of Eternity, we'll fully focus on the Lord and join him in all His Glory. We'll see him appear, just like the sun burns off the fog.

PRAYER: We know, Dear Lord, that death is but that portal we must pass to see You in your bright radiance, when we will see you face to face, in all your Glory, for all Eternity. AMEN.

AUGUST 23

HAVING A FRIEND IN JESUS

(Scripture to ponder: John 15:13–15)

What would you do if the girl you were to marry accidentally drowned the evening before the wedding? Would it drive you far from God or bring you closer to Him? That happened to a man named Joseph M. Scriven, and not long thereafter he left his native Ireland for Canada. The loss of his future wife brought him closer to the Lord. In writing home to his mother, he enclosed a poem he had written, one that was destined to become the beloved and familiar hymn, "What a Friend We Have in Jesus." Its second stanza gives some insight into Scriven's life, how he handled sorrow:

Have we trials and temptations?
Is there trouble anywhere?
We should never be discouraged,
Take it to the Lord in prayer.
Can we find a friend so faithful
Who will all our sorrows share?
Jesus knows our every weakness,
Take it to the Lord in prayer.

In St. John's Gospel—our Scripture selection for today—we hear what Jesus said about friendship:

"Greater love has no one than this, that a man lay down his life for his friends. You are my friends if you do what I command you. No longer do I call you servants, for a servant does not know what his master is doing; but I have called you friends, for all things that I have heard from my Father I have made known to you."

And what is it that Christ has commanded us to do? Here is what John quoted Christ as saying:

"This is my commandment, that you love one another as I have loved you"

Jesus called himself the Good Shepherd, the one who lays down his life for his sheep. Indeed, that is just what Jesus has done for us. He has laid down his life for us and has become not just our friend, but our crucified Lord, whom God raised from the dead, that we, too may have life eternal. Jesus is a friend indeed.

PRAYER: Thank you, Lord, for showing us the nature of true friendship, which is sacrificial love. Help us love one another as you have loved us. AMEN.

AUGUST 24

DESTROYING OUR ENEMIES

(Scriptures to ponder: Romans 12:14; Matthew 5:44)

Once when President Abraham Lincoln spoke some kind words regarding the enemy, he was rebuked by an elderly lady, who said that instead of speaking kindly of them, he should destroy them. He replied, **"Why madam, do I not destroy them when I make them my friends?"**

In our Scripture for today, St. Paul instructs the church at Rome to *"Bless them which persecute you; bless and curse not."* And the Lord Jesus, in our second selection from the Sermon on the Mount is even more explicit:

You have heard it said, love your neighbor and hate your enemy. But I say unto you, love your enemies, bless them that curse you, do good to them that hate you, and pray for them which despitefully use you; that you may be the children of your Father which is in heaven.

Christ specifically enjoins us to do good to those who seek to harm us, and to pray for them. Throughout the centuries many have been won to Christ by those who were persecuted, by the Christ-like behavior of Believers.

PRAYER: Help us, Dear Lord, to love those who do not love us and to pray for those who would do us harm. Help us do Your will. AMEN.

AUGUST 25

FOLLOWING A SAINT ABROAD

(Scripture to ponder: Matthew 13:57)

When I was a medical student I heard a wonderful address by Dr. Paul Brand, who was a missionary on furlough from India. He described his work with leprosy patients at the Christian Medical College in Vellore, South India. I resolved to go see his work, and the next summer I did so. It was an inspiring and educational experience.

I was recently reminded of that summer in India when our pastor told the story of a man who heard Mother Theresa speak in New York about her work in Calcutta among the poor and destitute. The man asked her if he might come visit her and see her mission. She perceived he was seeking meaning, fulfillment, and happiness in his life. She replied to him, **"If you'd take the money you'd spend for the round trip air fare and give it to the poor, you'd stand a better chance of finding happiness than in listening to me."**

In our Scripture selection for today, Jesus said:

"A prophet is not without honor, except in his own country."

He said this at the time he returned to his boyhood home of Nazareth and rose to speak in the synagogue. He had done mighty works as he began his ministry, but when he returned to his boyhood home, Matthew records, *"he did not do many mighty works there, because of their unbelief."*

We need to recognize the saints among us and support their work in our own neighborhoods! The Kingdom is here among us.

PRAYER: Help us, Dear Lord, see the Saints around us and show us ways to support and serve and love those who have needs, right here at home. AMEN.

AUGUST 26

HAVE MODERN RUNNERS GONE SOFT?

(Scripture to ponder: 1 Corinthians 9:25)

That was the title of a recent newspaper article I read that lamented the decreasing numbers of high school and college athletes taking up running. The author, a track coach, feared that lost runners—those who never gave it a real try—would never learn *The Secret*. He said the secret could never be taught, but only "discovered" by the athlete who was willing to make the sacrifices and take the chances. *The Secret*, he said, is this: **"There is inner pride, quiet joy and a personal victory in any struggle, regardless of the outcome."**

In today's Scripture, St. Paul speaks in a similar vein about the Christian life:

Run your race to win. To win the contest you must deny yourself many things that would keep you from doing your best. An athlete goes to all this trouble just to win a blue ribbon or a silver cup, but we do it for a heavenly reward that never disappears.

Christ himself never said the Christian life would be easy. Indeed, St. John records his words to his disciples:

"Here on earth you will have many trials and sorrows. But take heart! I have overcome the world!"

[John 16:33]

PRAYER: Strengthen us, O Lord, as we run the race of life, that we may do Your will and win the crown of glory. AMEN.

AUGUST 27

POVERTY, CHASTITY AND OBEDIENCE

(Scripture to ponder: Luke 20:19–25)

Vows of *Poverty, Chastity and Obedience* were—and still are—taken by persons who choose to devote their lives to Holy Orders. The Christian writer and commentator Richard J. Foster believes these three were chosen because they dealt with the three great ethical issues of human life: *Money, Sex and Power*. Throughout history these three areas have formed a stage on which the epic drama of human life has been played out.

For *Money*, we could substitute *Possessions*, and for *Power*, substitute *Authority*. *Sex* is splashed all over the media, and encompasses some of the greatest temptations of our time.

What should be our attitudes toward *Possessions* and *Sex* and *Authority?* We cannot all become monks, or live in cloisters, nor do I believe God wants us to. But certainly it's clear from the life and teachings of both Christ and St. Paul that our lives should be characterized by simplicity, not complexity or opulence. As regards *Sex*, the New Testament model is: chastity when single, fidelity in marriage.

Concerning *Power* or *Authority*, The Biblical perspective is summed up well in two of Christ's teachings. First, we are to *love God and love our neighbor [Luke 10:27]*; and second, from today's scripture selection, we should *"render unto Caesar that which is Caesar's and to God that which is God's"*—that is, we owe the government what's due to it; but our ultimate allegiance—and our worship—is to be given unto God.

PRAYER: **Through Your Spirit, O Lord, help us discern a right attitude toward possessions, sex and authority. Through Your Word, teach us Your Way and show us Your Will. AMEN.**

AUGUST 28

WHY DID HE DO IT?

(Scriptures to ponder: Galatians 6:2 and John 15:12)

On August 28, 2002 a 41 year old man from Tucson who was a nursing student at the University of Arizona shot and killed three of the professors of nursing, then turned the gun on himself. There was much speculation in the newspapers about why he would do such a heinous thing, and certain failures—during his military service, in two marriages that ended in divorce, and in his nursing class work—were cited as possible reasons for his rampage. It would be easy to write him off as a paranoid n'er-do-well. But for me, that's too pat an answer.

It's surely true that the ubiquity of firearms and our obvious endorsement of violence as the way to solve problems in our society—both in real life and in the make-believe world of movies and television—contributed to the problem. It happens that the man who killed the nursing teachers and then himself sent a long letter to the *Arizona Daily Star* giving the reasons for what he did.

That letter revealed a man who felt increasingly isolated and cut off from his classmates and even from life itself. In many respects, his life was a failure, yes. But I wonder, if St. Paul or Jesus were here, would either perhaps say it was also a failure of Christians who did not get involved?

Our Scriptures for today speak to these issues. St. Paul wrote to the Ephesians: *"Bear one another's burdens and thereby fulfill the law of Christ."* And what is the law of Christ? Jesus said, as related in John's Gospel, *"This is my commandment, that you love one another."* Christ's law is quite simple: *Love God and love each other.* Share each other's burdens, help one another out. In Robert Flores' case, I suspect there were many ways we could have helped out: help with the rent, help with his car insurance, help him cope. Maybe just be there, to listen and not judge. But nobody did that.

Desperate, cornered, trapped by his life, he went on a rampage. Although he did the awful deeds, we are all responsible, for we are all God's children: Christ calls us to love one another.

PRAYER: All around us, Dear Lord, people are hurting, even desperate. Make us see and hear and be willing to help in your name. AMEN.

AUGUST 29

SCRIPTURES THAT TRUMP

(Scriptures to ponder: See below)

There are 52 cards in a deck. In most card games, the high cards—either those with the high numbers, or face cards, the Jack, Queen, and King, plus the Ace—are the winning cards. But in the game of *Bridge,* low cards can sometimes be winning cards, because they can be *trump* cards. If a certain suit (spades, hearts, clubs or diamonds) is declared *trump*, then a lower card in that suit can win over a higher card in another suit that's not trump.

I am not a good bridge player. Although I know enough to play, I'm not good at it. My wife, on the other hand, is an excellent bridge player. Recently when we were reading through the New Testament in our devotions, she said, "There are so many different verses in the Bible with so many different meanings! Sometimes they contradict each other."

She has a point. But I believe there are certain key scriptures—to continue the bridge playing analogy, one might call them *scriptures that trump*—that I believe all Christians should be familiar with. Here are thirteen of mine.

1. *John 3:17–18. "God so loved the world . . ."*
2. *Philippians 2:4–11. "Have this mind among you . . ."*
3. *Isaiah 40:31. "They that wait on the Lord . . ."*
4. *Romans 8:31–32. "If God is for us . . ."*
5. *Psalm 91:1–2. "He who dwells in the shelter of the most high . . ."*
6. *Colossians 1:19–20. "In him was all the fullness of the Godhead . . ."*
7. *Psalm 23. "The Lord is my shepherd . . ."*
8. *Matthew 24:31–46. The Parable of the Last Judgment.*
9. *Luke 10:29–37. The Parable of the Good Samaritan.*
10. *Luke 15:11–32. The Parable of the Prodigal Son.*

11. Luke 6:31. The Golden Rule.
12. Matthew 6:7–13. The Lord's Prayer.
13. 1Corinthians 13. Paul's "Hymn to Love."

The Bible contains thousands of verses, but all are not equal. I've selected thirteen key scriptures that I believe are worth memorizing. They're like trump cards.

PRAYER: **There is salvation and solace in your Word, O Lord. Help us read it, learn it well, take it to heart and commit it to memory. AMEN.**

AUGUST 30

WELCOMING AND WRESTLING WITH ANGELS

(Scripture to ponder: Genesis 28:11–17; 32:24–32)

Here's a poem entitled "Welcoming Angels," by contemporary writer Pat Schneider, founder of Amherst Writers and Artists, and a faculty member of the Graduate Theological Union in Berkeley, CA:

Between the last war
And the next one,
Waiting for the northbound train
That travels by the river,
I sit alone in the middle of the night
And welcome angels.
Welcome back old hymns, old songs,
All the music, the rhyme and rhythm,
Welcome angels, archangels,
Welcome early guesses
At the names of things,
Welcome wings.

I have grown tired of disbelief.
What once was brave is boring.
Welcome back to my embrace stranger,
Visitor beside the Jabbok.
Welcome wrestling until dawn,
Until it is my hip thrown out of joint,
My pillow stone, my ladder
Of antique assumptions.
Welcome what is not my own;
Glory on the top rung, coming down.

In the poem she alludes to two episodes in the life of Jacob, described in our selections for today. The first is his dream of a ladder extending from earth to heaven, that later became the subject of the lovely spiritual, "We Are Climbing Jacob's Ladder." The second event was Jacob wrestling with God in the form of an angel beside the brook Jabbok. Jacob would not let go until the angel blessed him. It was there that Jacob was given a new name, Israel, which means "he who strives with God."

Reflecting on the poem, it does seem that as we grow older, we do welcome back the angels we have known from our youth. We recall old hymns and old songs, and I suspect that many who are not Christian grow tired of disbelief and find what was once brave is now boring. I suspect also that many wait and long for glory to descend from on high, for God to intercede in this woeful world.

But *He has already come*, has come incarnate in Jesus. Through the Lord Jesus, God has told us and showed us how we ought to live. When he comes again—which He promised—it will not be as a suffering servant, but as judge of all the earth.

PRAYER: **We bless You, O Lord, that You visited the mighty men of old, and that in Jesus You became one of us to offer salvation to all the world. AMEN.**

AUGUST 31

WHAT BOOKS WOULD YOU TAKE?

(Scripture to ponder: Hebrews 4:12)

When I was growing up there was a parlor game called "Desert Island" in which each person had to choose three books to take to a desert island, and had to tell why.

What books would you take? I was an English major in college and would certainly make one of the selections the *Complete Works of William Shakespeare*. A second would be Webster's *Unabridged Dictionary*. But if I had but one choice, the one I'd be sure to take is the *Bible*.

Not only is the Bible a treasure trove of fascinating stories and a great book of wisdom, it is alive and it's eternal. The writer if the book of Hebrews put it well in our Scripture selection for today:

For the Word of God is living and active, sharper than a two-edged sword, piercing to the division of soul and spirit or joint and marrow, discerning the thoughts and intentions of the heart.

Behind the text, beneath the actual words, is a force and a spirit that gives the Bible life, the Spirit of the Living God, that can quicken our human spirits to respond to the divine call. No other book is like it, no other book comes close. It speaks anew to the hearts of each generation.

PRAYER: We're grateful for your Word, O Lord. May we read it every day. AMEN.

SEPTEMBER 1

PRIORITIES

(Scripture to ponder: 1 Kings 3: 5–14)

Some commentators in the media have called September 11, 2001 a "Wake-up Call" for America, and it certainly changed the Bush administrations priorities for the coming federal budget. And that now infamous date has led many to rearrange their personal priorities.

You may recall the story from our Scripture selection that relates the priorities of the young King Solomon. The Lord appeared to him in a dream, asking Solomon what his wish was, what God should give him. Of all the things that he might have asked for—long life or riches or triumph over his enemies—Solomon chose to be granted *an understanding heart to judge his people.* God was pleased with Solomon's priorities, and granted him not only wisdom, but all the rest as well.

And in the New Testament, Jesus counsels his disciples not to be anxious about what to wear, or what to eat, ore what to drink. He suggests a different priority. *"Seek ye first the kingdom of God and his righteousness."* And then he adds—much as in Solomon's case—*"and all these things shall be added unto you." [Matthew 6:33]*

In a letter my father wrote to me in college, he made a statement that has stuck in my memory ever since. He wrote, **"There are only 24 hours in a day—but there are never less."** How we use them depends on our priorities.

PRAYER: Help us, O Lord, make our priorities Your Priorities. In Jesus' name we pray. AMEN.

SEPTEMBER 2

CLAIM YOUR INHERITANCE

(Scripture to ponder: Luke 15:11–31)

Over the years I have worshiped in many different churches and participated in a variety of denominations. It's been my impression that sometimes long-term Christians in main line churches can get brought up short and even become resentful when they see the excitement and rejoicing that occurs in more fundamentalist churches with the repentance and acceptance of long-time sinners who turn their lives over to Jesus. We secretly feel that we—who perhaps have been Christians all our lives and faithful Church members from our youth—should be entitled to more than someone who has just come to the Lord.

Indeed, in three well-known parables that occur together in Chapter 15 of Luke's Gospel, Christ emphasizes that Heaven rejoices when sinners repent: First, in the parable of the lost sheep; next in the parable of the lost coin; and finally in the parable of the Prodigal Son. In that third parable—our scripture for today—the emphasis is on the prodigal son who returns, and his joyous welcome by the waiting, longing father.

We who have been Christians all our lives may identify with the elder brother and resent that this younger son—who chose to take his part of the inheritance and went off and squandered it—is being welcomed back with hugs and robes, rings and banquets. We who've been thankless toilers here at home, do we get any recognition or praise?

But long-time Christians need to be reminded of the Father's words to his elder son: ***"You and I are very close, and everything I have is yours!"*** We should ask ourselves, "Do we appreciate all we have, and take joy in a close relationship with God the Father?" For the *Joy of the Lord is truly our strength. [Nehemiah 8:11]*

PRAYER: **Dear Lord, may we rejoice always that while we were yet sinners, Christ died for us. Through him we have fellowship with you. Draw us ever nearer and give us your strength and your joy. AMEN.**

SEPTEMBER 3

WHEN THEY FIND THE WALKMANS

(Scripture to ponder: Luke 10:30–37)

I have only a superficial acquaintance with archaeology. I'm amazed when I visit a museum of natural history to see how scientists reconstruct a society based upon the artifacts they've dug up.

Have you ever thought about what archeologists of the future might conclude about our contemporary society, based on what they encounter in digs several centuries from now? What do you suppose they'll think when they encounter a bunch of Walkmans, each with its own set of earpieces?

I suspect they'll deduce what I surmise when I look about our society: many folks choose—when they are on the bus or jogging, for example—to shut out others and keep to themselves. Do you suppose future observers of the past will infer that isolation and loneliness existed in our society?

What a contrast is given by the teachings of Jesus of Nazareth. He taught—in parables to the crowd, and by example to his apostles—that we must be involved with those around us, that our neighbors are not just those who live next door. In the Parable of the Good Samaritan, the Lord says our neighbor is any person who needs our help.

When we encounter the man who fell among thieves on the road from Jerusalem to Jericho, will we turn up the volume of our Walkman to drown out his cries for help? Will we pass by on the other side?

PRAYER: **In our inmost hearts, Dear Lord, we know your will. Help us always be mindful of the needs of others, and serve those needs. In Jesus' Name we pray. AMEN.**

SEPTEMBER 4

REDWOODS HAVE SHALLOW ROOTS

(Scripture to ponder: Galatians 6:2)

The summer before I entered medical school I spent three weeks backpacking in the mountains of California with my cousin. We visited the Yosemite Valley, hiked the John Muir Trail and finished by climbing Mt. Whitney.

My cousin's father was the retired president of Long Beach State College whose major area of research was dendrology, the study of trees. In connection with my visit I got to see and learn about some of the oldest trees in the world.

The *Sequoia gigantea* or Bigtree is the largest of all living things. Its close relative, the *Sequoia sempervirens* or coastal redwood is the tallest of all trees. Both these marvelous, immense living structures are found in stands in Northern California.

It's not by chance that they exist in stands. For the sequoia have very shallow roots. An isolated sequoia can be blown over in a storm. But standing together, these trees can weather the fiercest of storms.

So it is with Christians: in isolation we cannot weather the storms of life. But as members of the body of Christ, in fellowship and in communion in the church, we are able to share one another's burdens and triumph over the storms of this life. St. Paul puts it well in our Scripture selection for today:

"Share one another's burdens, and so fulfill the law of Christ."

PRAYER: Help us, dear Lord, to stand together, to seek the company and fellowship of our Christian brothers and sisters in the Church, to do the work you have for us to further your Kingdom. In Christ's name we pray. AMEN.

SEPTEMBER 5

GAINING PEACE THROUGH THE HOLY SPIRIT

(Scripture to ponder: John 14:25–27)

Over fifty years ago an American Rabbi named Joshua Liebman wrote a book entitled *Peace of Mind.* It became a best seller, for at that time—during the cold war between Russia and the United States—there was widespread anxiety and fear of a nuclear holocaust.

Although since 1945 atomic bombs have never again been used in warfare, the world is today probably a less peaceful place than it was when *Peace of Mind* was written. Warfare and violence are ubiquitous, and nowadays the airways and paperback racks are full of all sorts of schemes to bring inner peace—usually for a price—as the quest continues. Television gurus preach transcendental meditation and the media call for peace, but there is no peace. Anti-anxiety and antidepressant medications are the drugs most prescribed by doctors in the U.S.A.

For the Christian familiar with the teachings of the Master, this comes as no surprise. Christ cautioned his disciples before he left them, *"In the world you will have tribulation."* But in the same breath, he said, *"Be of good cheer, I have overcome the world." [John 16:33]*

How do we overcome the world and get peace of mind? It is through the Holy Spirit, as taught in our Scripture selection. On the night before he died, Christ said:

"These things I have spoken to you while I am still with you. But the Counselor, the Holy Spirit, whom the Father will send in my name, he will teach you all things and bring to remembrance all that I have said to you. Peace I leave with you; my peace I give to you; not as the world gives do I give to you. Let not your hearts be troubled, neither let them be afraid."

PRAYER: We thank you, O Lord, for the gift of your Spirit, through which we have the peace which passes all understanding, that keeps our hearts and minds stayed on You and not the troubles of this world. AMEN.

SEPTEMBER 6

AIR TRAFFIC CONTROL

(Scripture to ponder: Isaiah 30:21)

I recently took a flight back to Phoenix from Philadelphia, and to have something to read on the trip, bought a small book authored by a pilot, entitled, *All About Air Travel,* which gave many interesting facts about travel by air. Some of these related to the control of air traffic.

When commercial pilots fly, they are required to follow closely the instructions given to them by the air traffic controllers who regulate the traffic across the country. The pilots, in the course of their flights, get handed off from one control zone to the next, so that arrivals and departures from the major America cities are coordinated. The pilots must submit to the discipline of the patterns established by the air traffic controllers. To do otherwise would be to produce absolute chaos and would greatly increase the risk of major collisions or accidents.

So it is with the Christian life. Christians believe that God is in control, and we believe the way to avoid chaos and to live harmoniously with one another is to follow the Way set up by Him in the Scriptures. We must listen to and follow the instructions of the Master, which come to us through God's Word. In the words of our Scripture selection for today:

And your ears shall hear a word behind you, saying, "This is the way, walk in it."

PRAYER: Dear Lord, help us acknowledge you in control of our lives, and help us listen to Your Word and do Your will in all things. AMEN.

SEPTEMBER 7

SPOTTING THE DACOITS IN LIFE

(Scripture to ponder: Proverbs 1:10–18)

When I was a medical student I spent a summer in India, living with five Indian families on a program called The Experiment in International Living. We ten American students were immersed in that culture and experienced far more that we would have as tourists—including getting sick from exotic diseases such as amebiasis and malaria!

About half way through the summer we went on a trip by train around the vast subcontinent, on which we had many exciting adventures. One of the most gripping occurred in the middle of the night amid the barrenness of South India.

As I sat in the discomfort of second class, trying fitfully to get some sleep, I felt the train come to a stop. The rest of our group was asleep, propped against one another or against our backpacks, but I was awake. Something seemed not right, so I got out of the compartment and walked along the tracks to the engine, where the engineer was just dismounting from his perch in the old fashioned steam locomotive.

I asked him what the matter was. He said he had seen some strange lights moving up ahead on the tracks, so he stopped the train. He was now going to investigate. He and I walked up ahead and discovered that the rails had been taken up just before they came to a trestle over a deep ravine!

"Dacoits have done this," he said, referring to roving bands of mounted robbers. "They planned to derail the train into the ravine and then rob it." We walked back to the engine where the fireman had already broken out two rifles. They stood guard until it was light and a rescue train came to repair the track. How fortunate we all were that the engineer had the wisdom and foresight to spot the dacoits as they rode away from the scene, and to stop the train in time!

PRAYER: Heavenly Father, give us the discernment to spot the dacoits of evil that may lie in wait for us along life's path. Help us to take action to prevent entrapment by the evil forces that can beset us in this life. In Jesus' name we pray. AMEN.

SEPTEMBER 8

SPIRITUAL FOOD

(Scripture to ponder: Deuteronomy 8:3; Matthew 4:4)

I was in Border's Bookstore the other day looking for a new cookbook. Just for fun, I asked the clerk if there were any new diet books. "Oh my, yes," she said, "there's a new one at least every week"

As a physician I know there is one essential secret to dieting, and all the rest is mostly fluff. The secret is: *you must burn more calories than you take in.* Doing that inevitably leads to weight loss. But to lose weight and still stay healthy means that we need to take, in addition to fewer calories, certain essential nutrients as part of out diet—essential amino acids and various vitamins and minerals, without which we would become deficient and malnourished. Although there are many foods, fads and diets out there, to remain healthy we need just the essentials to stay fit or to lose weight.

Likewise in our spiritual lives, we need to be nourished with the essentials from the spiritual realm. What we take in through our eyes and ears is the food for our mind and our spirit: to keep healthy, given the tremendous variety presented to us by the media today, we need a diet that contains the essentials, and limits the fluff and fat. Foremost of these essentials—the vitamins, minerals and essential amino acids of our Spirit, so to speak—is *God's Word.* We need to partake of it every day as our daily bread.

PRAYER: Dear Lord, help us find daily sustenance in your word, for not by bread alone do we nourish ourselves. Let us feed daily on the scriptures so a new, right spirit will be within us. AMEN.

SEPTEMBER 9

DRAFTING AND THE CHRISTIAN LIFE

(Scripture to ponder: 1 Corinthians 3:5–9)

In 2002 Lance Armstrong won the grueling Tour de France for the forth year running. The victory was a tribute to his training and his stamina. The Tour de France is the most demanding of all bicycle races, lasting 23 days and covering over 2100 miles. It's been likened to running a marathon—and then following it with another 20 marathons back to back. Armstrong's feat is all the more remarkable, considering he came back from the ravages of testicular cancer and its arduous treatment to repeatedly win this tough race.

But he didn't win the big race all by himself. As crucial as his own conditioning and drive were to success, he couldn't have won without the efforts of his teammates, who shielded and protected him. They let him conserve his energy, by using a method called *Drafting.*

In *drafting,* individual members of a cyclist's team take turns in the lead, in the hardest-working position, while the others pedal in his draft, avoiding much of the wind resistance by staying in the wake of the leader. Various members of Armstrong's team would successively lead, letting him draft to save his energy.

Saint Paul alludes to a phenomenon similar to drafting, in our selection from his first letter to the church at Corinth. He speaks of efforts by him and his co-workers to spread the Gospel, likening them to a farmer raising crops: one plants, another nurtures the seedlings, someone else waters and another harvests. So we modern Christians not only sow seeds; we also receive the harvest of our forbears, the saints who have gone before us, preparing the way.

PRAYER: We thank You, O Lord, that we can draft in the path of those great saints who have led the way, of whom Your Son Jesus is foremost and first. AMEN.

SEPTEMBER 10

SAVED—BY TECHNOLOGY ?

(Scriptures to ponder: Acts 4:12)

I'm writing this on Tuesday, September 10, 2002, and I'm sitting in a barber shop waiting to get a haircut while the T.V. blares the *Today Show*. On the first anniversary of the terrorist attack, replays of the drama are being discussed. An expert in cellular telephones is being interviewed, the pretext being the several phone calls made from the Twin Towers of the World Trade Center, and calls from the plane that crashed in Pennsylvania just after the passengers overpowered the hijackers to prevent them crashing the aircraft into the White House or the Congress.

As the expert extolled the virtues of the newest technology; the dialogue was soon transformed into an advertisement for the latest generation of cellular phones. I was saddened to see how secular the approach was, and what great saving faith was being placed in the latest technology.

But reflecting on the issue by stepping back a bit, one sees that contemporary America seeks salvation in all sorts of diverse technology: from our medical care, through our communication systems, to our defense department: the emphasis is ever on the latest high-tech treatments, on cellular telephones or on laser-guided weapons. It's an orientation I don't accept.

It is true that our Christian Faith does not reject progress and technology; but it always keeps it in perspective. Our Hope is not in science, nor is it in technology. No, our Hope and our Salvation, as our Scripture for today declares, are in *God:* not in the Twin Towers, nor in any other man-made creation, no matter how awesome, but rather in the Name of the only true God, our Lord, the King of the Universe. As Peter declared just after Pentecost (our selection for today) there is no other name by which we can be saved.

PRAYER: May we always put our trust in You, O Lord, and not in man or in technology. Help us to do Your Will in all things. AMEN.

SEPTEMBER 11

WHAT IS YOUR GOAL?

(Scripture to ponder: Philippians 3:13–14)

In our Scripture selection from his letter to the Church at Philippi, St. Paul speaks of pressing onward toward a goal—which for Paul was the *high calling of Jesus Christ.*

What is *your* goal? What do you strive for in this life? Do you press onward for wealth, to accumulate money so you can retire? Or are you, in the words of the Declaration of Independence, seeking the *pursuit of happiness?* Or maybe you're a teenager who desires above all else acceptance by peers?

Christ Himself in the Sermon on the Mount *[Matthew 5]* speaks of what our goals ought to be. These are his priorities: *"Seek ye first the kingdom of God and His righteousness, and all these things will be added unto you."* By all these things he meant the material things of life, such as what we should eat or what we should wear. Hear his words:

"Lay not up for yourselves treasures on earth, where moth and rust corrupt and where thieves break through and steal. But lay up treasures in heaven; for where your treasure is, there will your heart be also."

Do you recognize the expression, **"Don't sweat the small stuff?"** I think it's relevant in the context of our life in Christ: If we love God and seek His Kingdom, He'll provide for all the rest of our needs. He'll provide for the "small stuff!"

PRAYER: We know, **"Dear Lord, King of the Universe, that you are able to provide for all our needs. Help us to seek first Your Kingdom. AMEN.**

SEPTEMBER 12

WITHDRAWING FROM THE WORLD

(Scripture to ponder: Romans 12:2)

The contemporary spiritual writer Thomas Moore has said, "withdrawal from the world is something we can, and perhaps should do every day." He urges it as a means of turning one's attention inward, toward meditation.

There is probably nothing more essential to preserve the dynamism of the Christian life. In the world we are all pulled in many different directions by our jobs and our responsibilities. If we do not take time to withdraw, to turn inward and to meditate on God, we will find that the world will have *"stuffed us into its mold,"* to use St. Paul's phrase as translated by C.S. Lewis. *"Do not be conformed to this world,"* Paul says, *"but be transformed by the renewal of your mind."* Those words were apt in the first century and they are apt today, as we look forward to a new century in a new millennium.

Renewal of spirit occurs when we set aside time—however brief—to withdraw from the world and to focus on our relationship with God.

An easy way to begin is to use the "959 Rule" suggested by Christian counselor Larry Burkett: devote nine minutes and 59 seconds each day to withdrawing from the world for meditation and prayer.

PRAYER: Help us, Dear Lord, set aside time each day to withdraw from the world to draw closer to you through reading of your word and meditation on it. AMEN.

SEPTEMBER 13

RESPONDING TO TRAGEDY

(Scripture to ponder: Romans 8: 35–39)

A friend was puzzled by the response of a Christian mother whose child died when the World Trade Center Towers went down on September 11, 2001. The mother, interviewed by reporters, was not angry or bitter. She said she was grateful for the years she had been given with her daughter. My friend could not fathom the mother's reaction.

I am sure this mother was stunned and saddened by the death of her daughter. But as a Christian, I understand the mother's response. For it seems to me, when faced with such devastating losses, one can respond in one of two ways. The unbeliever responds with bitterness—*How can God let such a thing happen?* The Christian knows God does not *will* such horror; but in an imperfect world, it happens. The Christian sees life as a gift of God, knows there is great peril and injustice in the world, and realizes life can be snuffed out at almost any moment. *But it's always been that way; we just aren't willing to acknowledge this truth until it strikes us personally.*

I'm sure that mother gave her child to God a long time ago. She was grateful for the years they had together. And she knew—as did her daughter—that *"nothing can separate us from the Love of God, which is in Christ Jesus."* That is the glorious reassuring message in our Scripture passage for today.

PRAYER: Help us cherish those we love, knowing that love is a gift from You, and nothing can separate us from that Love. AMEN.

SEPTEMBER 14

DIVINE DETACHMENT

(Scripture to ponder: Philippians 1:21–23)

When I visited India as a medical student and lived with several families in the course of a summer, I became familiar with some of the tenants of Buddhism. One of these is the cultivation of detachment, through the use of yoga and special meditative mantras.

Whereas in the West, the approach has been to overcome nature and disease, in the East, there has been an approach of *acceptance*. Because life is seen as an endless cycle of suffering, release is sought by overcoming one's cravings and passions. I found that in the Eastern religions there was not only a greater acceptance of things as they are, but also a greater acceptance of disease and of one's station in life. It explained much of the disease and poverty I encountered.

On my return from India, I was glad to be back in our great country, but more aware of how attached we in the West are to our material possessions.

If you read the New Testament closely, you find there are strong themes of detachment there as well. In writing to the Philippian Church, St. Paul asserts that he is indifferent as to whether he lives or dies. If he lives, he lives unto the Lord, to do His will, working for His kingdom; if he dies, he goes to be with Christ, which is even better. Even Paul, who could be so zealous for the Lord, could also manifest divine detachment, for he knew his salvation was secure.

PRAYER: While we work to do your will and further your kingdom, Lord, grant us divine detachment, so that whether we live or whether we die, we are secure, knowing we are yours. AMEN.

SEPTEMBER 15

PIGGY BANKS, GREED AND O.P.M.

(Scripture to ponder: Romans 3:23)

Many kids are taught the rudiments of thrift using piggy banks. When I was growing up, my folks used a more modern version called a "Three Coin Register Bank," a metal bank that looked like a small cash register, that progressively tallied the nickels, dimes and quarters I inserted. It unlocked only when the contents totaled $10.00. With such a bank I saved my paper route earnings and bought my first (used) gearshift bicycle.

Believing it's good to teach children frugality, I pricked up my ears when a local newscaster called a Pennsylvania cable T.V. company *"the private piggy bank of the Rigas family."* Mr. Rigas was a Pennsylvania businessman who progressively bought up movie theaters in the 1950s. With the advent of television, he then began to buy T.V. stations, and more recently, cable networks. So far, all were legal undertakings—in the entrepreneurial spirit of America.

But then Mr. Rigas succumbed to one of the seven deadly sins—Greed—that's recently seemed to characterize American businesses such as Enron, Global Crossing and WorldCom. The Rigas empire—called *Adelphia*—followed a downward spiral fed by avarice: 1) Extensive borrowing, using other people's money (O.P.M.); 2) Non-disclosure of loans to executives to feed 3) A high and mighty lifestyle that required ever more money; 4) Altering the company books to report increased earnings through "creative accounting," to keep investors buying the stock. Finally, the house of cards collapsed. It was, of course, neither ethical nor Biblical.

What's it all mean? For me, it confirms what St. Paul wrote to the church at Rome: *"All have sinned and fall short of the glory of God."* It reaffirms my belief that truly we can put our trust only in God.

PRAYER: We see from the current scandals that sin is still rampant in the world, no matter what we call it to sugar-coat it. Help us always to put our trust in You, O Lord, and not in frail humans. AMEN.

SEPTEMBER 16

HOW SHOULD WE PRAY?

(Scripture to ponder: Romans 8:26)

As I witnessed the shocking and ghastly unfolding of the terrorist attack on the World Trade Center Towers, a whole host of emotions arose within me—as I am sure happened to many other Christians who saw the horrors play out on television. Denial, disbelief, anger and rage welled up within me.

At such times, amid the rush of emotions, it's hard to know what to pray. For surely in the Psalms, we see formulations of anger and revenge. Our initial response is to want to lash out, to strike back.

But in his letter to the Church at Rome, I think St. Paul speaks of another response. In our selection from chapter eight, he says,

"We do not know how we ought to pray, but the Spirit himself intercedes for us with sighs too deep for words."

In such agonizing moments we must simply let go; in the face of such tragedy, acknowledging that we indeed don't know how we should pray, we simply let the Spirit pray through us.

I believe that's what Jesus did, as St. Luke records in chapter 22. As He knelt in the Garden of Gethsemane the night before His death, He prayed in great anguish, and He gave himself over to God's will.

PRAYER: In times of tragedy and loss, Dear Lord, we know not how we should pray, and we ask Your Spirit to intercede for us. AMEN.

SEPTEMBER 17

COMING TO GET THE FOOD

(Scripture to ponder: John 6:25–27)

Much of my professional life has been spent teaching medicine and surgery. I was involved in bedside teaching, in giving lectures and planning conferences. One year, as chairman of the hospital cancer committee, I led a discussion among my colleagues about how we could increase attendance at our weekly cancer conference. I was struck by what one of the older physicians suggested to induce the interns and residents to come to the conferences. He said, **"Be sure to have the conference over a meal—serve some good food and they'll show up—if not to hear the message, they'll come to get fed."** We followed his advice and, sure enough, attendance improved. Afterward I wondered how many came to get instruction, and how many just to get food.

It reminded me of what Jesus says in today's scripture:

"The truth of the matter is that you want to be with me because I fed you, not because you believe in me."

The crowds had followed Jesus across the Sea of Tiberius from the place where he'd miraculously fed the five thousand. Jesus said they came after him because they wanted to be fed—they wanted bread—but Jesus wanted to give them bread from heaven, namely *himself*. But, alas, they couldn't accept him as God's son: they saw only the son of Mary and Joseph.

Although Jesus fed the crowds, multiplying the five loaves and two small fish, he was anxious that they—and he's anxious that we, too—hear and digest his words, for they are spirit and life. Jesus wants us to feed on him, that is, to believe on him, that he is the Son of God.

PRAYER: **Feed us, O Lord, with the spiritual food of your body and blood, that we man believe you are truly the Son of God, the Savior of Mankind. Help us always do your will. AMEN.**

SEPTEMBER 18

THE UNFORGIVING NAIL

(Scripture to ponder: 1 John 2:1–2)

When I was a college student I worked as a carpenter's apprentice. One day when knocking down a stud, I hit my left thumb a terrific blow with my hammer and immediately developed a large, painful bruise beneath the nail. Although the doctor drilled a hole in the nail to release the blood under pressure, there was irreparable damage to the nail bed. I was left with a wave-like, unsightly scar in the nail.

Later as a surgical resident, when I found out there was no way to fix or restore the original flatness of the nail, I jokingly labeled it "my unforgiving nail," for it was forever damaged and scarred. I was told that nobody—not even the most skilled of plastic surgeons—could restore it.

I have made a few mistakes in my life and have suffered a few other, non-physical scars. But I am full of joy that there is forgiveness through Jesus Christ. In Him there is no such thing as being unforgiven. In today's Scripture the Apostle John says:

"If we sin, we have an advocate with the Father, Jesus Christ, the Righteous, and He is the propitiation for our sins, and not for ours only, but also for the sins of the whole world."

Through confession and forgiveness, He can restore us to wholeness. With our God, there is no such thing as an unforgiving nail.

PRAYER: Dear Lord, we praise you that You forgive our sins against others and against You, if we but come and ask. AMEN.

SEPTEMBER 19

ENCOURAGEMENT

(Scripture to ponder: Acts 13:46–52)

Alexander Solzhenitsyn, the Nobel prize winning novelist, tells of time he spent in the Gulag, the dreaded Russian prison camps. He was doing forced labor and was starving. Exhausted and despairing, he determined to end his life by non-cooperation with the authorities. That day he was cold and weak as he was herded out to a work detail. He resolved to fall down and not get up, even if he were beaten to death.

As he slumped and fell out of line, one of the guards yelled and approached with a whip. Another prisoner marched past, and with the handle of his shovel made the sign of the Cross in the snow. Solzhenitsyn realized he was not alone, and with that encouragement he gained strength and heart to keep going. That Hope, offered by a fellow prisoner, was a turning point in his life.

To be an *encourager* is to manifest one of the most blessed Christian attributes. Such a one was Barnabas, St. Paul's companion on his missionary voyages, whose name means, literally, Son of Encouragement.

How does one become an encourager? By getting out of one's self, by listening to and befriending other people.

A story is told of the two famous English Parliamentarians, William Gladstone and Benjamin Disraeli. It's said that Queen Victoria once had dinner with each of them on consecutive evenings. After dining with Gladstone, she remarked, "**I felt as though he was the smartest man in the world.**" But after spending the evening with Disraeli, she said, "**I thought *I* was the cleverest woman in the world!**" One man talked about himself, to display his knowledge; the other had drawn *her* out.

PRAYER: **Help us, Dear Lord, to be encouragers of those around us, befriending and lifting them up. Through Jesus Christ we pray. AMEN.**

SEPTEMBER 20

REJOICING IN THE RIGHT

(Scripture to ponder: 1 Corinthians 13: 4–6)

In his famous Hymn to Love in the 13th chapter of his Letter to the Corinthians, St. Paul says: *"Love does not rejoice in the wrong, but rejoices in the right."* It's our selection for today.

Pick up any daily newspaper in the country and odds are you will find much "rejoicing in the wrong"—accounts of lawbreaking, crime and evil. Publishers, editors and reporters appear to rejoice in printing all that is wrong with society, for it is what they call "*the News*," and it sells newspapers.

But as Christians we are called to a vastly higher standard. We are, to use St. Paul's phrase, "*to rejoice in the right.*" Jesus in the Beatitudes *[Matthew 5:6]* said, *"Blessed are those who hunger and thirst after righteousness"*—that is, those who long for the right, not the wrong to prevail—*"for they shall be filled."*

Similarly, in another contrast with the news media, St. Paul urges us to think on those things that are beautiful and true and of good report. *"Fill your mind with good things,"* he counsels in his Letter to the Philippians. *[Philippians 4:8]*

What a difference it would make if we all would follow the teachings of Christ and of St. Paul., if we would hunger after righteousness and fill our mind with good things! Let us always rejoice in the Right!

PRAYER:　　Dear Heavenly Father, help us fill our minds with good things so that in loving our neighbor we may rejoice in what is right. We ask through your son, Jesus Christ our Lord. AMEN.

SEPTEMBER 21

SUBMISSION

(Scriptures to ponder: Ruth 1:16)

I have some friends—Christian friends—who bristle at the word *submission*. I think they interpret it as meaning being under someone else's thumb, being subject to or a slave of another person's will. Certainly in the English language, the word *submit* has some overtones of that, and in modern America we don't believe in the concept of feudal fealty. That is as it should be.

But as our Scripture selections for today reveal, in the dedicated Christian life there's another meaning of *submission*, one that's crucial to understand and to incorporate into our lives if we're to fully know God's will for us.

Submission in that context means aligning our will to do the will of another, of taking on someone else's values and acting on them, rather than asserting our own independence.

Ruth was submissive when she chose to stay with her mother-in-law Naomi, who was the widow of the Israelite Elimelech. Ruth was not a Jew, she was a Moabite, but because she chose to stay with Naomi, Ruth came to the attention of Elimelech's kinsman, Boaz, who loved her because of her devotion to Naomi. Their son, the offspring of their marriage, was Obed, who became the grandfather of King David.

Similarly, the submissive obedience of Samuel in the Old Testament *[1 Samuel 1:9–10]* and of Mary in the New Testament *[Luke 1:37–38]* resulted in their being greatly used of God, Samuel as a prophet and Mary as the Mother of our Lord.

What do you suppose would have happened if either one of them had balked or refused?

PRAYER: Help us be willing to will Your Will, O Lord, so we may serve you, that Your Kingdom may come. AMEN.

SEPTEMBER 22

LISTENING WITH OUR HEART

(Scripture to ponder: Luke 17:20–21)

When movie director George Lucas put together his *Star Wars* series, he was quite aware of its spiritual overtones. It's apparent in the struggle of the good of The Force against the evil represented by Darth Vader. In one memorable scene, ObeWan Kenobe is teaching young Luke Skywalker how to use his light saber. The old warrior urges his protégée to let go, to follow his intuition, not his reason.

We, too, often seek answers using our deductive reasoning powers instead of using our intuition. Spiritual discernment most often comes when we listen with our *hearts* rather than our heads. The eighteenth century Jesuit cleric Pierre de Caussade, wrote of the way monks perceive God's will:

Their hearts tell them what God desires. They have only to listen to the promptings of their hearts to interpret his will in the existing circumstances. God's plans, disguised as they are, reveal themselves to us through intuition rather than through our reason. [32]

Our Scripture selection gives Christ's reply when his disciples asked about when the Kingdom of God would begin:

"The Kingdom of God isn't ushered in with visible signs. You won't be able to say, 'It has begun here in this place or there in that part of the country.' The Kingdom of God is within you."

[Luke 17:20–21, TLB]

If we listen with our heart, we will hear the voice of the master within.

PRAYER: Help us listen with our hearts to hear your voice within, that we may do your will and help your kingdom to come. AMEN.

SEPTEMBER 23

THE TONGUE AS A FIRE

(Scripture to ponder: James 3:5–10)

In The summer of 2002 the American West experienced some terrible forest fires. Dry conditions rendered the National Forests in Colorado and Arizona especially at risk, and two fires broke out which became two of the largest ever recorded, consuming thousands of acres of trees and forcing hundreds of people from their homes.

Now it happens that forest fires are often natural phenomena, touched off by lightening from summer thunderstorms. But the two huge fires in Colorado and Arizona this summer were not caused by nature. Each was deliberately set by a Forest Service employee, and each caused untold grief.

In today's Scripture the Apostle James exclaims,

"How great a forest is set ablaze by a small fire."

James goes on to liken the tongue to a fire. It's perhaps the smallest member of our bodies, yet what destruction it can produce.

When I consider the power of the tongue to stir passions, I think of the way two statesmen—Hitler and Churchill—used oratory to stir the passions of their people. The historian John Lukacs has likened the contest between Germany and Great Britain to a duel between their leaders, in which the chosen weapons were words. [33] With his tongue, Hitler whipped the German Volk to a frenzy of passion and hatred, while with *his* oratory, Winston Churchill inspired courage and endurance to his island race during the Battle of Britain, when London was being consumed by the inferno of the Blitz. Two tongues, one used for evil, one for good.

PRAYER: We know the tongue can both inflame and bless. Help us always to bless and edify others by speaking the truth in love. In Jesus' name we pray. AMEN.

SEPTEMBER 24

A PEBBLE IN MY BOOT

(Scripture to ponder: James 3:3–5)

I went out hiking in the desert the other day. Usually I fold my sox down over my boots to prevent any pebbles from getting in. I guess I forgot, or the sox worked up, for coming down a sandy slope something got in between the sock and the boot. At first I felt just a slight rub, but as it worked its way down under my heel, I felt pain, which steadily got worse as I hiked.

I was forced at last to take off my boot and shake it out. With all the discomfort I'd had, I thought I'd find a rock as big as a pea. But it was a tiny pebble, scarcely larger than a grain of sand. Yet it had caused great distress.

The Apostle James tells a similar story in today's Scripture selection. He warns us about the tongue:

We can make a large horse turn around and go wherever we want by means of a small bit in his mouth . . . so also the tongue is a small thing, but what enormous damage it can do!

Just as a tiny pebble under a sock can cause great distress, so the tongue, a small organ, can be the cause of great grief.

PRAYER: **Help us to curb and control our tongue, that what comes out of our mouth may lift others up and glorify You, Dear Lord. AMEN.**

SEPTEMBER 25

WHY THE GUN IN CHURCH?

(Scripture to ponder: James 1:19)

I had a comeuppance recently. I had planned an overnight hike and would miss the Sunday service at my church, so I attended the Saturday afternoon service. I usually go to the eight o'clock Sunday service so I didn't recognize anyone on Saturday.

When it came time for greeting and passing the Peace, I turned to greet the man in the pew behind me. As I extended my hand, before I could say hello, he pointed to a black, leather pouch on my belt and said sharply, **"Why the gun in church?"**

I was taken aback. I smiled and said it was a Swiss Army Knife, unsnapping its cover to show it. He mumbled something but he did not take my hand.

For a few minutes after the incident, as the service continued, I pondered what had happened, and wondered how often I had mistaken or misinterpreted someone else, or had judged them prematurely. Not rarely, I suspect.

In our Scripture passage for today, St. James urges us to *"Be swift to hear but slow to speak."* As someone once remarked, not merely in jest, God gave us two ears and two eyes, but only one mouth, so we should look and listen before we speak.

PRAYER: Help us, O Lord, always to see the best in others and not jump to judgment. AMEN.

SEPTEMBER 26

IS MONEY THE ROOT OF ALL EVIL?

(Scripture to ponder: 1 Timothy 6:9–10)

On several occasions I've heard folks say that money is the root of all evil. Once I asked a person who made that statement if he knew where it came from. He said the Bible. It does indeed come from the Bible, but he had *misquoted* scripture.

The words are St. Paul's, written to Timothy, in his first letter. It is our scripture verse for today. Paul writes:

But they that will be rich fall into temptation and a snare, and into many foolish and hurtful lusts, which drown men in destruction and perdition. For the love of money is the root of all evil.

So it's not money, per se, that is evil. Money is merely a medium of exchange for goods and services. It is *love of money*—that is, *cupidity* or *greed*—that's the root of evil of which Paul speaks.

Money, in itself, can do much good. With it we can purchase the necessities of life, and using it we can help meet the needs of others. But if our goal is to grasp for more and more money, that indeed is greed, and is a root of evil.

PRAYER: Help us O Lord, to see that it is the love of money that is evil. Help us love only You, and spend our money wisely to further Your kingdom and to help others. In Jesus' Name we pray, AMEN.

SEPTEMBER 27

LETTING THE BIRDS NEST

(Scripture to ponder: Proverbs 5:15–23)

Recently, while working on a Habitat for Humanity project sponsored by our church, I was nailing in place the little headers that had small holes in them to allow ventilation under the eves. Back of each hole was a piece of screen, to prevent birds and insects from entering and building nests.

I was reminded of a time in my life when I was struggling with sexual temptation. I consulted my pastor, who listened intently to my story and then remarked, "There's an old saying: You cannot keep the birds from flying overhead, but you can keep them from building a nest in your hair."

The pastor went on to elaborate that although our thought life is important—and God does see into the heart, he remarked as well, our *actions* are equally important. Self-control, whether it be of our eating habits, our anger, or our acts, is often an issue of controlling our *actions*, is spite of our desires. And our actions are under the control of our will. He suggested I read today's Scripture selection.

Purity of Heart, said Kierkegard, is *to will* one thing: obedience to God.

PRAYER: Dear Lord, when we struggle with our desires, help us to will to do your Will and follow Your Law and example. Give us the strength to resist temptation, and deliver us from evil. AMEN.

SEPTEMBER 28

MOTHER'S INDOMITABLE SPIRIT

(Scripture to ponder: Galatians 5:22–23)

While reading the other day, I encountered a quote by the French poet Paul Claudel, who on his eightieth birthday, wrote in his diary:

Eighty years old. No eyes left. No ears, no teeth, no legs, no wind, and, when all is said and done, one does without them.

I thought at once of my mother, who died two weeks after her one hundredth birthday. She lived in a life-care facility near Philadelphia. Throughout her long life, she was a most gracious person, whose indomitable spirit always was an inspiration to me. It was hard to watch her decline physically over the years. But in spite of eyesight severely impaired by macular degeneration and markedly diminished hearing, her spirit remained undaunted.

For her 80th birthday I composed a sonnet for her based on Saint Paul's letter to the Galatians (Our Scripture selection for today), in which he describes the fruit of the spirit, which throughout her life, she personified so well:

For the fruit of the Spirit is love, joy, peace, patience, kindness, goodness, faithfulness, gentleness and self-control.

In spite of declining strength and failing eyesight and hearing, mother soldiered on, cheerful and appreciative, seeing always the bright side of life. She, within a body that was steadily declining, was proof of Christ's words,

"It is the Spirit that gives Life."

[John 6:63]

PRAYER: We praise You, O Lord, for the gift of the Spirit that quickens our mortal bodies. Though they decline with age, Through You we have Eternal Life. AMEN.

SEPTEMBER 29

THE EMPEROR'S NEW WINE

(Scripture to ponder: Ephesians 5:18)

I spent my last two years of high school at a New England prep school. In the fall of my first year I was invited to a special "corridor party" with a number of fellow students. It was special occasion because it involved the uncorking of a gallon jug of cider into which, a few weeks earlier, one of the boys had placed raisins and some yeast. It was, of course, breaking the rules and was done in secret.

When I entered the room the cork had already been popped and several boys were imbibing the cider in paper cups, behaving quite tipsy. They passed me some, which I drank. It had a sharp taste, which I recognized. But no one else seemed to realize what the taste meant, and they all acted drunk.

Probably it was because I'd had science the year before and knew about the fermentation reaction, which starts with sugar (from the raisins) and produces first alcohol, and then goes on, if not stopped, to produce *vinegar*. My friends were downing vinegar, believing it to be alcohol, and were acting accordingly.

When I watch the commercials on T.V. nowadays, I'm reminded of that experience from high school.

How often advertisers try to convince us that their products are the real stuff—keys to lasting happiness—when they really are poor imitations, perhaps turning sour later! Rather than accept their vinegar, let us seek and obtain the pure wine of the Gospel, that our lives may be fulfilled.

PRAYER: Give us the gift of discernment, Dear Lord, that we may recognize your true new wine. AMEN.

SEPTEMBER 30

SPANGLED HEAVENS

(Scripture to ponder: Psalm 8)

I recently went out into the superstition wilderness east of Phoenix for an overnight hike. I hiked for about two hours and then camped on a large, flat rock near a babbling brook. It was about 85 degrees while I was hiking, but as soon as the sun set it cooled off rather quickly. As night approached, I blew up my air mattress and lay on my back in my down sleeping bag, gazing up at the heavens.

Venus was the first heavenly body that became visible, almost an hour before darkness was complete. I was far enough from the city so there was no glow from city lights to diminish the brightness of the stars as they came out.

I slept out under the stars and awoke about every two hours to see the progress of the Big Dipper, which slowly turned with the earth's motion. I was camped in a ravine, and the pole star was just above the horizon.

What a splendid night it was, cool and calm. As I gazed upward I was reminded of the hymn, "The Spacious Firmament on High" with its second line, "And spangled heavens, a shining frame, their great original proclaim." It also brought to mind the words of our Scripture selection:

When I consider thy heavens, the work of thy fingers, the moon and the stars, which thou has ordained, what is man, that thou art mindful of him? And the son of man, that thou visitest him?

God has given us dominion over all of His wondrous creation! And incarnate in Jesus, He has visited us!

PRAYER: **Thank you O Lord, for the marvelous heavens that declare Your glory, and the firmament that shows Your handiwork. We praise and love You, that You are mindful of us! AMEN.**

OCTOBER 1

PERSUASION . . . OR PAIN?

(Scripture to ponder: Exodus 19:26)

I go to the dentist about twice a year. For the last six visits he has urged me to have my wisdom teeth taken out—they aren't badly impacted, but the space around the gums is tight and forms pockets where small particles of food can lodge and fester.

I've so far put off the decision to follow his advice, hoping to get by with more regular flossing and brushing.

But what could not be achieved by *persuasion* has been effected by *pain!* A few days ago I began to have a toothache in my lower right wisdom tooth. I brushed and flossed harder, but the pain persisted and got a bit worse. I made a date with my dentist, who again recommended dealing with my wisdom teeth. This time I followed his advice.

PERSUASION or *PAIN?* As humans we often and repeatedly face the choice. When the Children of Israel were on their Exodus journey in the wilderness, God gave them the same options (our Scripture selection for today):

If thou wilt diligently hearken to the voice of the Lord thy God and will do that which is right in his sight and wilt give ear to his commandments and keep all his statutes, I will put none of those diseases upon thee which I have brought upon the Egyptians: for I am the Lord that healeth thee.

For having all my "wisdom" teeth, I wasn't very good at following sound advice, was I? I suspect I don't always heed the good advice that the Lord gives us in the scriptures, either.

PRAYER: Dear Lord, we know that true health and happiness are gifts from you. Help us always to do your will and follow your word. AMEN.

OCTOBER 2

LEAVING THINGS UNDONE

(Scripture to ponder: 1 John 2:1–3)

My wife and I are fortunate to have a home near Philadelphia, where we grew up, and a condominium in Phoenix, where I practiced surgery before I retired. We spend summers in Pennsylvania and winters in Arizona.

In mid February one year, when we were in Arizona, I had to come back to see my mother who had been hospitalized. I arrived in the evening and stopped off at out home to turn on the heat and the water, then went directly to see her. When I returned to the darkened house I noticed, on closing one of the window drapes, that several small picture frames on the windowsill had been knocked off on to the floor. I wondered if we'd been robbed.

But there was no sign of a forced entry, and nothing was disturbed in the house. But in looking around, I found a large, dead gray squirrel on the floor in the den. And in the living room I found a decorative brass fan in the fireplace was knocked over. The damper was open. It was apparent that when we left Pennsylvania after spending the Christmas holidays with our families, I left the chimney damper open. I ought to have closed it, and if I'd done it, perhaps the squirrel would have scampered back up the chimney and not have been trapped in the house where he died.

I should have shut the damper before we left the house in January. I was reminded of the words of the *General Confession*:

> *We have done those things we ought not to have done and We have left undone those things we ought to have done . . .*

How often I do things I should not, or leave other things undone! But thanks be to God: as our scripture selection for today indicates, we have an advocate with the Father for the forgiveness of sin. Praise God, we can confess our sins and be forgiven. In Him we will have Eternal Life, not death.

PRAYER: We often sin by leaving things undone, or by doing things we shouldn't do. We ask your forgiveness, Lord. AMEN.

OCTOBER 3

THE ESSENCE OF THE GOSPEL

(Scripture to ponder: Matthew 25:31–40)

How would you respond if you were asked to state the essence of the Gospel? I suspect the late Mother Theresa would have replied, "**The essence of the Gospel is to love the unlovable.**" That mission characterized her way of life and brought solace, comfort and relief to thousands of the poor and helpless around the world.

Our pastor recently told a relevant story, one related by the noted children's television host, Mr. Rogers, who sounded a similar note when he told this account at graduation exercises at a California college. During a Special Olympics held in Seattle, there were nine participants in the 100 yard dash. As they all got off at the starting gun, one young man was struggling to run, then stumbled and fell, skinning his knee. He sat on the track and began to cry, holding his leg.

Another runner in the race, a small girl with Down's syndrome, turned back, ran up to him, kissed his knee, and said it would soon be all better. The other racers turned back, too, and then all of them linked arms and walked across the finish line, as if to say to the spectators, "**It's not so important that we win the race, as that we all finish together.**"

Christ calls us to minister unto and to love the unlovable. In the parable of the Last Judgment, related in today's scripture from the twenty-fifth chapter of Matthew's Gospel, the Lord Jesus says:

"If you have done it unto the least of these my brethren, you have done it unto me."

PRAYER: Through your Holy Spirit, O Lord, grant us the ability and the desire to love the unlovable of this world, that we may do Your Will and further Your Kingdom. AMEN.

OCTOBER 4

GROWING IN LIKENESS

(Scripture to ponder: Ephesians 4:15)

In our Scripture passage for today, St. Paul urges us to grow up into the likeness of Christ. But just how do we do that?

Have you ever noticed how children tend to mimic or imitate the adults they see around them? It is one of the most common ways that we learn as we grow up. What is true in daily life is also true in the spiritual life as well. We need to read about Jesus with a child's trust.

When a professional actor seeks to portray a historical character, he first studies the life of that person, immersing himself deeply by assimilating all the available information about the one he wishes to emulate. He learns all about the attributes and habits and characteristics of the one he will model and by practice, consciously takes them on.

Likewise, if we would take on the attributes of Jesus, we must study Him by becoming utterly familiar with his life and his teachings as found in the New Testament, particularly the Gospels, and incorporate Him into our lives.

One of the most famous devotional books was written by the XV century monk, Thomas à Kempis. Its title is *The Imitation of Christ.* In it the saint shows us how to draw near to God and reflect His Love in our lives. The book reflects à Kempis' utter familiarity with the Scriptures and reading it is an excellent way to deepen our understanding of the Lord Jesus Christ. It's an excellent companion to the Bible.

PRAYER: **Help us, O Lord, to be imitators of your son Jesus Christ, that we may grow into his likeness and do Your will on earth. AMEN.**

OCTOBER 5

PRODUCTIVE BRANCHES

(Scripture to ponder: John 15:1–4)

One summer my wife and I visited Switzerland. As we took the cog railway from Brig to Zermatt through steep alpine meadows, we passed through a small village. Out the train window we saw orchards near the tracks. The apple trees had been carefully pruned so that they were laden with fruit. Many of the branches bore scores of apples and were arched out from the trunk, gracefully lowering their burden of fruit almost to the ground.

When I was a boy we had an apple tree in our back yard. It was not well-pruned and did not bear much fruit. By comparison, the Swiss apple trees, which were carefully pruned, produced several times as much fruit as ours had.

Jesus speaks of the pruning that God does in our lives. God causes those who are his own to be more productive by careful pruning. The branches that are cut back in pruning a tree or a vine will wither and die, but the remaining branches grow stronger and bear more fruit.

PRAYER: Thank You, O lord, that you have chosen us to bear fruit. Help us cheerfully and gladly bear pruning so we may become more productive for Your kingdom. AMEN.

OCTOBER 6

HAPPINESS AND TEARS

(Scripture to ponder: Psalm 13)

Do you remember the song from *Fiddler on the Roof,* "Sunrise, Sunset?" It's sung at the wedding of one of Tevye's daughters, and its refrain sums up the whole play:

Sunrise, sunset, sunrise, sunset, Swiftly fly the years; One season following another Laden with happiness and tears.

It's also a reflection of life itself, which has happiness mingled with tears, joys mixed with sorrows.

The Scripture for today is one of the Psalms of Lament, a form of psalm usually involving four parts: a complaint to God; a call for help; an affirmation of trust; and a vow to praise. The psalmist fears that God has forgotten him, and calls on the Lord for help, lest his enemies prevail over him. It concludes with an affirmation of trust in God and praise for His bountiful provision. It reflects feelings we all have, at times.

We know life is composed of joy and tears. When sorrow and defeat come, we need to remind ourselves of God's ongoing mercy and love.

The contemporary writer Ellie Wiesel tells [34] of a young Jew who struggled with many questions about the evil in the world. Consulting his rabbi, he was told to go study the Torah and the Talmud, which he did. But answers eluded him. Hearing that a famous rabbi was to speak in a faraway city, the young man journeyed to hear him. As he sat in the audience, though he knew it couldn't be so, it seemed the rabbi was looking right at him, speaking directly to him. After the message, he joined in the prayers and the praise of the fellow believers.

After he came home someone asked if he'd found any answers. He replied,

"My questions have remained questions, but somehow, now I can go on."

PRAYER: Dear Lord, we have many questions about the evil in the world for which we have no answers. But when we trust and praise You, we get strength to go on. Thank You for your blessings. AMEN.

OCTOBER 7

LOOK UP—AND LIVE!

(Scripture to ponder: Exodus 14:28–29)

When I read the today's account of the wanderings of the Children of Israel in the desert after the Exodus and before the entry into the Promised Land, one thing struck me: The people were constantly complaining! They complained there was no water. They complained about the mana that God sent to nourish them. When spies were sent into Canaan, ten of the twelve sent out complained about the size and might of the Canaanites. The people grumbled against Moses and against God, so much that God vowed that the generation who left Egypt would never see the Promised Land.

Because of their constant complaining the Lord sent lethal fiery serpents among the people. Many of them were bitten and died. When the people repented of their sin of anger and ingratitude, God had Moses make a bronze serpent and lift it up on a pole, so that anyone who had been bitten could look upon it and live.

It is significant that God did not take away the lethal serpents, but rather provided an escape for the people who had been bit.

In the New Testament, when Jesus is talking to Nicodemus, he alludes to the serpent that Moses lifted up:

And as Moses lifted up the serpent in the wilderness, even so must the Son of Man be lifted up: that whosoever believeth in him should not perish but have everlasting life.
[John 3:1–21]

It's instructive: God does not take sin out of the world—we must live in an imperfect and sinful world—but He provides a way to survive. We are to look at Jesus lifted up: believing in him, we have salvation and eternal life.

PRAYER: **In the midst of this sinful world we praise you, Lord; for we can look up to Jesus, who gives us eternal life. AMEN.**

OCTOBER 8

JOHN THE BAPTIST

(Scripture to ponder: John 1:6–18)

Really great men have a curious feeling that the greatness is not in them, but through them.—Ruskin

As I look at the life of John the Baptist as recorded in the Gospels, I am struck not only by his forcefulness, but also by his humility. Although he was being praised by the masses as a prophet, he always knew that greatness was not in him; rather it was *through* him. To those who hailed him, he continually pointed to Jesus, saying another was coming, one whose sandals he was unworthy to untie. When the two met on the banks of the Jordan River, where John was baptizing, John protested that it was *Jesus* who rather should be baptizing *him*. But Jesus insisted that John baptize him, *"to fulfill all righteousness."* *[Matthew 3:15]* As John was obedient and proceeded to baptize the Christ, he saw the heavens open and the Spirit of God descend on Jesus, and heard a voice from heaven proclaim, *"This is my beloved son in whom I am well pleased." [Matthew 3:17]*

If we, like John, can resist the temptations all around us, the voices of advertising and the media, that proclaim that we are masters of all and are all-deserving, if we can resist their siren-song and put ourselves in proper perspective before God, we too will hear His voice.

PRAYER: **In our lives, dear Lord, may we always show, like John the Baptist, that we must decrease that You may increase and be glorified through us. AMEN.**

OCTOBER 9

IS THERE A DIFFERENCE?

(Scripture to ponder John 3:1–22)

Pollster George Gallup has determined that a majority of Americans believe that Christ rose from the dead and is a living presence today. But he also discovered from his extensive research that there was little difference in ethical *behavior* between the churched and the unchurched. He found as much pilferage and dishonesty among Christians as among non-Christians. There appeared to be little difference between the two groups. It appears that for many, religion is not really life-changing.

What did the Lord Jesus have to say about this, about the need for change? In our Scripture selection for today, he asserted to Nicodemus—who was one of the pillars of the synagogue—that he needed to be born again. Nicodemus didn't understand, supposing Christ meant he'd once again have to enter his mother's womb. But Jesus explained that one is born again through water—that is, through baptism—and the Spirit, that is, through regeneration by the Spirit of God, when we acknowledge Jesus as Lord and Savior.

As Christians we confess our imperfections and recognize the role of sin in our lives, and we ask forgiveness of God. That acknowledgement—that sin exists, and that Jesus is Lord—distinguishes us. Through the Holy Spirit, it can be life-changing.

PRAYER: We do acknowledge our sinfulness, O Lord, and call upon Your grace and forgiveness for our salvation. AMEN.

OCTOBER 10

CONVERSING WITH GOD

(Scripture to ponder: John Chapter 9)

"We know that God does not listen to sinners; but if anyone is God-fearing and a worshiper of Him and does His will, He listens to him."

[John 9:31]

Those words were spoken by the man born blind, whose sight Jesus restored, described in our selection for today. The fellow was being interrogated by the Pharisees. Those stuffy leaders had already questioned his parents, and were not satisfied with the answers they got. So they quizzed the man himself. He confounded them with his answer. He said that *Jesus had to be of God, or he could not have done such a miracle as bringing vision to a man who was born blind*. The Pharisees were so mad, they cast him out.

But this man, who had newly received his sight, had great insight. He gives us the key to conversing with God, to a fruitful prayer life, namely, *God listens to those who fear and worship Him and who seek to do His will*.

If it seems that God is not listening to you, there may be an answer in the counsel of the man born blind. Ask yourself several questions. Is there is any sin in your life? Are you fearing God and worshiping Him? Do you seek to do his will? Scripture does not lie. Following its precepts will put you in touch with God.

PRAYER: Help us to confess to You our sins and reverently worship You and do Your will, that our prayers may be heard. AMEN.

OCTOBER 11

WHAT DOES IT TAKE TO BELIEVE?

(Scripture to ponder: Matthew 16:1–4)

You've probably heard the expression "**It made a believer out of me!**" which usually refers to some memorable or traumatic experience. It's apparent that different folks require different levels of proof before they will believe.

In today's Scripture verse, the Pharisees and Sadducees came to Jesus seeking proof he was the Messiah. They asked for a sign from heaven. Can't you just hear Christ as he mocks them, quoting the age-old jingle, "**Red sky in morning, sailors take warning / Red sky at night, sailors delight,**" saying they were adept at reading the signs in the sky, but couldn't interpret the *signs of the times*. He said the only sign he'd give them was the sign of Jonah. He was referring to his resurrection, of course: Just as Jonah was in the belly of the fish for three days, so Jesus would be three days in the earth before he rose from the dead.

Later, when his disciples asked him about signs of the end times, he mentioned wars and rumors of wars and famines and earthquakes *[Matthew 24:3–8]*—signs we're seeing in our own times—but he said even then, that was not the end. It raises two questions: First, **Just when will Jesus return?** And Second, **Just what does it take for us to believe?**

To answer the first, Christ said *no one knows except God.*

Regarding the second question, after the resurrection, Christ told Thomas (who required the hard physical evidence of seeing and feeling his wounds): *"Blessed are those who have not seen, and yet believe."* We are indeed blessed if we believe in the Lord Jesus, even though we have not seen him in the flesh.

PRAYER: In this confused, complex world, we cry out to You, O Lord, as did the man who brought his son to be healed: *"We believe; help Thou our unbelief!"[Mark 9:24]* Give us discernment to interpret the signs of the times, to do Your will and work toward Your Kingdom, as we await your glorious return. AMEN.

OCTOBER 12

SLIPPING INTO SIN

(Scripture to ponder: Jeremiah 17:9)

As a college freshman, I had three rather noisy roommates, so I chose to study in the library, which was situated next door to our dorm. I discovered in the secluded library stacks there were study carrels. A few of these had some books and belongings in them, but most did not, and some even had doors that locked.

I found an empty cubicle where I could leave my books and began to study there regularly. But so far as I could tell, the lock had no key. So to protect my books, and to insure I'd have the carrel to myself, I did a very simple thing: I unscrewed the lock tumbler, took it downtown and had a key made. For several weeks I enjoyed my private "study hall."

One day I went over to "my" study carrel to prepare for an exam and found it locked as usual, but this time my key didn't work. Moreover, looking over the top of the partition, I saw my books were gone. I went down to the librarian's office and made inquiry.

My books had been impounded. I was indignant and angry. The librarian called me in and told me that the stack carrels were only for graduate students and that I had done something very wrong. The upshot was I got suspended from college for a week. I had seven days at home to think about what I'd done.

On reflection, I realized I'd been wrong, but each step of the way had been so subtle, and my rationalizations had been so smooth that I didn't really think I was doing wrong as went along. I just slipped into it. Of course the administration at Wesleyan didn't see it that way.

So it is with sin. We can easily just slip into it, excusing and explaining it away to ourselves. But it's still sin and still wrong.

PRAYER: **Make us ever mindful, Dear Lord, how easily we can slip into sin. Keep us always on the right path. We pray in the name of Jesus. AMEN.**

OCTOBER 13

GOD FOR US, WITH US, IN US

(Scripture to ponder: John 14:18)

If we take an overarching view of the Bible, we can see that God has progressively revealed Himself to man down through history. In the Old Testament, especially in His dealings with Israel and in the Psalms, we see *God for us.* He is our defender and our rock, and we take refuge under his wings.

In the Gospels, Jesus is *Emmanuel, God with us.* The Holy, Almighty One became incarnate in the Lord Jesus Christ. Whereas before, we knew Him from afar, now He has come among us, living our life, walking our paths. Fully divine, fully human, He knows our sorrows and our joys. He is God with us.

And, finally, there is God within us. On his the last night on earth, Jesus spoke the words of our selection for today: *"I will not leave you comfortless."* To be our comforter and our counselor, God sent the Holy Spirit, to fill us and be with us always. He is *God within us.* One of the attributes of God within us is joy. Indeed, the word *enthusiasm* comes from the Greek roots that mean God within us!

PRAYER: **We praise You, O Lord, that you are for us, that You came among us as our savior Jesus Christ, and that Your Holy Spirit fills us and dwells within us, enabling us to do Your Will. AMEN.**

OCTOBER 14

BEING KIND

(Scripture to ponder: Ephesians 4:32)

Over the past few years there has been a series of outbreaks of violence in high schools across the country. The media are full of vivid accounts of the slaughter of classmates by students who appear to be retaliating for being picked on, bullied or ostracized.

The phenomenon is not new; I recall similar incidents from my own high school years. But the stakes are much higher because the means have escalated. In my school it was bare knuckles or a knife. Now it's automatic weapons and handguns.

The violence that permeates our society and the ubiquity of weapons are both contributing factors. But the root cause, I'm convinced, is *a lack of kindness and forgiveness.*

In our Scripture selection for today from St. Paul's Letter to the Church at Ephesus, he gives advice that would stop such violence by preventing it:

Be kind to one another, tenderhearted, forgiving one another, just as God in Christ has also forgiven you.

If kindness instead of bullying ruled the hearts of teens and if forgiveness instead of retribution was the reaction of those picked on to, I believe the slaughter in our schools would end.

PRAYER: Heavenly Father, just as we ask forgiveness in the Lord's Prayer, help us to forgive those who have done us wrong. And help us always to be kind to one another. AMEN.

OCTOBER 15

GOD'S QUICKENING SPIRIT

(Scripture to ponder: Genesis 1:26)

Helen Keller, born deaf, dumb and blind, learned to speak by a tedious process of discovery and practice by her tutor, Miss Annie Sullivan. It's said that when Helen Keller was taught the name of God, she replied, **"I knew Him, but I did not know His name."**

The Bible says we were created in the image of God. We have a body, a mind and a spirit, and the Spirit of the Living God can resonate with our spirit and respond with outpourings of Love.

When we respond in love to the need of our neighbor, God's Spirit is working within us to do His will.

Just as quickening occurs when a woman is pregnant, giving her that first awareness that something is alive within her, so through the Word, the Spirit of God quickens our spirits to help us grow into the likeness of Christ.

PRAYER: We thank you, Lord, that within each of us you have placed the seed of the spirit. Help us to nurture it so we may grow into your likeness. AMEN.

OCTOBER 16

THE PRUDENT MAN

(Scripture to ponder: Proverbs 27:12)

The Proverbs contain many verses that are excellent guides for living. Our Scripture selection for today asserts *"A prudent man sees danger and hides himself; but the simple pass on and are punished.*" I recall a good example of the wisdom of this proverb from my own family.

In the 1960s my brother-in-law was an officer on the aircraft carrier *Saratoga*, where he regularly drew the watch on the bridge. The officer of the deck on the bridge of a naval ship has control of the vessel, and is responsible for all that happens on his watch. When the watch changes, a standard protocol is employed.

Coming on duty, the new officer salutes and calls out, "**I am ready to relieve you, Sir.**" This is acknowledged by the Officer of the Deck, usually by a nod. But control of the vessel is not officially transferred to the new officer until he has said, "**I relieve you, Sir.**" At that point he officially takes the con. Until that happens, the responsibility for the ship remains with the other officer.

One morning, in the waters off Newport News, Virginia, my brother-in-law was scheduled to take the watch. As he arrived on the bridge, he called out, "**I am ready to relieve you, Sir,**" then walked across the bridge and looked out ahead of the ship. Off the port bow a tanker was headed in their direction. Although the two ships weren't exactly on a collision course, he thought he'd best wait until they were past one another to take the con. So he held off saying, "**I relieve you, Sir.**" He stepped to the back of the bridge and just waited until the incident was resolved.

Well, darned if the two ships didn't collide! It was not only an embarrassment for the Officer of the Deck; it led to a Court Martial and ruined his career in the Navy. My brother-in-law, simply by being prudent, was spared much grief, for, officially, he was not in command.

PRAYER: **Your wisdom, O Lord, can truly guide us in this life, if we will but read Your Word and heed its messages. Help us to do this every day. Help us do Your Will. AMEN.**

OCTOBER 17

SPEAKING THE TRUTH

(Scripture to ponder: Ephesians 4:15)

Once, in preparation for a trip to China, I read a book about that vast land written by a knowledgeable author. She was China section head at the British Library. By reading the book I hoped to learn some facts and figures about that country and gain some insight into its people, who comprise about one quarter of the population of the planet. However, I was brought up short in the very beginning of the book .

The introduction began as follows:

Why visit China? The question may seem academic; perhaps you have already decided you want to go there, *because it is there*. When Sir Edmund Hillary was asked why he wanted to climb Mount Everest (which is within China's contemporary boundaries), he answered, "Because it is there . . ."

I thought as I read that, Hmm. I've done some mountain climbing and a lot of reading about mountaineering, and I recognize that quote—**"Because it is there."** That response was actually made by British mountaineer George Mallory, who perished on the slopes of Mount Everest in 1924.

Knowing that fact, and the author's error, undermined my faith in this author as an expert, for she hadn't gotten her facts straight. She wasn't speaking the truth.

It made me wonder about myself and about my own witness for the Lord. How many times do I think I am speaking the truth, when actually I am misquoting? Or how many times do my own selfish actions, observed by others, undermine my claim that I am a Christian? How many times do I fall short of the mark? Yet I want to be a reliable ambassador for Christ. It gave me pause.

PRAYER: **Make us mindful, Dear Lord, of how we come across to others. Keep our actions faithful to our words. Help us always speak the truth in love. AMEN.**

OCTOBER 18

LOVING THE LORD

(Scripture to ponder: Matthew 22:34–40)

Our Scripture selection relates an encounter with the Pharisees. When Jesus was asked by a teacher of Jewish Law, "Which commandment is the first of all?" He replied by quoting the Book of Deuteronomy:

Hear O Israel, the Lord our God is one Lord. Love the Lord your God with all your heart and with all your soul and with all your mind and with all your strength.
[Deuteronomy 6:4–5]

What did Christ mean by his answer? I believe the four aspects that he mentioned—the heart, the soul, the mind and the strength—comprise the totality of a person's being.

To love with all one's heart means to love enthusiastically, imaginatively and sympathetically; to love with all one's soul is to love to the depths of one's inmost spirit; to love with all one's mind is to fully exercise one's intellect; and to love with all one's strength is to love with one's entire body. So, I believe, Christ wants us to love God totally and completely, with all our being.

But Christ did not stop there. He immediately went on to say:

And the second is like unto it: You shall love your neighbor as yourself: on these two commandments hang all the law and the prophets.
[Matthew 22:39–40]

Since the guide for living for a Jew of Jesus' time was the Old Testament, composed of the five Books of Moses (The Law) and the books of prophesy (The Prophets), he was saying that all we need to guide our life is to love God and love our neighbor. By his answer, Christ established the great vertical (toward God) and horizontal (toward our fellow man) axes of human life, which in his own life culminated in the Cross.

PRAYER: Give us the will and the desire and the strength to love you and love our neighbor, Dear Lord, that Your will may be done in our lives. AMEN.

OCTOBER 19

SETTLEING DOWN AT NIGHT

(Scripture to ponder: Psalm 127)

Do you recall the childhood prayer that goes: "**Now I lay me down to sleep, I pray the Lord my soul to keep?**" I suppose most of us moderns would say that prayer has a simplicity that borders on naïveté. But the quiet and innocent handing over of our selves to God's protection is one of the keys to inner peace. And to do it in the simple manner of a child—recalling that Christ said that *"of such is the Kingdom of Heaven" [Matthew 19:14]*—is another key.

How do you settle down at night? I'm sure there are many ways to do it. The well-respected Christian devotional writer Henri Nouwen does it by following a daily lectionary of Bible readings and meditating on them. He comments:

> "**It is often helpful to take one sentence or word that offers special comfort and repeat it a few times, so that, with that one sentence or word, the whole content can be brought to mind and allowed slowly to descend from the mind into the heart.**"

Nouwen's approach makes use of the well-recognized phenomenon that what we read or recite just before sleep, we retain best.

As we settle down for sleep at night it helps to divest ourselves of the cares and worries of the day. At bedtime, thank God for His blessings and mercy, and meditate on a portion of His Word.

PRAYER: Thank you, O Lord, for our daily protection and for the wonderful healing power of Your Word and the marvelous restorative power of restful sleep. AMEN.

OCTOBER 20

BECOMING A SERVANT

(Scripture to ponder: John 13:3–11)

In modern life great emphasis is placed on competition, on being first. In the business world that often means embracing a fierce competitiveness, with phrases like "Look out for Number One!" and "Cover your backside!" being common. It's often been called a "dog eat dog" world.

But Jesus' teaching is that to be true leaders we must become the servant of others:

"Whoever would be first must become last and become a servant of others"
[Matthew 9:35]

One who has truly given his life over to, and is controlled by the Holy Spirit, has been freed from the rat race of the world's competition. That person is freed to do God's will because he knows he is under God's protection and is therefore free to be a servant of others.

The world in which Christ lived and moved, like our own, was stratified. In the lowest stratum were servants who did the menial household tasks such as sweeping and cleaning up. If you went to a friend's house for dinner, you left your sandals at the door, and a servant would wash your feet. It was the most menial of tasks, removing the accumulated dirt and dung from the feet.

Yet Jesus, on the night in which he was betrayed, as described in today's Scripture passage, took a basin and a towel and washed his disciples feet, as an example of what they should be doing for one another and as an example for us of the role of servant.

PRAYER: Help us, O Lord, to worship You in our lives by becoming servants to the world, for the sake of Jesus Christ our Lord. AMEN.

OCTOBER 21

PREPARING FOR DROUGHT

(Scripture to ponder: John 4: 7–30)

I heard recently about a plan that the city of Tucson, AZ, was using to combat drought. Tucson is situated in high desert where the water table drops quickly, particularly in the hot summer season. The city arranged to buy water from Phoenix, and instead of storing it, simply pumped it into the ground, replenishing the water table so that in times of drought it would not run dry.

In a similar way, getting into the habit of reading scripture helps us prepare for arid periods in our lives. The Bible is a marvelous storehouse of wisdom, but it is not always easy to read. Yet by reading it faithfully and regularly, we stow it away in our subconscious. It becomes a vast subterranean resource for our spirit to draw on in times of spiritual dryness. As our selection for today notes, if we drink of the water that Christ provides, we will thirst no more.

(Parenthetically, I don't like the taste of Phoenix water. The people of Tucson discovered that once Phoenix water got filtered by passing through their water table, it had the same good taste as their own water!)

PRAYER: **Give us grace to spend time regularly reading your Word, that it may give us wisdom and strength in dry periods, and sweeten the dull taste of much that we read and hear in everyday life. AMEN.**

OCTOBER 22

SAVORLESS SALT CAN BE A SMILE

(Scripture to ponder: Matthew 5:13)

Biblical expositors, when dealing with the segment of Matthew in which Jesus calls his followers 'the salt of the earth,' often talk about two properties of salt for which it was used in the ancient world. These are its ability to add flavor and zest to food, and its use as a preservative for food. Christ says that if salt has lost its savor, it's good for nothing, but is to be cast out, to be trodden under men's feet.

Over my lifetime I've heard several preachers declare that Christians are to add zest and flavor to life or how they can act as preservers of sacred traditions for society, and thereby act as salt, in the manner in which Christ means, when in today's selection he calls us the salt of the earth.

That makes me think of an additional use for salt that Christ did not mention, perhaps because they rarely get snow in the Holy Land, at least in the towns and cities where he walked.

During the time I attended Medical School, I lived for five years in Rochester, New York. Rochester winters were severe, with lots of snow and ice in the weather coming down off Lake Ontario. Large trucks from the roads department in Rochester spread salt on the streets after storms, to melt the snow and the ice.

I am reminded of this use of salt when I see the effect a smile has on a person who is angry or hostile: it often helps thaw them out, melting chilly emotions, helping making peace where tempers might flare. We Christians can be salt in that way, too.

PRAYER: **As you have proclaimed, Dear Lord, we are indeed the Salt of the Earth. Through our faith, may we add flavor to life, preserve the great traditions of the Church, and melt coldness wherever we find it, as we seek to do your will. AMEN.**

OCTOBER 23

PRAISE FOR THE PRESERVERS

(Scripture to ponder: Acts 1:1–5)

When I spent a weekend on Catalina Island and visited the Botanical Gardens built in memory of William Wrigley, Jr., I was reminded of how much we Americans owe to those who've had the foresight to preserve the natural splendors of our great country.

I had the same feeling of praise and gratitude for the two men who discovered the lovely Karchner Caverns of southern Arizona, who had the patience and prescience to preserve in their pristine state those lovely caves so future generations could see them unscathed.

Likewise, I praise those Saints who took the time and trouble to preserve God's message to man, recorded in the Psalms of David, the Proverbs of Solomon, the Letters of St. Paul and the accounts of the Lord Jesus recorded in the Gospels.

Our Scripture selection for today is the opening of The Acts of the Apostles. St. Luke, who wrote the Gospel of his name, also wrote the exciting book of Acts.

Without these writers, inspired by the Holy Spirit, preserving the traditions and wisdom of the Faith, we would not have the Church as we know it today.

Perhaps the greatest preserver of all was the Lord Jesus, who chose twelve diverse men to preserve His teachings and his life, so we can come to know him today.

PRAYER: **We praise You, Lord, for selecting those who have preserved the beauty of Your creation and those who have given us Your word. AMEN.**

OCTOBER 24

DEALING WITH DEPRESSION

(Scripture to ponder: 1 Kings 19: 1–8)

It is not uncommon that people experience depression. Abraham Lincoln and Winston Churchill, both renowned leaders, suffered bouts of depression. Churchill called it his "black dog."

In the Bible we read about Moses' depression in Numbers Chapter 11, and our selection today describes Elijah's depression following threats from Ahab and Jezebel. Many of the Psalms relate King David's pain and despair.

It is ironic—and hard for many to believe—that when things seem most hopeless and we feel most helpless, God seems to act. I think it's because the condition of brokenness and contriteness allows us to abandon our own agenda and fully submit our will to the Lord.

The writer of Psalm 130 calls out in despair,

"Out of the depths have I cried unto Thee, O Lord!"

But he ends the psalm on a hopeful note:

"Hope in the Lord, for with him is mercy and plenteous redemption."

We all have times of being down; it's part of the sine wave of human life. But rather than allow those times to drag us into despair, we need to turn our feelings and our inadequacy over to God.

Then with the psalmist, we can declare,

"Hope in God, for I shall again praise Him, my help and God."

[Psalm 43:5]

PRAYER: You are indeed our Hope, our Savior, and our Provider. We turn our fears and our discouragement over to you, and pray in Jesus' name. AMEN

OCTOBER 25

IN QUIETNESS AND CONFIDENCE

(Scripture to ponder: Isaiah 30:15)

Recently at breakfast, in connection with devotions, my wife and I read in the 30th chapter of Isaiah the selection for today,

"In quietness and confidence shall be your strength."

It so happened that within he past few years I experienced a brief period of complete quietness, so I asked her if she could guess where it took place. Her first guess was when I backpacked into the Superstition Wilderness near Phoenix to spend a night alone. It was a good guess, for it was quiet out in the desert, but not completely quiet, for I'd camped beside a babbling brook.

Her next guess was the top of a mountain I'd recently climbed. That too was a good guess, but again not right. Although it was isolated on the mountaintop, it was noisy, with gusts of wind buffeting my ears.

She gave up on the third guess, so I told her. It was in a special chamber in a doctor's office where I'd gone for an audiogram to test my hearing. I was put in a comfortable armchair in a small sealed-off room, isolated from all external noise. I was asked to listen for certain tones played by the technician and was asked to press a button when I heard a sound. The utter quietness of the test setting was eerie and strange.

Most of the time, the background noise that's part of modern urban life surrounds us constantly, or we have a radio or TV set on. But we need quietness to commune with the Lord and to pray. We don't need an audiogram chamber, but we do need a special, quiet time.

PRAYER: **Help us set aside times of quietness and confidence, Dear Lord, so we may commune with You every day. AMEN.**

OCTOBER 26

AN EVERLASTING LOVE

(Scripture to ponder: Jeremiah 32:3)

Love has been the subject of many poems and sermons throughout history. Elizabeth Barrett Browning was an invalid when she wrote one of the most famous love poems in English, a sonnet to her husband Robert, the future poet laureate of England:

How do I love thee? Let me count the ways.
I love thee to the depth and breadth and height
My soul can reach when feeling out of sight
For the ends of Being and ideal Grace.
I love thee to the level of every day's
Most quiet need, by sun and candlelight.

I love thee freely, as men strive for right;
I love thee purely as they turn from praise.
I love thee with the passion put to use
In my old griefs, and with my childhood's faith.
I love thee with a love I seemed to lose
With my lost saints—I love thee with the breath,
Smiles, tears of all my life—and, if God choose,
I shall but love thee better after death.

But as wonderful as human love can be, God's love is even greater, more longsuffering and faithful. The prophet Jeremiah records God's words in our Scripture selection:

"Yea, I have loved thee with an everlasting love."

Our human love ends with death. God's love transcends death and goes on forever. There's a touching story about Prime Minister Winston Churchill when he attended a dinner party. Over coffee the conversation turned to a parlor game in which each person was asked to state, if he or she were able to come back after death as a famous person in history, who would it be? When Churchill's turn came, he thought a moment, turned, and gently taking his wife Clementine's hand, said, "**I should like to come back as Lady Churchill's second husband.**"

PRAYER: **Your Love for us is indeed everlasting, transcending this mortal life. We praise You for Your care and Your many blessings. Help us to do Your will. AMEN.**

OCTOBER 27

UNCONVENTIONAL RESPONSES

(Scripture to ponder: Matthew 15:21–28; Mark 7: 24–30)

I'm always fascinated when I hear of unconventional responses that provoke action. I read, for example, of a high school senior named Emilie Dubois from Rhode Island, who wanted to attend William and Mary College in Virginia. She had applied, but was put on a waiting list—with 800 other applicants. Her unconventional response was to go to William and Mary and walk around the campus for three days wearing a sandwich board that declared, "Hi! **I love this school, and I'm here to remind Admissions how thrilled I'd be to attend.**" [35]

The result? She was taken off the waiting list and given a place in the upcoming freshman class.

Or perhaps you've heard the story of the man waiting in a long line to interview for a job during the great depression. Just one among many, he resorted to an unconventional response to bolster his cause. Before the doors opened, he counted the number of men in line and wrote out a note that he got passed to the head of the line, to be given to the interviewer. It read, "**Don't make any decision until you've spoken with #28!**" The man conducting the interviewing, of course, gave special attention to #28, and he got the job.

In today's scripture, both of the Gospel writers tell of another unconventional response, that of the Syrophoenician woman who came to Jesus to plead that he heal her daughter. She was not a Jew, and Jesus responded that he'd been sent only to the lost sheep of the house of Israel, that is, to the Jews. He said it wasn't right to take the children's bread and throw it to the dogs. Her unconventional response, one that induced him to act to heal her daughter, was,

"Yes, Lord, yet even the dogs eat the crumbs that fall from the master's table."

We should never fear to approach God with our soul's sincere desires, even approaching Him unconventionally.

PRAYER: **We know from your Word, O Lord, that You are never too busy to hear us when we call our in need. Help us not refrain from sharing our heart's desires with You. AMEN.**

OCTOBER 28

THE PAST AND THE PRESENCE OF THE PAST

(Scripture to ponder: Acts 1:4–8)

The Christian apologist and poet T.S. Eliot once wrote:

> **"The historical sense involves the perception not only of the pastness of the past, but of its presence."**

For Christians, that enigmatic quote has great meaning. The Christian Church, though possessed of a glorious past, is also, through the Holy Spirit, very much in the present. For ours is not a dead faith, memorialized in ancient Mideastern ruins or towering European cathedrals; no, it's a faith, a hope and a doctrine that is very much alive.

There is much to learn from the past history of the Church. First there are the teachings and the historical record of the Old and New Testaments. Second, there are the lives of the saints and the record of the Church as it has evolved through the ages. The Bible is the best selling book of all time, and more books have been written about Christ than about any other person in history.

But it's in the "Presence of the Past" that the power and the vibrancy of the Christian Faith become manifest. For not only have the life of Christ and the and the presence of the Church changed history, the power of the Holy Spirit has transformed countless lives down through the centuries. It continues to do so today.

The Spirit that empowered the miracles of Jesus, that raised him from the dead, is today still alive and active in the world, changing and transforming lives. In our Scripture selection we read of its dynamism in the early church. The presence of the Holy Spirit was *the* distinguishing factor of the early Church. It's what makes, for me, the *Acts of the Apostles* the most dynamic book of all.

PRAYER: Grant us, O Lord, to be empowered by Your Holy Spirit to do Your will, that Your Kingdom may come on earth. AMEN.

OCTOBER 29

NO PRIZE FOR SECOND PLACE

(Scripture to ponder: 1 Corinthians 9:24)

When I was a sophomore in high school I was coxswain on a crew team that rowed a four-oared shell. One of our mottos, which kept us striving to work hard was *"There's no prize for second place!"* Unlike the in the Olympics, the Schoolboy Rowing Association gave only one prize—to the winner.

St. Paul, in our scripture Selection for today, wrote to the church at Corinth:

"In a race everyone runs, but only one person gets first prize. So run your race to win. To win the contest you must deny yourselves many things that would keep you from doing you best."

As a coxswain, I wasn't pulling an oar, so in that sense I was extra weight. My team thought it important that I keep my weight down, so every day I rode nine miles on my bike from our school to the boathouse on the Schuylkill River where we kept our shell. That was my contribution to our success, for later that spring we won the national championship on the Potomac River in Washington, D.C.

I discovered a few years later when I was on the varsity wrestling team in college that the same effort, the same discipline and denial, was needed to win in that sport. I always had a struggle to make weight, and once each season for the big match with a rival school, the coach had me drop to a lower weight to have an additional advantage.

Likewise in the Christian life, doing our best for the Lord often means discipline and denial, running the race of life to win.

PRAYER: Help us, O Lord, to always do our best for You, even when it means denying ourselves. Help us press onward to the prize of the high calling of the Lord Jesus Christ. AMEN.

OCTOBER 30

A SOFT SPOT FOR THE BAD

(Scripture to ponder: Luke 7:36–40)

Anglican Bishop Desmond Tutu of South Africa was instrumental in setting up The Truth and Reconciliation Commission that investigated the abuses of the Apartheid era in that nation's history. At one point when he was being interviewed by a reporter, a man who pressed him regarding the perpetrators of apartheid getting their just deserts. The bishop turned to him as they sat together, tapped him on the knee, and whispered in a conspiratorial tone, **"Our God has a soft spot for the bad."**

God does indeed have a soft spot for the bad. In fact, it was that attribute of Jesus that irked the religious authorities of the day—that he, who was supposed to be a prophet and a holy man, would sit down and eat with sinners and with publicans, those hated, turncoat Jews who collected taxes for the Romans.

In revealing his soft spot, Jesus had a lesson for the Pharisees, and for us as well. In today's scripture Christ is invited to lunch at the home of a proud Pharisee named Simon. His host gave him no water to wash his feet nor did he anoint his head with oil or greet Jesus with a kiss, all hospitable social customs of the day.

In the course of the meal a woman came up to Jesus and washed his feet with her tears, dried them with her hair, then kissed and anointed them with costly ointment. Now she was a notorious sinner—tradition has it that she was a prostitute—yet Jesus forgave her sins. To his hard-hearted host, he told a parable about forgiving debts, concluding,

"To whom little is forgiven, the same loves little."

In his first letter, St. John writes *"If we confess our sins, He is faithful and just and will forgive our sins and cleanse us from all unrighteousness." [1 John 1:9]* God does indeed have a soft spot for all repentant sinners.

PRAYER: O Lord, You have forgiven us so much. May we, who rely on your mercy for our salvation, forgive others as well. AMEN.

OCTOBER 31

ONE NATION UNDER GOD

(Scripture to ponder: Psalm 33:12)

Recently the Ninth Federal Circuit court of Appeals handed down a judgment that the words "under God" in the American pledge of Allegiance rendered it unconstitutional. It was not the last word on the issue, which will doubtless be submitted to the U.S. Supreme Court for review. It made me smile, though, for the decision seemed to ignore the place of God in American history.

Historically, the Founding Fathers, although they represented a variety of sects and beliefs, were certainly united in their belief in God. The Declaration of Independence alludes to "**Nature's God**" in the opening paragraph. The second paragraph asserts that the unalienable Rights on which the new nation will be founded—"**Life, Liberty and the pursuit of Happiness**"—are endowed upon all men "**by their Creator**," an obvious reference to God.

Finally, our Declaration of Independence ends with this:

". . . **with a firm reliance on the protection of** *divine Providence,* **we mutually pledge to each other our Lives, our Fortunes and our sacred Honor.**"

Aside from the lack of an historical perspective, I find it ironic that the suggestion to remove the words "under God" should come from a United States courtroom, for there every witness who testifies swears to "tell the truth, the whole truth, and nothing but the truth, *so help me God."*

PRAYER: Forgive us, O Lord, when we behave as though we were our own creator, protector and sustainer. We know that we have been blessed because *You* are our God. Help us to acknowledge and proclaim You as our Strength, the Source of all Creation and of all Virtue. AMEN.

NOVEMBER 1

DOUBLE-BITTED AXES & TWO-EDGED SWORDS

(Scripture to ponder: Hebrews 4:9–12)

When I was fourteen, I took a four-week canoe trip in the Maine Woods. I had a favorite camping axe called a Hudson Bay Cruising Axe, which was light-weight and very sharp. It had a single blade, and opposite the blade was a solid hammer-like head useful for pounding in tent pegs. The axe was handy around camp, for cutting up firewood, but it wasn't much good for chopping down a tree.

That same summer we ran into some lumberjacks who were felling the huge trees found in the North Woods. Their axes were much larger and heavier than mine and were double-bitted, that is, they had sharp blades at both ends of the head. I showed my Hudson Bay Axe to one of the lumberjacks, who held it up next to his own axe. He smiled and said, "Yours is good for small jobs around camp, but mine's good for the real work in the woods, felling big trees. And it stays sharp twice as long!"

Good for the real work, I thought to myself as I looked at his heavy, double-bitted axe. Years later, I was reminded of that axe and that encounter, when I read the words of St. Paul in Hebrews:

> **"For the word of God is living and active, sharper than any two-edged sword, piercing until it divides soul from spirit, joints from marrow; it is able to judge the thoughts and intentions of the heart."**
>
> [Hebrews 4:12]

God's word is good for the "real work" of life: it is as sharp and useful as a two-edged sword or a double-bitted axe. For through the word of God we gain the insight and discernment we need for this life.

PRAYER: Help us spend time each day reading Your word, Lord, which is sharper than a two-edged sword or a double-bitted axe, to help us judge the thoughts and intentions of the heart. AMEN.

NOVEMBER 2

SAVED BY THE FLOOD

(Scripture to ponder: Genesis 6:11–22)

Recently, re-reading the story of Noah and the Flood in chapter seven of Genesis, it occurred to me that Noah was *saved* by the same force that *destroyed* the rest of mankind: the deluge that inundated and drowned the others caused the ark to be buoyed up and saved Noah, his family, and all the animals. What made the difference?

The difference was that Noah believed God and obeyed Him. When told to build an ark, he did. That the rest of humanity neither believed nor obeyed God is evident in the previous chapter of Genesis:

"The Lord saw that the wickedness of humankind was great in the earth and that every inclination of the thoughts of their hearts was evil continually."

[Genesis 6:5]

The scripture is silent as to how Noah's neighbors reacted, but it's not hard to imagine, for the ark that God asked Noah to build was gigantic (by modern measurements it was about 500 feet long and 93 feet wide), and it was put together on dry land. Noah must have been subject to a lot of ridicule. Moreover, Jesus implies that it was life as usual at the time Noah built the ark. In Matthew 24 (in telling how it will be when he returns), Christ describes Noah's time:

"In those days before the flood, they were eating and drinking, marrying and giving in marriage, until the day that Noah entered the ark, and they did not know until the flood came and swept them all away."

[Matthew 24:38&39]

The obvious difference was that while Noah believed and obeyed, the rest of mankind neither heard, nor cared, to do God's will, and was oblivious, caught up in its own activities. Do you suppose this story has relevance for us today? What should be our response? As Count Leo Tolstoy asked, **"How then should we live?"**

PRAYER: As Noah obeyed and was lifted up by the waters, so may we hear and obey Your word, to be lifted into Your presence and saved. AMEN.

NOVEMBER 3

ASKING JESUS TO LEAVE

(Scripture to ponder: Mark 5:1–20)

When we look at how people encountered Jesus in the New Testament—and how they encounter him in life today—there appear to be three responses. One response is to follow him, as the disciples did, and as did the crowds, composed of those who wanted to be healed or to hear him preach.

A second response was elicited from those who saw Jesus as a threat, people like the Pharisees or the Sadducees, who saw Jesus' popularity as a challenge to their position and their authority. Their response was to get rid of him, to destroy him.

The third response is perhaps the most common response to Jesus today. It's illustrated by those who witnessed his confrontation with the strong, wild man with an unclean spirit who roamed the tombs. That story is related in today's selection from Mark's Gospel. Jesus cast out his demons, sending them into a herd of swine, that plunged down a steep hillside and drowned in the lake. The townspeople who were told of this miracle came and saw the demoniac in his right mind. What did they do? *They asked Jesus to leave.*

It's not a rare response, is it? Confronted with the power of Jesus to alter their lives, many don't want to make the change. They'd prefer to go on in their old ways. *So they ask Jesus to leave.* The intriguing thing is, *he does,* for he never takes us by storm. But they miss the chance to have the Lord transform their lives.

PRAYER: How easy it is, Dear Lord, to avoid an encounter with you. Instead of responding to your call, we ask you to leave. We pray you'll change our hearts, so we always welcome you. AMEN.

NOVEMBER 4

CONSCIENCE—AND PARENTHOOD

(Scripture to ponder: Proverbs 22:6)

What is our conscience? The dictionary defines it as the sense of right or wrong within an individual. A wag once defined conscience as "that little voice that tells you someone is watching." Shakespeare's Hamlet said: "conscience doth make cowards of us all," meaning that we're restrained in our behavior by our consciences.

Here's a story about a cafeteria line in a parochial school that gave me a chuckle. Next to a bowel full of juicy red apples on the counter there was a printed sign that read: "**Take only one: God is watching.**" Farther down the line, in front of a platter of jelly-filled doughnuts appeared a smaller, hand-written sign that said: "**Take all you want— God is watching those apples!**"

The Bible is silent as regards the issue of conscience, but there is no question where it stands on moral issues. Ethical choices are important, and a moral sense must be imparted to children if they are to lead virtuous lives and develop a conscience to guide them in Godly ways.

"Train up a child in the way he should go; and when he is old he will not depart from it."

That's today's selection from the wisdom of the Book of Proverbs. I'm convinced that much of the evil and crime we see in the world is the result of children *not* being brought up to have Godly values. Left to their own devices, or left to be nurtured by television, children will learn, certainly; but they'll learn what the world—not the Scripture—has to teach.

PRAYER: Grant us the grace and the wisdom and the energy to teach our children Your ways, O Lord. Help us set aside time to pray with them and read the Bible together, teaching and training them in how You would have us live. AMEN.

NOVEMBER 5

BEHIND THE FAÇADE

(Scripture to ponder: Proverbs 14:12)

Everything is not always as it seems. We can be deceived by facades of dress or manners, and by how the slick magazines present life to us. Our Scripture for today says,

"There is a way that seems right to a man, but its end is the way of death."

Do you recall the four-stanza poem by New England writer Edward Arlington Robinson (1869–1935), about a man named Richard Cory? Here's how it reads:

Whenever Richard Cory went down town,
We people on the pavement looked at him:
He was a gentleman from sole to crown,
Clean favored, and imperially slim.

He was always quietly arrayed,
And he was always human when he talked;
But still he fluttered pulses when he said
"Good Morning," and he glittered when he walked.

And he was rich—yes, richer than a king—
And admirably schooled in every grace:
In fine, we thought that he was everything
To make us wish that we were in his place.

So on we worked and waited for the light,
And went without the meat, and cursed the bread;
And Richard Cory, one calm summer night,
Went home and put a bullet through his head.

PRAYER: Help us see below the surface, Dear Lord, beneath the glitter that so often masks what's real in this world. Help us put our trust in You, the One true source of Reality. AMEN.

NOVEMBER 6

ENCOURAGEMENT AS A GLIMMER OF HOPE

(Scripture to ponder: Luke 22:31–34)

Encouragement—one of the great Christian attributes—can come in many different forms. I've found there are many different ways to encourage another person. Often the greatest encouragement comes when, despite difficult circumstances, someone offers us a glimmer of hope.

It happened to me when I went off to prep school and got in with the wrong crowd. I broke one of the rules, and smoked at a dance on a trip to a girl's school. Afterward, I fessed up to it, and with several others was placed on a special program of punishment called *Special Discipline*, that involved a six-week loss of privileges. For a teenager, it was a severe, discouraging sentence.

We met with the Headmaster, who told us of our fate. He related what was in store for us under *Special Discipline*—no sports, in study hall for all our free periods, no Saturday night movies, no going into the town—and then he dismissed all but me and another boy new to the school. When the others had left, he turned to us and said, "**I know your fathers, and I know you are not a part of that bunch. But you're going to have to take your medicine like the rest of them.**" That's all he said, and he let the two of us go. But he'd offered a glimmer of hope, one that for me was a beacon of brightness over the ensuing six weeks, which were otherwise rather bleak, as you might imagine, for a fifteen year old boy.

Jesus offered a similar hope to the Apostle Peter, as St. Luke relates in his Gospel, our selection for today. Christ knew Peter would deny him. The Lord did not change that circumstance. But He did offer Peter the hope and the encouragement that his faith would not fail, and that thereafter, he would be able to strengthen his brethren.

It's an important lesson in encouragement, worth reading and pondering. Is there someone we could encourage today?

PRAYER: Help us to encourage our fellow Christians—not by denying the reality of their difficulties—but by giving them hope, affirming the power of Christ to work in their lives. AMEN.

NOVEMBER 7

GOD SPEAKS TO US IN HISTORY

(Scripture to ponder: Luke 13:1–5)

The prominent theologian, George A. Buttrick, once wrote that

"History is a dialogue between God and human beings in the language of events."

If history is indeed what Dr. Buttrick asserts, a way God speaks to us, what do you suppose is the message to be learned from the terrorist attack on the United States in September 2001?

No one can deny it was a dastardly deed that ranks with the sneak attack on Pearl Harbor in its awesome magnitude. Both were surely manifestations of Evil, and both required a response to bring justice. But I wonder—in the context of a divine—human dialogue—what would God say?

In our selection from Luke, Jesus speaks to the issue of innocent people dying at the hands of evil men. Herod had killed men of Galilee and mingled their blood with sacrifices. One might think Christ would have something to say about Herod, who perpetrated the deed. But rather, Jesus speaks about what should be done lest others have a similar fate befall them. For Jesus calls his listeners to *repent*.

Do you suppose if Christ were here today, and we asked him about the events of September 11th, he would ask us also to repent? What if he asked us to examine *ourselves*, in our efforts to explain such a tragedy? Are we without sin? Would we acknowledge our own sinfulness? It is a question worth pondering prayerfully.

PRAYER: Forgive our sins, O Lord, our casual, callous and isolated enjoyment of life, while most of the world suffers in grinding poverty. We have not loved our neighbors as we have loved ourselves. Rescue us from our own sinfulness, we pray. AMEN.

NOVEMBER 8

REPLACING OUR "IF ONLYS"

(Scripture to ponder: John 11:1–40)

The two words, "If only!" are among the saddest words in our language. Often they are expressions of regret—as I experienced recently after I got robbed: "If only I had not left the garage door open!" Or they can verbalize a special wish, contrary to reality, as in "If only I had a better job!"

Today's selection from St. John's Gospel can teach us how to deal with the "If onlys" in our lives, namely to replace them with faith and hope. John relates the death of Lazarus, who with his sisters Mary and Martha, were beloved friends of Jesus.

After Lazarus has died and been in the tomb four days, Jesus comes to Bethany and is greeted on the road by Martha, who exclaims poignantly, *"If only you had been here, my brother would not have died."* When He tells her that her brother will rise again, she replies that she knows that he will rise again in the resurrection at the last day. When Jesus replies, *"I am the Resurrection and the Life,"* Martha confesses her belief: *"You are the Christ, the Son of God."* She has replaced "If only" with a bold statement of faith and hope.

Likewise we, when faced with the "If onlys" of life—which lead to blame and anger and guilt—need to replace them with faith and hope in God's power and goodness.

PRAYER: So often, Lord, we murmur "If onlys" as we go through our lives. Help us replace them with faith in You, that we may experience the power of Your resurrection. AMEN.

NOVEMBER 9

A ROUND TUIT

(Scripture to ponder: Mark 12: 41–44; 2 Corinthians 9:6&7)

Once during a worship service I saw a new card in the pew rack. It was different from the visitor registration cards or the offering envelopes. It was gray, made of stiff paper, and showed a picture of what looked like a quarter-sized ancient coin, on which were inscribed the words: *A ROUND TUIT*. Its margin was perforated so you could punch it out.

I was puzzled until the sermon. It was time for the annual every-member-canvass, and the pastor's message went something like this:

"As you well know, this is the time of year when we make our annual pledge drive. One would hope that every member of the church would make a pledge, but that doesn't turn out to be the case. A study done last year in our denomination showed that many folks who did not pledge reported that although they got the cards to make a pledge, they never got around to it.

"In the pew racks in front of you are the pledge cards for this year. Each has a small, punch-out section—*A ROUND TUIT*. So this year nobody will be able to say they never got around to it."

I had to admire the cleverness, even if it was a bit corny. But it got me thinking: Each of us pays ten to thirty per cent of our income in taxes, yet most of us give less than five per cent to the church. Granted we can get in trouble if we don't pay taxes, and we do get schools, fire and police protection in exchange.

It's also true there's no penalty for *not* giving to the church. But I believe God loves a cheerful giver, one who like the widow in today's Scripture selection, gives from a grateful heart. For we are richly blessed by God, who gives us all things, even Life Eternal.

PRAYER: May we always recognize and respond to your great bounty, O Lord, especially the gift of Eternal Life through Your Son, our Lord Jesus Christ. AMEN.

NOVEMBER 10

I AM WITH YOU ALWAYS

(Scripture to ponder: Matthew 28:16–20)

The great focal point of the Christian Faith is the Resurrection, and the great fact of Christian life is *we are not alone*. St. Matthew relates at the end of his Gospel how Jesus took leave of his apostles on the mountain in Galilee. He sent them out into the world to make disciples of all nations, baptizing them in the name of the Father and of the Son and of the Holy Spirit. And as He parted from them, Jesus said, *"I am with you always, even to the end of the world."*

Over twenty centuries, many have predicted the end of the world, but it has not come. Yet down through the ages, thousands of witnesses have attested to the presence of the Risen Lord in their lives.

One such occurrence happened to the wife of Peter Marshall, related in her book, *A Man Called Peter.* He was the Chaplain of the U.S. Senate and a superb preacher. Late one night he had a sudden heart attack and was taken to the hospital in the early morning. Catherine Marshall did not know, as she waited at the hospital while they worked on him, that she would never again see her husband alive. As she prayed for him to be spared, she says she was filled with an indescribable peace and enveloped by love.

About eight o'clock AM, she was told of his death and was shown into the room where his body lay. She tells, as she looked at the bed, she saw with her spiritual eyes two warm presences—her husband and the Lord Jesus—who lingered, then faded away. But the glory of that moment—which she said was the most intense experience of her life—remained her life long.

PRAYER: We bless you, Lord, that you are with us always, and through the power of Your resurrection, we have eternal life. AMEN.

NOVEMBER 11

THE GOOD SAMARITAN

(Scripture to ponder: Luke 10:25–37)

In Old Testament times Samaria was part of the Northern Kingdom of Israel, stretching from the Jordan River to the Mediterranean Sea. It was the site of much wickedness at the hands of people like King Ahab and Jezebel, as related in First Kings. When the Israelis were conquered and deported to Babylon, non-Jewish colonists settled in Samaria.

The Samaritans were a people who eventually cast off their idols and accepted the Pentateuch, but they believed God was to be worshiped not in Jerusalem, but at a temple built on Mt. Gerazim. Samaria became the capital city of an Assyrian province that was later conquered and destroyed by the Romans. It was rebuilt in 126 B.C by Herod the Great, who renamed it Sebaste in honor of Emperor Augustus [Augustus in Greek is Sebaste].

The Jews despised the Samaritans and there was great enmity between the two peoples. Jews had little to do with the Samaritans, and it's significant how Jesus replied when asked by a lawyer how to inherit Eternal Life. Jesus asked him what was written in the law. The lawyer, quite familiar with the law, summed it up, and quoted the commandments exactly as Jesus himself cited them once before [Matthew 22:37]:

"You shall love the Lord your God with all your heart, with all your soul, with all your strength and with all your mind, and your neighbor as yourself"

[Luke 10:27]

But being a lawyer, the man wanted a specific definition of *neighbor*. Jesus replied with today's scripture, a parable about a man who'd been robbed and beaten and needed help. Jesus was addressing **Jews**; but the worldwide importance of his teaching is shown by his choice of the helpful neighbor. It was not the Priest nor the Levite, members of the religious establishment, who stopped. Instead it was a despised Samaritan, who bandaged the wounded man and took him to the inn..

So Jesus is saying our neighbor is anyone—regardless of color, or creed, or nationality—who needs our help, not just the person who lives next door.

PRAYER: Embolden us, O Lord, by your Spirit, to act as neighbors to those who need us most, no matter where we encounter them. AMEN.

NOVEMBER 12

THE GRATEFUL SAMARITAN

(Scripture to Ponder: Luke 17: 11—19)

A second place Jesus singles out Samaritans—a people despised by the Jews—is in the healing of the ten lepers. Jesus and his disciples were headed for Jerusalem, passing along the border between Samaria and Galilee. Our selection describes how in a certain unnamed village ten lepers came to Jesus to be healed. In verse 14, Christ instructs them what to do—*"Go and show yourself to the priests"*—and they leave and are healed on the way. But only one of the ten, a Samaritan, returns to thank Jesus and to praise God for the healing.

Jesus asks, *"Were not the ten cleansed? But where are the nine?"* Jesus singles the Samaritan out for praise, and says, *"Were there none found that returned to give glory to God, save this stranger?"*

I've always wondered about the other nine lepers. Were they headed for the priests, carrying out Jesus' instructions? Or were nine of the ten so excited and overjoyed to be healed, that they hurried off to change their clothes and once again join the mainstream of humanity? Or maybe the other nine, being healed and no longer outcasts, went off at once to be again united with their families? But regardless of how one chooses to question it, the fact remains that only one out of ten returned to thank Jesus.

Could it be that maybe in this parable Jesus is telling us about *ingratitude?* Is he teaching us bout human nature, about what we should expect? Perhaps he's saying that if we do something nice for someone else, even something wonderful, then 9 out of 10 times we shouldn't expect thanks.

For in the Bible, this episode in Luke follows right after Jesus has taught his disciples about servanthood: when we serve others we are really serving God, responding to *his* love, mercy and blessings, and should not be expecting thanks. Is that perhaps what Jesus is driving home?

PRAYER: You have blessed us, O Lord, so we can be a blessing to others. Help us serve You as we serve others, not expecting thanks, for Your Love is thanks indeed. AMEN.

NOVEMBER 13

A SPECIAL WOMAN

(Scripture to ponder: John 4:4–42)

A third time a Samaritan is singled out by Jesus occurs as he and his disciples are journeying back from Judea to Galilee. They must go through Samaria, and Jesus stops to rest at Jacob's Well in Sychar while his disciples go into the town to buy food. A woman of Samaria comes to draw water and Jesus asks her for a drink—a doubly surprising request, because a Jew didn't talk to a Samaritan, least of all to a strange woman. It's a peculiar and fascinating encounter, worth reading and re-reading in John's forth chapter, and it's laden with meaning.

I am struck by two aspects of this meeting that are often overlooked in most commentaries. First, this is a conversation in which Jesus reveals who his identity—that he's *the Messiah*—to a person who is not a Jew. Christ tells her that the time is coming when God will be worshiped in Spirit and in Truth, and it will not be a matter of being in Jerusalem, as the Jews held, or on Mount Gerazim, as the Samaritans asserted. When she replies that she knows that Messiah is coming, Christ tells her openly that he is the Messiah.

A second peculiarity of this encounter is that, for Christ, it's nourishing. When the disciples come back, they're surprised that he's speaking to a woman. When she leaves to tell other townspeople about Jesus, and the disciples urge Jesus to come and eat with them. But he replies he has meat that they don't know about, and explains that his meat is to do God's will and to accomplish God's work. He has derived sustenance from his encounter. It is an important principle, still true today, through the power of God's Spirit.

When we do God's work, when we serve others, there is indeed divine nourishment for us, special sustenance that God provides.

PRAYER: **We bless and praise you, O Lord, that You reveal Yourself to us through Your Holy Spirit and that through that same Spirit, You sustain us to do Your will and Your work. AMEN.**

NOVEMBER 14

HE'S COMING! HE'S HERE NOW!

(Scripture to ponder: Matthew 25: 31–46)

Advent is the season when we prepare our hearts for the coming of the Lord Jesus. We can do this in a number of ways. One is to reflect on the story of Jesus' birth, the account we know so well, from the Gospel stories of Matthew and Luke that tell about the journey to Bethlehem, about the manger and the angels and the wise men. Another way we prepare is by singing the Christmas carols we all love, such as Silent Night, O Little Town of Bethlehem, Joy to the World.

Or perhaps at this season we long for the *Second* Coming of Christ, and see Advent as preparation for that, for we're drained by the poverty and hunger in this poor world, this globe where nations ever seem to take up arms against one another, where terrorists disrupt lives, destroy buildings and sow tragedy. We long for God's Kingdom to come on earth, for the time, as the hymn puts it, "**when the darkness shall turn to the dawning, and the dawning to noonday bright.**"

But if we believe the words of our Lord in today's Scripture, (the Parable of the Last Judgment), *Christ has indeed already come.* For he comes continually to visit us. If we would truly do God's Will and follow God's Way, will we not see the face of God in every needy person we encounter this Advent Season? Listen to our Lord's words from our Scripture selection for today:

For I was hungry and you gave me food, I was thirsty and you gave me drink, I was a stranger and you welcomed me, I was naked and you clothed me, I was sick and you

visited me, I was in prison and you came to me . . . .Truly I say to you, as you did it unto the least of these my brethren, you did it unto me.

Do we truly, earnestly wish to inherit the Kingdom? Do we really look for Christ's Advent? Then should we not follow his urging, and love him in everyone we meet?

PRAYER: Thank you, O Lord, for the unsearchable riches of Joy that we have in Your Love. Help us to love one another as You have loved us. May we meet you face-to-face each day. AMEN.

NOVEMBER 15

HAVING ENOUGH FOR RETIREMENT

(Scripture to ponder: Luke 12:22–31)

"WILL YOU HAVE ENOUGH FOR RETIREMENT?" was the title of an article in a copy of the *Reader's Digest* I was leafing through by the pool. It was March, and my wife and I were down in San Carlos, Mexico, for a week's vacation, relaxing. I had to smile as I glanced through the article, which was obviously pitched at someone who was not yet retired. We were, and our retirement funds were hard hit after the stock market's drop over the past year, dropping even further after the terrorist attacks of September 11, 2001.

Looking out over the bay, I saw birds—literally hundreds of them—of all varieties and shapes and sizes, from the huge pelicans diving at steep angles, wings akimbo, into the bay, followed by smaller birds anxious for a chunk of the snatched fish, to tiny swallows nesting in the dried mud of the cliffs above the sea. Everywhere we looked during our week on the Sea of Cortez, we saw birds.

"Where do you suppose they get all their food?" I asked my wife. The countryside was Sonoran desert—not much there—but the sea's full of fish, and the birds seemed well provided for, whether the small ones scavenging from the pelicans, or the gulls that watched beside the pier as fishermen cleaned their catch, eagerly snapping up discarded parts. Jesus' words from our selection in Luke 12 came to mind. Speaking of birds, he said:

They neither sow nor reap; they have no storeroom nor barn; and yet God feeds them; how much more valuable are you than the birds!

I smiled again as I thought of how God's great bounty had provided for us during our working years; He'd continue to do so all our days. For God is the same yesterday, today and forever.

PRAYER: **We bless you, O lord, for Your infinite bounty. You provide for the birds of the air and You likewise take care of us, Your children. Help us always to do Your will. AMEN.**

NOVEMBER 16

FLYING HIGH—OR PLOUGHING STRAIGHT

(Scripture to ponder: Luke 9:62)

You may be familiar with the painting *The Fall of Icarus* by the XVI Century Flemish painter Pieter Bruegel. It's based on an ancient myth and depicts the fall of Icarus, who with his father Dedalus escaped from a tower where they were imprisoned on an island in the Aegean Sea. Using wax, Dedalus had carefully attached feathers to his arms and to the arms of his son, which enabled them to fly like an eagle over the sea to escape. Dedalus warned Icarus not to fly too low, to avoid the waves, nor to high.

But Icarus, delighted that he could soar on his new wings, flew higher and higher, close to the sun, and the warm rays melted the wax so the feathers fell off. Icarus plunged to his death.

Off to the left in the painting—which is a vast landscape—the artist showed a farmer at his plough, who's looking over his shoulder at Icarus. The contrast between the fallen Icarus and the farmer is reminiscent of the words of Jesus in today's passage:

"No one who puts his hand to the plough and looks back is fit for the Kingdom of Heaven."

I think Bruegel had a double lesson for us in the panting.

Any farmer who has ploughed with a horse or a tractor knows that to make a straight furrow you must keep his eyes fixed on something straight ahead, and particularly, not look back. Likewise, the Christian life is one of looking steadily at the Master as we press onward, not looking backward, nor flying so high that we loose our wings and plunge to destruction.

PRAYER: Help us always to keep our eyes on You, Lord, so we may be fit for Your Kingdom. AMEN.

NOVEMBER 17

INDIA AND ISRAEL

(Scripture to ponder: John 10:7–18)

When I was a medical student in 1961, I spent a summer in India. The program I was a part of stressed understanding the culture, and we had five homestays with families around the subcontinent. We lived with Hindus and Muslims and had the chance to meet many of the government leaders, including Nehru. Through reading, I learned much about Mahatma Gandhi and the independence movement of India's recent past.

I have been struck by similarities and contrasts between what happened in India then, and what's occurring in Israel now. The people of India wanted independence and achieved it under Gandhi's leadership. Guided by the soul force of *satyagraha*, they were willing to lay down their lives in passive resistance to British occupation.

The Palestinians, too, it seems, are willing to lay down their lives, but in a vastly different and more violent way. Suicide bombing has become an almost daily event in the State of Israel nowadays, and it is quite apparent that violence only begets more violence.

The Lord Jesus spoke about the good shepherd who lays down his life for his sheep. He was speaking of Himself, but also of sacrificial love. We know from Gandhi's statements that he was greatly influenced by the teachings of Jesus. I am sure if Jesus were here today He would still teach sacrificial love, but surely not the sacrificial suicide we witness in the Near East. Nor do I believe he'd endorse the eye-for-an-eye retribution it provokes among the Jews. I expect if Jesus looked over the Holy Land today, he'd weep just as he did when he arrived and looked over Jerusalem the final week of his life.

PRAYER: We bless you, O Lord, for your sacrificial shepherd-love. Inspire us always to respond in love, even to violence. AMEN.

NOVEMBER 18

TWO RESPONSES TO THE CHRIST

(Scripture to ponder: Matthew 2:16–18; 3:13–15)

In the beginning of the Gospel of Matthew, we see two different responses to encounters with Jesus, one temporal and one spiritual. They're our selections for today. The first response, related in Matthew 2, was from the wicked King Herod, who tried to trick the three Wise Men from the East, who'd come to worship the infant Jesus, into telling him where Jesus was to be born—so he could pretend to go and worship Him, too. We know by his actions when the Magi failed to return, what kind of a reception he was actually planning for the Lord, for in his desperation he had all the male children in Bethlehem under age two killed. Herod could tolerate no threat to his kingship.

Contrast that account with what Matthew relates in the next chapter, his description of the encounter between John the Baptist and Jesus. John was, by the time Jesus came to be baptized, a popular figure who drew great crowds to his exhortative preaching. He at once recognized who Jesus was, and he humbled himself before him, saying, "I have need to be baptized by *You!*" John asserted that he himself was unworthy to even remove Jesus' sandals, a servant's job. But at Jesus' request he went ahead and baptized the Lord. John later said, alluding to Jesus, *"He must increase while I must decrease."* Quite a contrast to King Herod.

As we ponder these accounts, we need to search our own hearts as to how *we* respond to the coming of the Messiah. Do we seek to do away with Him, to preserve our own dominance and control? Or will we, like John, humble ourselves before God incarnate and do his bidding?

PRAYER: Grant us grace, Dear Lord, to recognize you and let You become Lord of our lives. AMEN.

NOVEMBER 19

PERSISTENCE THAT PAID OFF

(Scripture to ponder: Hebrews 10:36)

Prior to about 1870, infection was the great scourge of surgery. Because wound infection so invariably followed operations, there was really no such thing as what today we call elective surgery. Almost all surgery was done for urgent or emergent conditions.

During the mid-eighteenth century, three physicians—the American Oliver Wendell Holmes, the Hungarian Ignaz Semmelweis and the Englishman Joseph Lister—made observations that began to unlock the secret of surgical infections.

Holmes was Professor of Anatomy at Harvard. He thought infection at childbirth might be spread by the unclean hands and instruments of obstetricians. He published a paper of his opinions in 1843 but did not pursue them further. The medical establishment scorned him.

In 1848 Semmelweis suspected that infection on the wards of his lying-in hospital in Vienna was spread by the hands of medical students who came straight from the autopsy suite to the bedsides of women in labor, whom they examined with unwashed hands. His hypothesis was correct and he proved it by making them wash their hands in a solution of chloride of lime, which dramatically cut the infection rate. But like Holmes, he too did not persist. His sensitive nature could not endure the ridicule of doctors who did not believe him. Despite his important discovery, he died in obscurity.

When Lister began using the antiseptic solution carbolic acid to treat the skin around compound fractures, he effectively eliminated infection in these wounds. He went on to apply the same technique to the skin over the site of operations, with the same good results, which he published in 1867. But Lister's discovery was derided by most of the medical establishment, and few in his native England believed in what he was doing.

Lister's reaction to the disbelief and abuse heaped upon him was far different from that of Semmelweis. Lister was a Quaker, imbued with an imperturbable spirit that kept him going in the face of opposition. He continued his work and kept publishing good results until eventually the whole surgical world was won over. To Lister we owe the safety of modern surgery, all because he was patient and persisted in his efforts.

PRAYER: **You tell us in your Word, O Lord, to persevere in prayer and in good works. Sustain us as we seek to do your will. AMEN.**

NOVEMBER 20

MOOD INDIGO—OR INDIGO BUNTING?

(Scripture to ponder John 1: 1–18.)

When I was a teenager and a member of the Glee Club, I sang in the school octet. One of our favorite songs was "Mood Indigo," a popular song at the time, written by the great Negro songwriter Duke Ellington. It had close harmony, and the title referred to the blue mood you got when your sweetheart was gone:

Always get that mood indigo, since my baby said goodbye. In the evening when lights are low, I'm so lonely I could cry!

Because of that song, I thought *indigo* referred to a blue mood of depression. But about a year later, in connection with obtaining Bird Study Merit Badge in the Scouts, I had occasion to see an *Indigo Bunting*, a lovely bird whose feathers give off a brilliant iridescent blue when caught by the sun. In the shade, however, the male Indigo Bunting can appear almost black! *So it depends on light.* In the bright sun, indigo is an azure, iridescent blue; in its absence, it's the somber, dark hue of mood indigo.

The Bible is full of references to the effects of light and darkness. Light is associated with virtue and splendor, and darkness with evil and corruption. The Gospel of John opens with these themes of light and darkness. Jesus is the Light of the world; but to Nicodemus, he proclaims,

"This is the condemnation, that Light is come into the world and men loved darkness rather than light, because their deeds were evil."

[John 3:18]

By contrast, Jesus calls *his* followers the light of the world. We who are Christians are those who've been called out of darkness, into his marvelous light. So in the Sermon on the Mount, Christ can urge:

Let your light so shine before men that they may see your good Works, and glorify your Father who is in heaven.

[Matthew 5:16]

PRAYER: By our lives O Lord, help us bring light into the world, dispelling mood indigo, to show forth the iridescent, blue of your love, that all mankind may glorify You. AMEN.

NOVEMBER 21

IN THE TIME YOU HAVE LEFT

(Scripture to ponder: John Chapter 14)

In my career as a surgeon, I've operated on many people with cancer. It's always been my practice to follow them afterward. Many were cured of their malignancies, but it was not rare that a patient would eventually succumb to their disease.

My Christian faith—belief in eternal life through Christ's resurrection—has enabled me to feel comfortable with death and be able to discuss it with my patients. I believe not all doctors feel comfortable talking about death, and many see it as a defeat in their battle against disease. Although I was not usually the primary physician for terminal cancer patients upon whom I'd operated, as they approached the end, I'd visit them and often spoke with them about death.

One question I ask patients who are nearing the end is, "What would you like to do in the time you have left?" When I asked that of a woman in her 50s who was dying of uterine cancer, she broke down and began to sob, telling me a wrenching story of alienation from her daughter, who lived two thousand miles away, and with whom she'd had a falling out over the grandchildren. I was touched by her remorse and her desire to be reconciled, and a thought occurred to me. "Why don't you get a cassette tape recorder and record just what you've shared with me, and send it on to your daughter, telling her that you love her?" She did.

When I returned about a week later, she greeted me with a radiant smile and exclaimed, "My daughter's coming to see me!"

Often it isn't until we are faced with death or serious illness that we ponder such things. But the awful events of 9/11/01 have made many realize how fragile our lives really are. Many have chosen to rearrange their priorities in the time they have left. St. John of the Cross made a statement that is a good reminder: "**In the evening of life you shall be judged on love.**"

PRAYER: **We love you, Lord, and seek your Love in our hearts. Grant us healing in our lives, that we may always love others. AMEN.**

NOVEMBER 22

BANKRUPTCY

(Scripture to ponder: Luke 16:1–9)

Did you know that in America a record number of bankruptcies—1.5 million individuals and 40 thousand businesses—were filed in 2002? Personal savings were at an all-time low, while credit card debt reached an all-time high.

One newspaper article[36] told about a woman who used a dubious method to get herself out of debts she'd incurred when she was pulling down a large salary, living "high off the hog." She compiled debts of over $20,000 on her six credit cards by buying $400 Prada sling-back shoes, $500 Gucci purses, and by visiting salons in New York City for hair styling and pedicures. Then she lost her job. When she saw a sign at the supermarket that read, "**Wanted: $7,000 to Pay Off Debt,**" she got an idea.

She set up a special web site that she called *www.savekaryn.com*, asking for donations. Her appeal brought in over $13,000 from hundreds of donors across the globe. She also auctioned off some of the high-ticket items she'd bought, and after she got a new job, established a budget. (Of course, she'd not had a budget before.)

It brought to mind my Dad telling me of a fellow who once placed an ad in the *New York Times*. It simply stated, **"Last Chance to Send a Dollar,"** and listed his address. He received thousands of dollars from the foolish people who answered his ad!

It also reminded me of today's scripture passage, in which a rich man commended his unjust steward, who, who when he got into trouble, befriended his master's creditors by reducing their bills. Jesus comments,

"The children of this world are wiser than the children of light."

PRAYER: **Help us be faithful stewards of the bounty you have given us, O Lord, and support your work, living within our means, debt free. Guide us by your Spirit. AMEN.**

NOVEMBER 23

PEACE—TO MEN OF GOOD WILL

(Scripture to ponder Luke 2: 9–14)

My sleep has been disturbed lately by the reports of all the killing and destruction in the Holy Land, as Palestinian suicide bombers blow themselves up trying to kill Israelis, and the Jews retaliate, smashing Palestinian settlements with tanks and rockets and armor.

Last night I had a dream and awoke to find myself reciting a passage from the King James Bible that I had learned almost passively as a boy, having heard it in successive Advent seasons. In my dream I pictured shepherds in the fields of Palestine on a dark and lonely night, and I heard a voice—it was my own—saying aloud:

"And lo, the angel of the Lord came upon them and the glory of the Lord shone round about them: and they were sore afraid. And the angel said unto them: Fear not: for behold I bring you tidings of great joy which shall be to all people. For unto you is born this day a savior which is Christ the Lord . . .

"And suddenly, there was with the angel a multitude of the Heavenly Host, praising God and saying Glory to God in the Highest, and on earth, Peace, Good will toward men!"

When I awoke, I recalled that after I grew up and went away to school, and I began to read the Bible in other versions besides the King James, I discovered that a truer rendering of verse 14 might be:

Glory to God in the Highest, and on earth Peace to men of good will!

That seemed, on reflection, to be a key to the violence in the Middle East: not only have the warring parties not accepted the Savior, which is Christ the Lord and his message of love and peace; but in addition, *there's a total lack of good will.* Instead, both sides have willed evil and retribution upon their foes. Peace will never come if that continues.

PRAYER: We pray for peace on earth, O Lord; but we know it will only come to men whose hearts are full of good will. We pray through our Lord and Savior Jesus Christ. AMEN.

NOVEMBER 24

FOUR LIKE MEN

(Scripture to ponder: Romans 8:28–30)

How would you respond if asked how these four men were alike: Lionel Hampton, Benny Goodman, Jackie Robinson and Branch Rickey? Could you guess? If you said that two were black and two were white, or that two were sports figures and two were musicians, you'd be right, but that's not it. What these four had in common was each assisted in breaking the color barrier. Each man was, in a certain sense, the firstborn among many brothers, for following their precedent, many blacks came to play in the Major Leagues or join the Big Bands.

Jackie Robinson was an outstanding athlete at UCLA at the time of the Second World War. After college he joined the military, and after his discharge in 1945, Branch Rickey, manager of the Brooklyn Dodgers, hired him to play for the Montreal Royals, a Dodgers farm team. The following year Rickey signed him on with the Dodgers. The two men will ever be remembered, Robinson for his talent, skill and grace despite racial taunts, Rickey for his courage in hiring him as a player.

Likewise, Lionel Hampton and Benny Goodman broke the color barrier of the Big Bands in 1936, when Goodman asked the talented vibraphone player to join his trio with Gene Krupa and Teddy Wilson, to form the Benny Goodman Quartet. Later Hampton formed his own band, but it was Benny Goodman's courage that gave Hampton the chance to show his skill and talent as a member of an all-white band.

So in a sense, each of these four men was the firstborn among many who followed.

In our Scripture passage from his letter to the Romans, St. Paul calls Jesus the firstborn among many brethren. He has broken the barrier of sin.

PRAYER: We praise you, O Lord, for those people of courage who have gone before us, and for the Saints, our Spiritual forbears in the Faith that have shown us the way to follow You. AMEN.

NOVEMBER 25

LOOKING TO GOD

(Scripture to ponder: Psalm 123)

Our scripture for today, Psalm 123, is one of the shorter Psalms. It's been classified as a "Psalm of lament," one of the many in the Book of Psalms that calls for help from the Lord.

The psalm opens with the psalmist lifting his eyes to God, who is enthroned in the heavens, and the petitioner uses three similes: the eyes of servants lifted to their masters;

the eyes of a maid to her mistress; and the eyes of the Lord's people lifted to Him. In each, one is seen as mighty, the other as humble. But each of these—God, the mistress, and the master—all also have the attribute of *caring*. We look to the Lord, high, lifted up, and mighty, as a source of mercy., as One who cares for us.

The psalm ends by speaking of *contempt and scorn*, and here I see two ways to interpret it. One is as a cry from the psalmist for release from the contempt and scorn of others who are proud and at ease, who taunt him. In this it's in keeping with Psalm 124 and a number of other psalms in which the petitioner feels set upon or persecuted by others.

But as I look into my own soul, I see another form of *contempt and scorn,* one for which I need rescue as much or more than from the contempt of others. It's my own contempt, when I'm tempted to look down on others, when I see my own blessings as special favor from God and I become proud and contemptuous, like the Pharisee in the temple looking down in scorn on the publican (described by Christ in *Luke 18:10*). Only confession and repentance will release me, so God can rescue me from myself, as I cry with St. Paul,

"Who will deliver me from this body of death?"

[Romans 7:24]

For only then can I serve God with my whole heart and soul and mind and strength, and only then can I truly love my neighbor.

PRAYER: We do look to you, O Lord, for mercy and for strength. But most of all, we pray that you would rescue us from our own selfishness and pride. We pray in Jesus' name. AMEN.

NOVEMBER 26

MAKING TOUGH DECISIONS

(Scriptures to ponder: Colossians 3:17; Philippians 4:6)

When faced with a difficult decision, how do we decide what's the right course of action? It's not an easy question, and there are no pat answers, but today's scriptures give Christians sound advice, I believe. In his letters to the churches at Philippi and at Colossi, St. Paul has a key. It's found in our selections for today:

Whatever you do, in word or deed, do it all in the name of the Lord Jesus, giving thanks to God the Father through him.

[Colossians 3:17]

Do not be anxious about anything, but in everything, by prayer and petition, with thanksgiving, present your requests to God.

[Philippians 4:6]

I had an interesting example of this recently. I'd given a lecture to a group in Phoenix, about a course on Shakespeare I'd attended in Oxford, England. (I'm a retired surgeon, but Shakespeare is one of my loves, and I was sharing my experience with a lay group.) After the talk, a woman came up to shake my hand.

"Aren't you a general surgeon?" she said, as she introduced herself and her husband. When I affirmed it, she continued, "I thought so. Six years ago you did my mastectomy. I want you to know I'll always be grateful for your advice." I recognized her face, but not her name.

She continued. "You see, I had advanced breast cancer—17 lymph nodes were positive in the specimen. You advised me to consider a bone marrow transplant, but my oncologist wanted to give me standard chemotherapy. I decided to go to L.A. for another opinion, and they agreed with you. I had it done four years ago. It was harrowing, but I'm doing fine now and feel great."

I began to recall her case. It was one of those tough decisions, where I'd given her my best advice and then turned things over to the Lord. I didn't know what was best for her, but God did.

In medicine, as in life, we never have, nor can we ever have all the answers. But if we stay close to the Lord and do our best and prayerfully consider things, with thanksgiving, we can entrust our decisions to Him.

PRAYER: Help us remain always close to you, O Lord, prayerfully bringing before you all the decisions of our lives, that we may have the Holy Spirit to guide us in this life. In Jesus name we pray. AMEN.

NOVEMBER 27

FREEDOM—FOR WHAT?

(Scripture to ponder: Romans 8:1–9 in the Living Bible)

We Americans are the most free people in history—never before have people had so many choice s and so many options. Our Declaration of Independence asserts the inalienable rights of life, liberty and the pursuit of happiness. Yet many in this affluent land of the free are not happy. For freedom itself does not always bring happiness.

Perhaps you are familiar with the movie, *The Shawshank Redemption*. It's about prison life. In it a man who has served time for many years under a regimented and repressive regime is finally released. He finds, as he tries to adjust to life outside, that with freedom, instead of feeling relieved, he's lonely and isolated. He ends up hanging himself from the light fixture in a boarding house room. His being set free has led to death.

Many people think that freedom means we can do as we please. But the Scripture says otherwise: Our natural state is one of being enslaved to sin and to selfishness. It's what the theologians call the unregenerate state, what the Bible calls walking after the flesh, trapped by our own desires, always looking out for #1. The Bible also gives the solution. Hear St. Paul in today's Scripture passage from his letter to the Romans:

There is now no condemnation awaiting those who belong to Christ Jesus. For the power of the life-giving Spirit—and this power is mine through Christ Jesus—has freed me from the vicious circle of sin and death . . . Those who let themselves be controlled by their lower natures live only to please themselves, but those who follow after the Holy Spirit find themselves doing those things that please God. Following after the Holy Spirit leads to life and peace, but following after the old nature leads to death, because the old sinful nature within us is against God. It never did obey God's laws and it never will.

[TLB]

PRAYER: We praise You, O Lord, that through Your Son and Your Spirit we are made free from the cycle of sin and death. Empower us to do Your Will and to serve others. AMEN.

NOVEMBER 28

LOOKING GOOD

(Scripture to ponder: Isaiah 53:2)

I am impressed, when I read the local paper or thumb through our glossy magazines, with the number of advertisements by plastic surgeons suggesting many ways that folks can improve their appearance. Special implants can be used to enhance lips or breasts, wrinkles can be erased and liposuction used to remove fat deposits or contour the shape of our bodies. It's all done for a price, of course.

Most health insurance doesn't cove cosmetic surgery, but plastic surgeons do very well because so many people want to change how they look, for our society extols beauty.

This is quite a contrast to the Biblical perspective. Speaking of the coming Messiah, the prophet Isaiah said in today's selection,

"He had no form or majesty that we should look at him, and no beauty that we should desire him."

At the time the Messiah arrived, pomp and ceremony were associated with the Roman Empire. Christ was heralded not by trumpets and drums, but by the preaching of John the Baptist, who was clothed in sandals and a camel skin. Of John, Christ asked the crowd,

"What did you go out to see? A man dressed up in soft garments? Behold, those who wear fine apparel and live in luxury are in the palaces of kings."
[Luke 7:24–25]

No, neither John the Baptist, the forerunner, nor Jesus, the Messiah, was what the crowds expected. For Jesus himself came as a servant and washed the feet of his disciples. Likewise, he calls *us*, not to make ourselves beautiful in the eyes of society, but to be servants, for his sake.

PRAYER: All about us O Lord, are altars to beauty and adulations of the self; but we have heard your soft call in the midst of society's noise. Help us serve one another in love, to do your will. AMEN.

NOVEMBER 29

THE PERIL OF OUTWARD APPEARANCES

(Scripture to ponder: 1 Samuel 16:7)

I'd been looking over some medical charts several years ago, reviewing them for accuracy and completeness in my capacity as Director of an Indian Health Service clinic on the Yakima Reservation in Washington. I noted a rarely used and hazardous antibiotic called chloramphenicol had been prescribed by one of the other doctors for a sick child. The medication was rarely used because it could cause a serious, even life-threatening bone marrow depression.

Reading on, I was even more surprised to discover the tentative diagnosis for which the drug had been prescribed: typhoid fever, a rare disease. So far as I knew, we'd never seen a case on the reservation. So I arranged to speak with the doctor involved. If it was indeed a case of typhoid, it was a real diagnostic find, and the disease was reportable to the state health department.

Figuring he must have noticed some of the diagnostic stigmata of typhoid, I asked him if he'd seen a rose-colored rash, or noted a pulse rate much slower than one would expect for the fever. He said, "No, these were not present." What was the basis for the diagnosis, I asked. He replied, well, the kid looked like a child that had typhoid that he'd once seen in his training in Baltimore. On more careful questioning, he meant that this Indian child *physically resembled* the other child. His diagnosis was based on nothing else. I was floored.

The diagnosis was wrong. The child turned out to have the flu, and we stopped the potentially lethal medication.

Our Scripture selection for today says,

"Man looks on the outward appearance but God looks on the heart."

We make superficial judgments of others at our peril, whether in medicine, or in daily life.

PRAYER: We praise you, O Lord, that you look on the heart. May we always seek to do so too, and seek to do your will. AMEN.

NOVEMBER 30

WHO KNOWS WHEN?

(Scripture to ponder: Matthew 24:36)

During the season of Advent, the arrival of Christ on earth—culminating in the story of his birth at Bethlehem—is celebrated. But it's worth pondering another aspect of Advent, namely the Second Coming of Christ.

I believe a close reading of the New Testament leaves no doubt as to the return of Christ. All of the Gospel narratives allude to it, and in reading the Acts and the Letters of Paul, it's apparent that Christ's imminent return was expected.

Down through the ages since Christ walked the earth, there have been repeated predictions of His return. Every few years another Christian cult proclaims the end of the world is near, usually presaged by the return of Christ. Yet it's obvious that in over 20 centuries, he has not yet come back. Does the Scripture give us any clues as to when he will return? I think it does.

There's an expression in common use today that I consider sacrilegious. It's the comment, **"God only knows!"** It seems it's most commonly used as a reply, meaning roughly, "I have no idea." But that same phrase, slightly rearranged, is exactly what Christ said about his return: "Only God knows!" For when asked about his return, Jesus confessed that nobody, not even he himself, knew. Matthew's entire chapter 24—well worth reading in its entirety—is devoted to the question. Verse 36 sums it up:

"But of that day and hour, no one, knows, not even the angels of heaven, nor the Son, but the Father only."

PRAYER: We recognize that You alone, O Lord, will determine the exact timing of our Savior's return. Help us to be faithful servants until then. AMEN.

DECEMBER 1

HOW MUCH TIME DO WE HAVE?

(Scripture to ponder: John 16:28)

Reading the New Testament—particularly Jesus' own words in the Gospels—leaves no doubt that He will return. He said the timing was up to God—that only God knows when it will be—and it's apparent that it will be associated with the so-called "end times," that is, with the end of the world, according to Scripture. (Matthew's chapter 24 deals with this.)

Many books have been written about the "End Times"—and many predictions have been made that the end was coming. But it has not yet happened, has it? Nevertheless, thoughtful people are apt to ask, "How much time do we have?" I think there is an answer to that question, and it hinges on the nature of time.

I believe there are two kinds of time: Temporal and Eternal. Temporal time is how we arrange our schedules and is essentially Greenwich Mean Time, related to the rotation of the earth on its axis—24 hours in a day. Temporal time's also measured in years, a year being 365.25 days, the time of the orbit of the earth about the sun. Temporal time is *finite*. We measure our lives in Temporal time from birth until we die.

The other time is Eternal Time: time which God keeps, and by which the universe is measured. Compared to Temporal Time, Eternal Time is *infinite*. I believe these two times, Temporal and Eternal, intersect at two points: at our death, and at the end of the world—which will be when Christ returns. So the answer to the question of how much time we have is simple: We have until Jesus returns, or until we die, which ever comes first. That's when time will end, and the Last Judgment will occur. We can make a decision for Christ any time before we die, for from him we receive Eternal Life.

PRAYER: Help us, O Lord, to number our days, so that whether we live or whether we die, we belong to You, and are safe in Your Love, always ready for Your return. AMEN.

DECEMBER 2

TWO WHO SAID "YES!" TO GOD

(Scripture to ponder: Luke 1:38)

Two teen-aged girls, one modern and one ancient, said "Yes!" to God. The modern girl was seventeen. She gave her answer in the library of Columbine High School in Littleton, Colorado. Cassie Bernall's mother tells the story in a book [37] published in 1999. Her daughter was confronted by a raging boy who asked her if she believed in God. When she said "**Yes**," he killed her by a shot to the head.

Cassie was martyred for her faith, a rare event in modern America, but not uncommon in the history of the Christian Faith. Countless followers of Christ have died because they have refused to renounce their faith in God. Would you be willing to give your life for your belief?

The other girl who said "**Yes!**" lived 20 centuries ago. She too was confronted by a man, but not one who was angry or raving. While she was an unmarried virgin, an angel sent by God appeared and told her she'd been chosen to be the mother of Jesus. But the child would be fathered not by her fiancée, but by the Holy Spirit. Mary responded to the angel Gabriel by saying, *"I am the handmaiden of the Lord: let it be according to thy word."* Giving her life for God in a different way, she too said "**Yes!**"

There weren't abortions in those days, so as the yet unmarried Mary grew great with child, the potential for scandal also grew. Joseph, to whom she was betrothed, was an upright man. He resolved to break things off and put her away quietly. But he too was visited by an angel, and Joseph said "**Yes!**" to God's plan.

God wants each of us to say "**Yes!**" to his question. He stands at the door and knocks. Will we let him in? Will we say "**Yes!**" to God?

PRAYER: We do indeed praise You, O God, for the faithfulness of Cassie Bernall and the Virgin Mary, the Mother of Our Lord. Empower us through Your Holy Spirit to say "Yes!" to You with our whole heart. AMEN.

DECEMBER 3

THE THONG OF A SANDAL

(Scripture to ponder: John 1:19–28)

When I was a medical student I heard a missionary surgeon, Dr. Paul Brand, give one of the best talks I've ever listened to. He spoke about his work in India where he was a surgeon specializing in hand rehabilitation. Many patients there who had leprosy were rendered both helpless and useless because the infection attacked the nerves to the muscles of their forearms, causing the so-called claw hand deformity.

Brand told about how, just after he first arrived in India, he was shown around the grounds of a leprosarium by another physician who was its director. They came upon a patient who was trying to tie the thong of his sandal, which he was struggling with because of the deformity of his hands. Brand stooped to help the man and the director introduced them. As the new doctor shook hands with the man, he was astounded, for the patient squeezed his hand in a crushing grip. As I sat in the listening audience at medical school, Brand told the assembled doctors, **"I'd been taught that the hands of such patients were paralyzed—but here this man was not only *not paralyzed:* he had tremendous strength. Only the muscles that *opened* the hand were paralyzed—not the ones used for gripping."**

Because of the insight from this encounter, Dr. Paul Brand went on to develop a special tendon-transfer operation that restored usefulness to the hands of thousands of patients with leprosy, enabling them to have meaningful lives—all because he knelt down to help a man fasten the thong of his sandal.

John the Baptist uses the same image in our scripture for today, saying he was not worthy of the menial task of untying the thong of the sandal of the Lord Jesus. Yet later, in St. Luke's Gospel *[Luke 7:28]*, Jesus says no one born of woman is greater than

John, reaffirming Jesus' teaching that those who humble themselves will be exalted. [Matthew 23:12]

PRAYER: May we always seek to serve others, Dear Lord, even if it means being willing to help them tie their shoes. Lead us in your paths and help us do your will. AMEN.

DECEMBER 4

JESUS MEANT WHAT HE SAID

(Scripture to ponder: Luke 7:11–17; John 11:1–44)

My mother tells a story of me when I was about six years old. When once I didn't want to do something, I stamped my foot and surprised her by backing up my "NO!" with these lines from Dr. Seuss:

"I meant what I said, and I said what I meant: an Elephant's faithful one hundred per cent!"

I suspect we adults don't always mean what we say—I know I've fallen short on that account not a few times. The old expression, "Put your money where your mouth is!" points up our tendency to say things we won't always back up with deeds.

Jesus, by contrast, did say things that he was prepared to follow with actions. For example, he did not merely say, *"I am the light of the world."* To prove it, he opened the eyes of the blind so they could see the light. Or another example, perhaps the most famous of all, in our Scripture selection for today: Christ proclaims, *"I am the resurrection and the life,"* and to show he meant what he said, he raised the dead, first the son of the widow of Nain. *[Luke 7:11–17]* Later, as John records, he raised Lazarus, who had been in the tomb four days. *[John 11:1–44]*

In his Epistle the Apostle James asserted,

"I will show you my faith by my works."

[James 2:18]

Our Christian life is made up of both faith *and* works. When we proclaim our faith in the Lord Jesus, we must back it up by doing his will. Indeed, we show forth our faith in how we act.

PRAYER: **We believe you are the Christ, the Savior of the world, O Lord, and we ask for the faith and the will to do your will. AMEN.**

DECEMBER 5

INVENTIONS AND LABOR SAVING DEVICES

(Scripture to ponder: Psalms 10 & 14)

Recently I wrote a book review for the *Journal* of the American Medical Association. The book's title was *Inventing Modern America: From the Microwave to the Mouse*. It described 35 inventions made by Americans during the twentieth century.

The list of inventions—many of them labor saving devices—was impressive, and most of them involved technology. Included were the bar code scanner, industrial robots, the assembly line, pacemakers, microwave ovens, computers and bullet-proof fabrics.

Reading the book made me proud to be an American and blessed to be the beneficiary of such splendid inventions. But despite the author's extolling the technology, and my own pleasure in reading about it, I was saddened as I reflected on the implication that technology would be the salvation of the world.

Rather, I fear, it may be the opposite. For although modern aircraft can span oceans and make travel easy, the same planes have been driven into tall buildings by terrorists. And although nuclear power furnishes huge cities with light and power, a single nuclear weapon can wipe out a huge city. Technology may be neutral, but the heart of man has devised fiendish ways to use it.

In our selections for today—Psalms 10 and 14—the Bible describes the heart of man and its wicked propensities. What is the answer? In chapter three of John's Gospel Jesus gave the answer to this dilemma in his conversation with Nicodemus: We must be born anew—that is, our hearts must be set aright by being transformed by God's Holy Spirit. Left to our own devices or controlled by evil, terrible things result. Controlled by God's Spirit, love and healing can prevail.

PRAYER: **We know the evil that can control the heart of man. Fill us with Your Spirit and transform our lives, so that by our doing Your will, Your Kingdom may come. AMEN.**

DECEMBER 6

STANDING ABOVE OR BESIDE THE FRAY

(Scripture to ponder: John 17: 15–16)

When I was in London one summer I encountered an interesting book, a collection of sonnets composed by contemporary poets in celebration of the two hundredth anniversary of William Wordsworth's sonnet composed upon Westminster Bridge in 1803. The original reads:

Earth has not any thing to show more fair:
Dull would he be of soul who could pass by
A sight so touching in its majesty:
This city now doth like a garment wear
The beauty of the morning; silent, bare,
Ships, towers, domes, theatres and temples lie
Open to the fields, and to the sky;
All bright and shining in the smokeless air.
Never did sun more beautifully steep
In his first splendor valley, rock, or hill;
Never saw I, never felt a calm so deep!
The river glideth at his own sweet will:
Dear God! The very houses seem asleep;
And all that mighty heart is lying still!

Now anyone who knows much about London in the nineteenth century knows that Wordsworth must have had a day that was extraordinarily clear when he composed his sonnet, for both fog and the smog from countless coal burning stoves and hearths continually beset that great city. It was notorious for both.

Phoenix, AZ sometimes has peculiar inversions when a pall of smog covers the city, especially in winter. But I recall early one day in February when it was cold and crisp and clear, when I climbed Squaw Peak before sunrise. From the summit, spread out before me like a jeweled garment, I saw the twinkling city shimmering in the darkness, and it reminded me of Wordsworth's sonnet.

Sometimes we need to climb above or step aside from the fray, out of the noise and smog of our busy existence, to get perspective. For we are in the world, but not *of* the world, as our text for today from John's Gospel asserts. The gospel records show that Jesus often stepped aside, often to the solitude of the hills, to commune, to pray, and to be renewed for his earthly ministry. So should we, too.

PRAYER: We praise you, O Lord, for the times we get away above the fray, to see the beauty of your world and to renew our spirits. AMEN.

DECEMBER 7

WILL WE BE READY?

(Scripture to ponder: Matthew 24: 45–51)

If we do not know exactly when Christ will return, and if we do not know the exact length of our days—that is, just when we will die—and further, if we believe as the Bible teaches, that there will be a judgment, then the logical next question is "Will we be ready?" "Will we be prepared?"

When I was a boy, I was active in Scouts. The Boy Scout Motto is "Be Prepared." In Scouting, the concept of being prepared usually applied to being ready, on a hike or a camp out, for adverse weather or for an unexpected accident. But broadly interpreted, as applied to life in general, I take the motto to mean *be ready for anything*.

Applied to our lives, as relates the Second Coming of Christ, *being prepared* means: we're ready at any time for His return. In a way, it's like having our affairs in order, with a will and a living will. Just as an attorney would advise us not to die intestate, so we should at all times be in right relationship with the Lord.

In the Gospels, Jesus tells several parables about His return. (See Matthew Chapters 24 & 25 for some examples, including the parable of the wise and foolish virgins, and the parable of the talents.) In our scripture selection for today, followers of Christ are seen as faithful and wise servants. It's clear that Christ's return will be unexpected, and equally clear that as Christians, we should ready for it. To me that means having our relationships well-mended, including our relationship with God and those with others on this earth. It means, in essence, that we must at all times love God, and love our neighbor as ourselves.

PRAYER: Help us always to be ready for your return, O Lord, by always whole-heartedly loving both You *and* our neighbor. AMEN.

DECEMBER 8

THE INFLUENCE OF IMITATION

(Scripture to ponder: Ephesians 5:1)

Isn't it interesting how children will imitate adults? I'm sure any parent can remember incidents that occurred when raising their kids, in which imitation was humorous or embarrassing, or both!

My wife Diane tells of a time when her oldest daughter was a two-year-old. There'd been a fly buzzing around the kitchen, and Diane went after it with a folded newspaper, exclaiming, "Oh, damn!" as she swatted and missed it against the window.

She forgot about the incident. Later as she was working in the kitchen, she was startled to hear her daughter exclaim, "Oh damn!" as she swung her little hand as the fly buzzed by. For Diane, it was a humbling and educational experience!

The innocence and imitation of children is indeed educational. They learn and grow by imitating what they see around them, often adult behavior. As regards children, I'm reminded of what a medical student once confided to me regarding his teachers, "**We are learning when you least suspect it.**"

St. Paul urges us to be imitators of Christ, as innocent children. Such child-like impersonation trusts implicitly that what is being mirrored is genuine and true. To imitate Christ, we must be familiar with how Jesus lived and how he interacted with those around him. And to do that, we need to become utterly familiar with his life, reading the scriptures every day.

PRAYER: **Help us, like little children, Dear Lord, to imitate you in all that we do, so that your kingdom may come. AMEN.**

DECEMBER 9

BUILDING SHELTERS IN ARID PLACES

(Scripture to ponder: Matthew 4:1–11)

Diane and I recently visited Taliesin West near Scottsdale, AZ, where Frank Lloyd Wright had the winter campus for his School of Architecture. Apprentices who came to work with him spent their first few months living out in the open, where they had to construct places to live in the arid atmosphere of the Sonoran Desert. We went on a fascinating two-hour guided walk called the shelter tour.

Wright made his students use indigenous materials to construct their shelters, then had them live in them for the duration of the time they were in the desert. Through first-hand experience, living alone in an arid environment, they found out how their designs held up.

Our human lives are often punctuated by arid places—times that seem dry and even barren. Such times can be as harsh as the desert, and such times in our lives can be unsettling. But I believe God allows us to experience such times to teach us and to draw us nearer to Himself.

There are—and always will be—empty and arid places in our lives and in our souls. The question we should ask is not *why*, but rather, *with what* are we going to fill them? Will we fill them with drugs or with alcohol, with our jobs or with hobbies? Or will we let them be filled with God? I believe we encounter such times so we will turn to Him. He has placed them there so we become restless and seek Him. Saint Augustine put it well:

"Our hearts are restless until they find their rest in Thee."

PRAYER: We know from the Scripture, Lord, that your son Jesus used the arid and lonely places to come away, to find rest and to commune with You. Let us do likewise. Let us find our rest in You. AMEN.

DECEMBER 10

RENEWING A RIGHT SPIRIT

(Scripture to ponder: Psalm 51)

My wife and I visited New York City three months after the terrorist attacks on the World Trade Center. I was impressed, and it confirmed in my own mind what I'd read by several commentators, about a change of spirit that seemed to have come over New Yorkers since the September 11th terrorist attacks: people we met seemed kinder, more helpful and less impatient than I remembered them from when I lived in the East.

On three occasions during our visit people went out of their way to be kind and helpful to us, a noteworthy change of attitude and behavior from the usual hustle and crush of that great city. It was almost as if a new spirit pervaded the populace.

King David, in Psalm 51, asks God to *"renew a right spirit"* within him. The Lord did just that. And He is able to do that for any of us, if we will but ask and allow it.

The change that takes place in all of our cities at this time of year is likewise the renewing of a right spirit. For a few days each December, the spirit that pervades society seems renewed, and people are indeed kinder, gentler, and more helpful. It's the spirit of unselfish giving, which of course, comes straight out of the Good News brought by the baby who was born in Bethlehem. It temporarily transforms the spirit of the populace.

But the marvel and the wonder is that the same Spirit can transform us daily, if we will return each day, in prayer, to the Source of that Love.

PRAYER: **Renew us day by day, Dear Lord, and put within us the right spirit of your Son Jesus. AMEN.**

DECEMBER 11

THE APPLE OF THE EYE

(Scripture to ponder: Psalm 17)

In Psalm 17, David implores God to keep him as *"the apple of his eye."* The phrase apple of the eye—which appears again in *Proverbs 7:2*—refers to the pupil of the eye, and the concept implies a careful guarding and attention. The simile has a sound basis in the physiology of vision.

Of all the sense organs, the eye is the most valuable and the most protected. Whereas the ear is shielded by having the eardrum deep within a bony canal in the skull, the eye is out in front and exposed. So the eye's been protected by three reflexes. First is the lid reflex, which causes the eye to flinch—to involuntarily close—when the lid or the eyelash is touched. In surgery we use the lid reflex as a measure of the depth of anesthesia. As long as flinching occurs when the eyelash is stroked by the anesthesiologist when a patient's being put to sleep, pain sensation is still present, and I cannot make a painless incision to begin an operation.

A second defense for the eye is the corneal reflex, which also causes flinching if the cornea is touched. The cornea has no blood vessels—which is why it can be transplanted without rejection—but it is amply supplied with nerves, so it's exquisitely sensitive, even to gusts of air or flecks of dust.

Finally, a flash of light or a sudden motion directed toward the eye will cause flinching to protect the eye from injury.

So when David in the Psalms calls for God to keep him as the apple of the eye, he knows he's well protected indeed!

PRAYER: We know how precious our sight and vision are, O Lord. We praise You and pray that you will keep us under Your protection as the apple of Your eye. AMEN.

DECEMBER 12

WHAT IS THE CHURCH?

(Scripture to ponder: Colossians 1:15–20)

Ernest Gordon was a Scottish officer in World War II, captured at the fall of Singapore. Interned by the Japanese, he was part of the labor force of prisoners who worked on the Burma-Thailand Railroad and built the Bridge over the River Kwai. In his book about that experience, he's given one of the best definitions of the Church that I've encountered, one based on the transforming power of God's love in the horrible environment of a jungle prison camp:

"So far as most of us could see, there were three definitions of the church. There was the church composed of laws, practices, books, pews, pulpits, stones and steeples; the church adorned with the paraphernalia of state. Then there was the church composed of creeds, catechisms, and theological professors, a church which was identified by words in great volume.

Finally, there was the church of the spirit, called out of the world to exist in it by reason of its joyful response to the initiative of God's love. Such a church had the atmosphere not of law court nor of classroom but of divine humanity. It existed wherever there was Christ's love. The physical temple and the doctrinal affirmation are needed—but both are dead without the church that is communion, the fellowship of God's people."

[Through the Valley of the Kwai, p. 174]

PRAYER: We easily see the church as a building, and we know the church of creeds and catechisms, O Lord; help us to become the Church of the Spirit, of love and service to one another. AMEN.

DECEMBER 13

A KEY CHRISTIAN SCRIPTURE

(Scripture to ponder: John 3:16–18)

Hear the words of St. John's Gospel from today's selection:

For God so loved the world that he gave his only Son that whoever believes in him should not perish but have eternal life. For God sent the Son into the world, not to condemn the world, but that the world might be saved through him. He who believes in him is not condemned; he who does not believe is condemned already, because he has not believed in the name of the only Son of God.

This passage of scripture is fundamental to the Christian faith because of its three crucial assertions. First, that God has provided eternal life for those who believe in his son, the Lord Jesus Christ. The old saying is there's nothing as certain as death and taxes. But through faith in Christ, eternal life is possible, and death no longer holds us in its sway.

Second, these verses assert that God sent Jesus into the world not to condemn the world, but rather so the world could be saved. It's a pretty messed up world, you have to admit. Reading the daily paper or listening to the nightly news forces one to conclude that evil, death, and destruction are rampant upon the earth. It's all too easy for Christians to pass judgment on the world, to condemn it because we despise the sin that's so prevalent. But this passage (verse 17) is a warning to us that we must not judge, for Christ came to save the world, not condemn it. We too must do likewise.

Finally, verse 18 of this passage deals with the condemnation issue, asserting that condemnation occurs because of a lack of belief. St. Paul wrote,

"By grace are you saved through faith, and not of ourselves, for it is the gift of God."
[Ephesians 2:8]

So we are saved because of God's gift of Christ, saved through faith in him. It's not because of wrong actions that judgment will come; it's because of a lack of belief in Christ.

PRAYER: Thank you, Father, for loving this world so much that you sent your son, not to condemn us but to save us. Help us do your will. AMEN.

DECEMBER 14

EXPECTING HIS RETURN

(Scripture to ponder: Matthew 25:31–46)

As we ponder God's gift of His Son during Advent, and as we think about Christ's Second Coming, how ought we to prepare for it? It's quite obvious how the world prepares for the celebration of His birth, for Christmas. The secular world has "cashed in" on it by what the Christian writer Wendy Miller has called "the propaganda of commerce." It is indeed the biggest sales time in the whole year for department stores.

But what shall we say about the other Advent, about the Second Coming of Christ, an occurrence about which the New Testament is simultaneously so specific, yet so vague? When I read the Gospels, particularly the words of Jesus about when He will return, I'm reminded of a watchword I learned when I first had the opportunity to travel abroad.

I had the chance to live abroad for two summers, first in Austria when I was in college and again when I was a medical student and lived in India. Our group of ten American students was part of a program called The Experiment in International Living, designed to promote international understanding. We each lived with a foreign family, not as a guest, but as a family member.

Our reliable watchword for those summers—and one that has validity for life, I've found—was *"expect the unexpected!"* It stood us well as we were immersed in a foreign culture, and it stands us well in everyday life, if we believe the words of Jesus. As related in our selection from Matthew 25, his return will be unexpected, and we should so arrange our lives and relationships to be ready for it. We should *expect the unexpected.*

PRAYER: We know that for the world, Your return will be unexpected. Help us always to be ready for it, by living our lives according to Your will. AMEN.

DECEMBER 15

CHARITABLE GIVING

(Scripture to ponder: 2 Corinthians 9:6–7)

It's that time of year—the Advent season—when we look forward to the coming of the Lord Jesus. But if you're like me, it's also the time of year when you receive all sorts of appeals from organizations that want your money before the tax year ends. I get a myriad of requests in the mail: everything from Public Radio to the Red Cross and the Boy Scouts, as well as requests from many Christian charities. How do we make wise decisions about which groups to support? I put first my local church.

To evaluate most of the other charities, I rely on a list published each fall in the *Christian Science Monitor,* an annual survey of the 50 largest charities in the United States. I find the information worthwhile, for they include not just the size of the organization, tallied by total income, but also the percent of their revenues that's devoted to programs (as opposed to administrative costs or fund raising), and the salary and benefits of the highest paid official.

Did you know that in 2002 the Red Cross, ranked third in size, spent 90% on programs, and paid its CEO over five hundred thousand dollars? Or that the Boy Scouts of America—ranked 13th—spent 89% on programs, but paid its CEO $1.5 million (which did include some back years of deferred salary)? I was surprised that Lutheran Services in America was listed as the largest organization (with $7.6 Billion in income). I was pleased to discover that almost 92% of its total revenue was devoted to programs, and that its CEO's salary was only $102,000.

Our scripture passage for today tells us that God wants us to be cheerful givers—and I am sure He wants us to be careful and wise, too. You may want to check out charities on line at these websites: *www.charitywatch.org,* for the American Institute of Philanthropy, or *www.give.org* for the Better Business Bureau's Wise Giving Alliance.

PRAYER: **You have urged us to be charitable, O Lord. Help us through Your Spirit to be wise in our giving. AMEN.**

DECEMBER 16

GIVING OUR UNDIVIDED ATTENTION

(Scriptures to ponder: Deuteronomy 6:5; Psalm 9:1)

Recently I accompanied a neighbor to visit her cardiologist to get the results from a coronary artery angiogram and to hear his recommendations for further treatment. I offered to be there with her and her husband because I knew how confusing medical jargon could be and I thought I might help with some questions she had about her care.

We were shown into a small exam room by a medical assistant. The husband and I stepped out as my neighbor put on a gown and had a cardiogram done to prepare for the doctor coming in. We came back in the room just before he arrived. It seemed a bit crowded with the four of us in a small room, she on the exam table, her husband and I in armchairs and the doctor sitting on a stool at a small writing table in the corner.

The cramped quarters of the examination room did not bother me, for I've often spoken with families in small rooms before or after surgery. What *did* bother me was that the doctor spent most of the time leafing through the chart. He didn't seem to be giving the patient his undivided attention, nor did he seem to really be listening as she responded to his questions. It's an occurrence all too common in these rushed days of modern medicine.

But it's a trap that's evident not just in managed medical care. It made me think of how I don't often give God my undivided attention when I pray. Rarely do I "close the book" on other, intrusive thoughts or on my activities, and pay attention only to Him. But God wants all of us. As our scripture texts assert, we are to love Him with all our heart and soul and strength, and we are to praise Him with our whole heart.

PRAYER: So often we give You our divided attention, O Lord. Help us love you wholeheartedly, and praise You with our entire being, with singleness of heart, soul and might. In Jesus' name we pray. AMEN.

DECEMBER 17

A CHRISTMAS CAROL

(Scripture to ponder: Romans 12:2; Ezekiel 36: 26–27)

Most of us are familiar with the famous story by Charles Dickens, *A Christmas Carol*. I recall as a boy our family used to sit by the fire and listen to it on 78 rpm records each Christmas Eve.

I also remember in particular one December in San Francisco when my wife and I attended a marvelous performance of Dickens' play, done by the American Conservatory Theater group. That performance occurred just four years after our two children were badly injured in a head-on collision, an accident that left our four-year old son partly paralyzed. He was just beginning to walk again at about age eight, when we saw the play.

In the production, Tiny Tim so reminded us of him. In the final scene—when Uncle Scrooge comes to have Christmas dinner and realizes Tim has not died after all—the tears streamed down our cheeks as we held hands and cried for joy that our son, too, had been spared.

Many folks think *A Christmas Carol* is a Christmas Story, which of course it is. But in a sense, it's not so much about Christmas itself, as it is about *Advent*—about the arrival of the Savior in a life. For when Scrooge awoke that morning after his three dreams, after being escorted through them by the spirits of Christmas Past, Present and Yet-to-Come, nothing around him had changed. The bedposts, the heavy drapes, the dark room were all the same. The street, the shops, the people he saw when he threw open the shutters were all the same.

What *had* changed was *Scrooge*. His heart of stone had been transformed, his spirit had been renewed. That transformation, that renewal, is what Advent is all about. It happened to Ebenezer Scrooge, and it can happen to each one of us, if we will but prepare our hearts for his coming.

PRAYER: **Help us prepare our hearts, O Lord, for Your coming; so that there, You may have a home. Transform our soul and spirit, so that this Advent, we may grow into your likeness. We pray in the Name of Jesus. AMEN.**

DECEMBER 18

GREED

(Scriptures to ponder: Psalm 49:16–20; 1 Timothy 6:10)

A recent Internet poll asked respondents to indicate which of the seven deadly sins they thought they were most guilty of. Of the seven (which include *Anger, Envy, Gluttony, Avarice, Lust, Pride,* and *Sloth*) the one that came in *last* was *Avarice,* that is, *Greed.* It meant the respondents thought themselves least prone to greed. That seemed strange to me, for nowadays it appears that greed is at the root of much of the corporate malfeasance that's brought down several large companies like Enron and World Com. I see it as one of the main motivating factors in our society. Maybe the wrong people answered the poll!

Columnist Jane Eisner [38] puts her finger on one of the causes of our societal greed, when she writes:

> **"Built deep into the foundations of the advertising age is the belief that we, as consumers, never have enough."**

In the same vein, it seems perfectly O.K. to want more and more; indeed, it's downright *unpatriotic* not to want more, to buy more, to consume more, for it helps prop up a sagging economy in lean times and it keeps the machinery humming when things are bullish. It's our duty!

I think we've been so brainwashed by advertising and so deceived by the reflections the media portray, that we overlook what the Bible says about *Greed.* The voice of Scripture gets drowned out by louder, more strident voices on the airways that command more of our time. But the quiet truth of the Gospel endures and prevails. God is not mocked.

PRAYER: Help us see everything from your perspective, O Lord; may we truly follow You and not be conformed to this world, but be transformed by renewal of our spirit by your Spirit. AMEN.

DECEMBER 19

THE RUSH FOR GOLD

(Scriptures to ponder: Proverbs 16:16; Psalm 19:10)

Which would you rather have: gold or knowledge? It seems like many folks today are engaged in the pursuit of gold—that is, making money. It seems almost as though avarice—the love of money, one of the "seven deadly sins"—was part of the human psyche.

In a creek near Sutter's Mill in Northern California gold was discovered in 1848, setting off a stampede into that state. About fifty years later on a branch of the Klondike River in the Yukon another gold discovery set off another flood of fortune seekers, most coming from Seattle and San Francisco.

The quest of those who set out for the Klondike was more arduous as than the California 49ers, for they had to endure passage on a cramped steamer to the Alaska panhandle, then climb over mountain passes into Canada in the winter, hauling the ton of supplies required for entrance by the Mounties.

A young man who set out from Oakland to make his fortune in the Klondike ended up returning home within a year, having endured a harsh winter in a cabin on Henderson Creek. He came back with no gold, but chock full of the Northland and of stories of the Sourdoughs and their sled dogs.

That man—who set out to find gold but returned instead with knowledge—was **Jack London**. His stories of the North and his longer pieces about animals, such as *The Call of the Wild* and *White Fang* became more valuable than gold or silver. He was for a time the highest paid author in America.

Our Scripture says wisdom is better than gold, and understanding than silver: the precepts of God are more to be desired than gold. If we seek God's Kingdom *first*, all things will be added unto us.

PRAYER: **Those who have found you, O Lord, have found treasure beyond measure. Help us to seek and do your will. By serving others, let us bring in your kingdom. AMEN.**

DECEMBER 20

LIVING IN COMMUNITY TODAY

(Scripture to ponder: Acts 2:44–45)

The scripture passage for today, from *Acts,* relates how the early Christians held all things in common, even selling their own property and possessions to be able to share with all. They lived a communal life, perhaps not unlike some monastic orders still do.

Reading the *Acts of the Apostles,* one of the most exciting books in the entire Bible, I'm impressed by the dynamism of the early Church. The early followers of Jesus, empowered and emboldened by the Holy Spirit, were an invigorated and energizing group. They had a sense of community that seems to be lacking in many churches today. Two things strike me as sources for the difference between the early church and the modern church. Both are related to *independence.*

The focus and emphasis in contemporary American society is on the *individual,* not on the *communal* life. It's a philosophy that tends to separate people rather than draw them together. We each have our own automobile, and although we do tend to live in families, we're prone to locked doors and gated communities. We cherish our privacy and our independence. Wanting to feel independent militates against community.

In a book entitled *Making All Things New,* the spiritual author Henri Nouwen has written:

> "The question is not simply, 'Where does God lead me as an individual person who tries to do his will?' More basic and more significant is the question, 'Where does God lead us as a people?' That question requires that we pay careful attention to God's guidance in our life together and that together we search for a creative response."

I think individually we often seek God's will, as we should. But in my experience, it's rare that we as congregations seek God's corporate, His communal will for us. Nouwen has a point: If we search together for what God wills for us as a church and as a people,

I suspect we will be drawn closer together, and perhaps rekindle what the early Church experienced.

PRAYER: **Help us seek your will in community, O Lord. May we share our possessions as we share our dreams. AMEN.**

DECEMBER 21

WHAT DOES GOD EXPECT?

(Scriptures to ponder: Micah 6:8; Titus 2:12)

In this series of Advent Meditations, as we have pondered the Second Coming of Christ as described in Scripture, we realize that:

1. (Nov. 30) Only God knows when Jesus will come again;
2. (Dec.1) We have time—until he comes, if we're alive, or until we die;
3. (Dec. 7) We can be ready, if we plan properly;
4. (Dec. 14) We should *"expect the unexpected,"* and assume the world will be conducting "business as usual" when He comes; and
5. (Today) There will be, as Scripture puts it, "weeping and gashing of teeth" as the world is caught unaware.

What does God expect of us? How ought we to behave to best be prepared for Christ's return? The Bible provides some answers. One answer is from our first Scripture selection in the Book of the Prophet Micah:

"He has showed you, O man what is good; and what does the Lord require of you but to do justice, and to love kindness and to walk humbly with thy God?"

[Micah 6:8]

Another answer, our second selection, St. Paul gives in Titus 2:12. We should

"We should live self-controlled, upright and Godly lives."

[NIV]

Perhaps the fullest expression of what God expects comes straight from the words of the Lord Jesus, in two relevant passages. First, when asked by a lawyer what he must do to inherit Eternal Life *[Luke 10:25]*, Jesus makes clear, using the parable of the good Samaritan, that we must love God and love our neighbor, pointing out that our neighbor is anyone who needs our help.

Secondly, in the parable of the Last Judgment [Matthew 25:31–46], Christ makes it clear that we'll be judged on how we minister unto him, and he asserts that he can be in anyone we meet. He says if we feed the hungry, assuage the thirsty, take in strangers, clothe the naked and visit those who are sick or in prison, we will be ministering unto Him, and will be judged accordingly. I think that's what God expects of us.

PRAYER: Help us see You in those around us, so that as we serve the needs of others, we are serving you, Dear Lord. AMEN.

DECEMBER 22

GETTING AND SPENDING

(Scripture to ponder: Psalm 8)

Getting and spending we lay waste our powers, Little we see in nature that is ours;
We have given our hearts away, a sordid boon.

—William Wordsworth

Those words are perhaps even more relevant today than they were two hundred years ago when the poet penned them. England was coming into prominence as a great imperial power, the Industrial Revolution was just getting under way, and the total population of the earth was less than one billion.

Today, America is the one great superpower that with five percent of the earth's population consumes almost fifty per cent of the world's resources. The industrial revolution has come and gone, it's a far more polluted world than Wordsworth knew, and our globe must now sustain six billion of us.

While it's true that in the book of Genesis, God instructs man to have *dominion* over all the earth and over all the beasts, in the full context of Scripture, I believe God would have us be *stewards* of His creation, responsible for nurturing and preserving the beauty of our planet. But we are consuming that creation at an alarming rate.

I believe it's significant that although we can see thousands of stars in the night sky and telescopes reveal billions more, nowhere else in the universe has there been proven a creation such as ours, nor is there any other evidence of human life in the vast cosmos. We've been made just a little lower than the angels, as our Scripture reading from Psalm 8 asserts, and for that great privilege we have a great responsibility.

PRAYER: **Help us be still and know that You are God. Let us ever be mindful of all that You have entrusted to us. Help us nurture and preserve it. AMEN.**

DECEMBER 23

LOVE CAME DOWN

(Scripture to ponder: Luke 2:1–7)

Our passage of scripture today tells of the birth of the Lord Jesus as St. Luke relates it in his second chapter. Caesar Augustus had issued a decree that a census should be made throughout the Roman Empire. In the Holy Land, Jews were required to go back to the city of their forefathers to be enrolled.

Joseph was descended from King David and it was to David's city—Bethlehem—that he and Mary journeyed from Nazareth for the enrollment. She was near term with child fathered by the Holy Spirit, and she went into labor when they reached the town. No rooms were available at the inn, so to have some shelter they settled for the night in the animal shed.

In Matthew's Gospel, however, the account of Jesus' birth begins with the adoration of the Magi, the Wise Men from the East, a fitting beginning for God Incarnate, the King of the Universe. But Luke, the physician, chooses to emphasize Jesus' *humble* beginnings: at his birth, Mary wrapped him in swaddling cloths, the way poor folks dressed and diapered their young. And instead of a cradle, the baby was placed in a manger, a feeding trough for animals.

I think Luke chose to emphasize these humble beginnings on purpose. For God came down—Love came down—at Christmas, to dwell among us as one of us. And Jesus would later wrap a towel around his waist and get down on his knees to humbly wash his disciples feet to show us the way of salvation and servanthood, so we could truly know God.

PRAYER: We thank You and bless You, O Lord, that You, the King of the Universe, became incarnate and lived among us to show us Your Love. Help us love others as You have loved us, so we may do Your Will and further Your Kingdom. AMEN.

DECEMBER 24

LETTERS TO GOD

(Scriptures to ponder: Mark 9:37; Matthew 19:14)

There used to be a radio program called *Kids Say the Darndest Things!* I'm pretty sure it's not still aired. It's been replaced by television shows like *America's Funniest Home Videos.* I got an e-mail recently that that cracked me up. It gave a bunch of letters to God from children. Let me share a few.

Dear God, I read the Bible. What does begat mean? Nobody will tell me. Love, Alison.

Dear God, What does it mean you are a jealous God? I thought you had everything you wanted. (signed) Jane.

Dear God, Is it true my father won't get in Heaven if he uses his golf words in the house? (signed) Anita.

Dear God, I bet its very hard for you to love everybody in the whole world. We have only 4 people in our family and I can never do it. (signed) Nan.

Dear God, Did you really mean Do Unto Others As They Do Unto You? If you did then I'm going to get even with my brother.

Dear God, My Grandpa says you were around when he was a little boy. How far back to you go? Love, Dennis.

Dear Mr. God, I wish you would not make it so easy for people to come apart. I had to have three stitches and a shot. (signed) Janet.

Dear God, Did you mean for giraffes to look like that or was it an accident? (signed) Norma.

Dear God, If you watch in Church on Sunday I will show you my new shoes.

Dear God, Is Reverend Coe a friend of yours, or do you just know him through the business? (signed) Donny

We read these and chuckle. It makes me think there will be humor in heaven, for Mark reports Jesus saying,

"Whoever receives a child in my name receives me,"

[Mark 9:37]

And Matthew records Jesus' words,

"Let the little children to come to me, for of such is the Kingdom of Heaven."

[Matthew 19:14]

The innocence and trust of children are dear to God.

PRAYER: Grant, O Lord, that we may have the innocence and trust of little children as we come to you in prayer. AMEN.

DECEMBER 25

ONE SOLITARY LIFE

(Scripture to ponder: Matthew 2:1–12)

One Christmas season Diane and I attended the "Christmas Spectacular" at New York's Radio City Music Hall. It's where the famous line dancers, the Rockettes, perform, and I expected to see lots of glitz and dazzle and special effects. I wasn't disappointed. But I witnessed something else, something that I did not anticipate in the current era of "political correctness."

The show began with a dizzying three-dimensional sleigh ride as each of us donned paper glasses and watched the big screen. Song and dance numbers followed this opener. It was all great fun, and frankly, I expected that the rest of the program would be quite secular and gloss over any references to Christ. But I was wrong.

The finale was moving and inspirational, a "Living Nativity" that acted out the journey to Bethlehem. Our Savior's Birth was reenacted as the orchestra played Christmas carols, and in a voiceover, the show concluded with this message:

"He was born in an obscure village, the child of a peasant woman. He grew up in another obscure village where He worked in a carpenter shop until He was thirty. Then for three years He was an itinerant preacher.

"He never owned a home. He never set foot inside a big city. He never traveled two hundred miles from the place He was born. He never wrote a book, or held an office. He did none of the things that usually accompany greatness.

"While He was still a young man the tide of popular opinion turned against Him. His friends deserted Him. He was turned over to His enemies, and went through the mockery of a trial. He was nailed to a cross between two thieves. While He was dying, His executioners gambled for the only piece of property He had—His coat. When He was dead, He was taken down and laid in a borrowed grave.

"Over two thousand years have passed, and today He is remembered as the central figure for much of the human race. All the armies that ever marched and all the navies that ever

sailed and all the parliaments that ever sat and all the kings that ever reigned, put together, have not affected the life of man upon this earth as powerfully as this ONE SOLITARY LIFE."

The show ended as we sat in awed silence.

PRAYER: We bless You, O Lord: for through the *One Solitary Life* of Your only begotten Son, we who believe on him have eternal life. May His Spirit dwell in our hearts forever. AMEN.

DECEMBER 26

THE HEART OF ALL TRUE HAPPINESS

(Scripture to ponder: Matthew 20:25–28)

Norman Vincent Peale was one of the most popular preachers and Christian authors of his generation. He died at age 94 in 1994. His wife, Ruth Stafford Peale, is still alive at age 96. She was her husband's closest friend and helper but was a great leader in her own right. She received several honorary degrees and currently heads a large organization, The Foundation for Christian Living. Mrs. Peale recently published her autobiography, entitled *A Lifetime of Positive Thinking*.

I was struck by her comments about happiness:

"Today more than ever, I believe the challenge has not grown stale: To serve God by trying to serve people lies at the heart of all true happiness. Once, I was asked at a ladies' luncheon what made me happy. I told my audience that there was no absolutely foolproof formula for happiness. Then I encouraged them to stop struggling to be happy, since happiness isn't something you can deliberately set out to achieve for yourself, like skill at typing or a college degree. In fact, the more you focus on your own happiness, or lack of it, the more it will continue to elude you. This is because preoccupation with self is the enemy of happiness. The more concerned you are with

your own pleasures and successes—or your own problems and failures for that matter—the less contented you are going to be." [39]

In asserting the key to finding happiness is in serving others, Ruth Peale is echoing
the words of Jesus, after he was asked by James and John to be placed on his right and
left hand in the coming kingdom (It's our Scripture selection for today):

> *You know that the rulers of the gentiles lord it over them, and their great men exercise
> authority over them. It shall not be so among you; but whoever would be great among
> you must be your servant, and whoever would be first among you must be your slave;
> even as the Son of man came not to be served but to serve, and to give his life as a ransom
> for many.*

With Jesus as our model, we can find true happiness serving others.

PRAYER: We thank you, O Lord, that you sent your Son, who, as a servant, gave
his life for us. Empower us through your Spirit to do likewise for others. AMEN.

DECEMBER 27

THE MYSTERY OF THE EMPTY TOMB

(Scripture to ponder: Matthew 27: 62–66; 28:1–25)

Albert Einstein once said, "The most beautiful thing we can experience is the mysterious. It is the source of all true art and science."

I suspect there is no greater mystery than that of the empty tomb on Easter morning. Our scripture gives one explanation, namely that Jesus' body was stolen. But the
Jews had been fearful of that very thing, and Matthew records that they asked, and were
granted by Pilate, to have a guard set out to prevent just such an event. So nobody
stole his body.

In Matthew's account, early on Easter morning, there was an earthquake and an angel rolled away the stone blocking the entrance to the tomb. The guards collapsed like dead men. The angel told Mary and the women with her that Christ was risen from the dead, and was going before them to Galilee.

We, too, who believe in Christ, are likewise partakers of that marvelous mystery. Hear what St. Paul says in chapter 15 of his First Letter to the Church at Corinth:

Behold I tell you a mystery: We shall not all sleep, but we shall be changed, in a moment, in the twinkling of an eye, at the last trumpet. The dead shall be raised incorruptible, and we shall be changed.

Praise God for the great mystery of the resurrection, by which we have Eternal Life!

PRAYER: Thank You, Dear Lord, for the great mystery of the resurrection, for the obedience of your Son, who suffered death on the cross, that we too may be raised with him to Life Eternal. AMEN.

DECEMBER 28

GIVINGUP AND GIVING OVER

(Scripture to ponder Matthew 10:39)

Recently I was reminded of an important lesson in prayer, one that that Lord has repeatedly taught me throughout my life. I call it *Giving up and Giving Over*. It is one way, I believe, that God uses to draw us closer to Him.

In this particular instance it related to a favorite pen that I wanted to take on a trip abroad. As I got ready to pack, I looked high and low for it, retraced my steps and searched all my coats and shirts, to no avail. It was not an expensive pen, but one whose heft I liked, and one I'd grown accustomed to. I was quite frustrated.

When it didn't turn up, I gave up and gave the matter over to God. On the trip I took an old "throwaway" Bic pen. It happened that we were headed for London, so I thought

I would buy a replacement at Harrods, the famous department store where I'd originally bought the pen two years earlier. So I looked for a replacement pen when we were there, but I couldn't get just what I wanted. The same pen was listed in the catalogue, but the store did not have any in stock at the time.

After we returned, as I sat at the breakfast table with my wife, I happened to open a notebook I keep handy to jot down ideas for writing devotionals, and Lo! stuck between the pages, there was my pen!

It reminded me of Christ's words in Matthew 10:39, that those who lose their life for his sake will find it. I am convinced that we release the power of God when we give up—that is, acknowledge our own weakness—and we give over—that is, commit ourselves to God's care, trusting Him.

PRAYER: Help us to give up striving on our own, Dear Lord, and give over all things to You in prayer. AMEN.

DECEMBER 29

BELAYED BY GOD

(Scripture to ponder: Psalm 37)

In mountaineering, one of the most important techniques is called belaying. It's a method of security that, although it doesn't prevent a fall, is designed to minimize its risk. When two climbers are roped together and are "on belay," only one of them climbs. The other holds the rope, securing it by fastening it to the mountain using a piton or a wedge driven into the rock, to which is attached a snap ring called a carabiner, through which the rope passes, almost like through a pulley.

As one climber proceeds, the other allows only a short amount of slack in the rope, so if the first climber should fall, he can be arrested by the rope, secured by the second climber.

I once climbed the Matterhorn with a Swiss guide. The day before our climb, he took me up a steep pitch of the mountain to be sure I understood the use of the rope, how to belay, and to be belayed. I was familiar with rope techniques, and checked out O.K. Things went fine the next day when we climbed that majestic peak. He was an excellent guide and I felt secure roped to him.

In Psalm 37, the Psalmist speaks of God almost as if He were an Alpine guide, when he extols the security we have in him:

The steps of a good man are ordered by the Lord, and he delighteth in his way. Though he fall, he shall not be utterly cast down, for the Lord upholdeth him with his hand.
[Psalm37:23–24]

In mountaineering, a climber is most secure when he is roped to another climber to whom he can entrust his life. And in life itself, there is no greater security than trusting ourselves into the hand of God.

PRAYER: **We do indeed delight in following Your way and doing Your will, O Lord. Uphold us with Your hand, all our days. AMEN.**

DECEMBER 30

"PLAN B"

(Scripture to ponder: Mark 10:28)

My neighbor and I swim laps at the YMCA. Last week he spotted one of his friends, a man who suffers from a gradual, wasting disease, laboriously coming up the stairs with a cane. They greeted one another and my neighbor asked how he was getting along.

"**They sure make it hard to get around this place,**" the man sighed. "**I have to come down those outside stairs from the parking lot, then up more stairs to get to the locker room. Then to swim, I have to go up and down another flight of stairs.**" He was puffing slightly as he finished speaking.

"**Why don't you go with Plan B?**" asked my friend, thinking there must be an alternative to all the effort. The man smiled and said,

"There *is* no 'Plan B'!"

For this man, bravely fighting a progressive disease, there was no alternative. It struck me that the same is true for the Christian. As the old hymn puts it, "I have decided to follow Jesus . . . No turning back, no turning back."

In our scripture text for today, Peter exclaims to Jesus,

"We have left everything and followed you."

Peter and the other disciples had given up their livelihood to become followers of Christ; eventually they would give up their very lives in his service. For them, too, there was no '*Plan B.*' Dietrich Bonhoeffer, the German pastor who was hung by the Nazis, once said,

"When Christ calls a man he bids him come and die."

And so he does—for through Christ's plan, we die to our old selves. But through Grace, we live in newness of life, for him.

PRAYER: We know, O Lord, that for those who confess and follow you, there is no "Plan B." But with you as Savior, we have the pearl of great price: Your Peace, which passes understanding. Help us always to do your will. In Jesus' name we pray. AMEN.

DECEMBER 31

A NEW YEAR'S THOUGHT ABOUT LONGITUDE

(Scripture to ponder: Galatians 6:9&10; 5:22–23)

It's New Year's Eve and I've just finished reading a fascinating book entitled *Longitude*. [40] It relates the saga of solving the problem of longitude, namely how a ship's captain could figure out just where on the high seas he was at any given time. It was a problem fraught with difficulty, but of supreme importance to maritime nations like England.

In the seventeenth century, when global exploration expanded and colonial trade was growing, there was no easy, accurate way to calculate longitude—that is, to know exactly where one was on the earth's east-west axis. Latitude, one's position on the north-south plane, could be determined from the heavens, but establishing longitude was much harder. The calculation required complex solar and stellar observations and elaborate tables, and the process took several hours.

At the time, the problem was there was no accurate timepiece for use on a ship: a pendulum clock was thrown off by rolling and pitching, and spring-wound ones were adversely affected by changes in temperature and humidity. After many years of trial and error, the British clockmaker John Harrison and his son finally perfected a chronograph that was impervious to changes in the weather, one that gained or lost only seconds per month. It at last permitted accurate calculations of longitude from the zero meridian in Greenwich, England.

Nowadays, using a hand-held, satellite-based system called Global Positioning, in about twenty seconds you can pinpoint your location on earth, accurate to within a few feet. As the old song goes, "You've come a long way, baby!" Technology and science, as in all areas of modern life, have made a tremendous difference. But in the moral realm we've not done so well, have we?

When we look about, or listen to news from near or far, we find we are no closer to peace than in Harrison's day. Is there an answer? If so, what is it? I cannot change much in the world, but I can change myself. So maybe the answer lies in the words of another song:

"Let there be peace on earth, and let it begin with me."

PRAYER: Through Your Holy Spirit, O Lord, may peace in this world begin with me. Help me manifest all your attributes: Love, Joy, Peace, Patience, Kindness, Goodness, Faithfulness, Gentleness, and Self-Control. AMEN.

REFERENCES

[1] Quoted in "Open Your Eyes to Opportunity," in *Positive Thinking Vol. 53, #5*, June, 2002.

[2] Burns, James McGregor, *Roosevelt: The Lion and the Fox.* Harcourt, Brace Jovanovich, New York, 1956.

[3] Yancey, Philip, *Soul Survivor.* Doubleday, New York, 2001, pp. 20–21.

[4] As quoted in *Imprimis,* a publication of Hillsdale College in Minnesota (December 1989).

[5] The story was told in a sermon given jointly by Pastors Margaret Ann Fohl and William Arnold on Sunday, August 11, 2002 at Bryn Mawr Presbyterian Church, Bryn Mawr, PA.

[6] By Roger Rosenblatt; New York, Harcourt, 2002

[7] By William J. Bennett; New York, Doubleday, 2002

[8] By Dinesh D'Souza; Washington, Regnery Publishing, 2002

[9] Foster's comments are from *Spiritual Classics,* Harper Collins, New York, 2000, pg. 182

[10] This account is based on one found in Philip Yancey's *Soul Survivor* (Doubleday, New York, 2001), pp 159–160.

[11] This account derived from Garrison Keilor's *Writer's Almanac* for 3 February, 2002.

[12] Pastor of the Allison United Methodist Church in Carlisle, PA, in a sermon on December 22, 2002.

[13] As cited in *Lincoln Talks: An Oral Biography,* Edited by Emanuel Hertz. Bramhall House, New York, 1939), pg 422.

[14] Kelly, Thomas, *A Testament of Devotion.* Harper Torchlight, New York, 1941.

[15] Kelly, Thomas, *The Eternal Promise.* Hodder and Stoughton, London, 1966.

[16] Carter, J. *Sources of Strength.* Times Books, New York, 1997, p. xvii.

[17] *The One Year Book of Hymns,* by R. K. Brown and M. R. Norton, Tyndale House, Wheaton, IL, 1995, entry for Feb 4.

[18] Kleeburg, MA and G Lemme, *In the Footsteps of Martin Luther* Concordia Publishing House, St. Louis, MO, 1964,, P. 106.

[19] *The One Year book of Hymns* by R.K. Brown and M.R. Norton, Tyndale House, Wheaton, Il, 1995, entry for March 24.

[20] *Spiritual Classics: Selected Readings for Individuals and Groups on the Twelve Spiritual Disciplines.* Richard J. Foster and Emilie Griffin (Eds.), Harper San Francisco, 2000.

[21] Ernest Gordon, *Through the Valley of the Kwai,* Harper and Row, New York, 1962.

[22] Miller, R.M., *Harry Emerson Fosdick,* Oxford U. Press, Oxford, 1985, pg 49.

[23] Quoted by William Barclay in the *Promise of the Spirit,* p. 47.

[24] *Bullfinch's Mythology.* The Modern Library, New York, Pp 85–86.

24 *Bullfinch's Mythology.* The Modern Library, New York, Pp 85–86.

[26] *Beyond the Walls: Monastic Wisdom for Everyday Life.* Doubleday Image Books, New York, 1999, p.117.

[27] Elliot, Elisabeth. *Through Gates of Splendor.* Tyndale House, Wheaton, IL, 1956.

[28] Quoted by Jere Van Dyk in an editorial, "Houses of Worship," in *The Wall Street Journal,* 17 January 2003.

[29] Quoted in Garrison Keillor's *Writer's Almanac* for 19 September 2002.

[30] Gomes, P. "Guidance for how to make a life, not just a living." *Christian Science Monitor,* 19 November 2002.

[31] This Story is related in *Positive Thinking, Volume 53,# 4.*

[32] Quoted in *Abandonment to Divine Providence* (New York: Doubleday Image, 1975) pg. 105.

[33] *The Duel: The Eighty-Day Struggle Between Churchill and Hitler.*

[34] As recounted in James Limburg's *Psalms.* Westminster John Knox Press, Louisville, KY, 2000, pp.37–38.

[35] As related in the *Christian Science Monitor,* 4 June 2001.

[36] "Web Panhandlers Tale," in *the Christian Science Monitor,* 25 November 2002.

[37] *She Said Yes* by Misty Bernall. Plough Publishers, Farmington, PA, 1999

[38] "Greed is part of the Nation's Psyche," in the *Philadelphia Inquirer,* 28 July 2002.

[39] Ruth Stafford Peale, *A Lifetime of Positive Thinking,* Guideposts, Carmel, NY, 2001, p.103.

[40] Sobel, Dava. ***Longitude: The True Story of a Lone Genius Who Solved the Greatest Scientific Problem of His Time.*** Penguin Books, New York, 1995.

To order additional copies of

A Surgeon's DEVOTIONS

Have your credit card ready and call:

1-877-421-READ (7323)

or please visit our web site at
www.pleasantword.com

Also available at: www.amazon.com

Printed in the United States
24884LVS00002B/95-114

9 781414 100821